W9-BGQ-853

The Songwriter's & MUSICIAN'S Guide *to* Nashville

Sherry Bond

THIRD EDITION

ALLWORTH PRESS
NEW YORK

OCT - - '05

© 2004 Sherry Bond

All rights reserved. Copyright under Berne Copyright Convention, Universal Copyright Convention, and Pan-American Copyright Convention. No part of this book may be reproduced, stored in a retrieval system, or transmitted in any form, or by any means, electronic, mechanical, photocopying, recording, or otherwise, without prior permission of the publisher.

08   07   06   05   04   5   4   3   2   1

Published by Allworth Press
An imprint of Allworth Communications
10 East 23rd Street, New York, NY 10010

Cover design by Derek Bacchus

Cover photograph by Marc Bell/Bellsphotography.com

Page composition/typography by SR Desktop Services, Ridge, NY

ISBN: 1-58115-397-X

Library of Congress Cataloging-in-Publication Data

Bond, Sherry, 1941-
    The songwriter's and musician's guide to Nashville/Sherry Bond.—3rd ed.
        p. cm.
1. Country music—Tennessee—Nashville—Vocational guidance.   I. Title.

ML3790.B66 2005
781.642'09768'55—dc22

                                                        2004021392

Printed in Canada

Contents

Acknowledgments

Thank you to my sons Jeff and Robert Weedman! Jeff, a creative visual and graphic artist, updated Robert Oermann's wonderful artistic rendering of Music Row. Robert, who works at Sony Music Nashville, served as my efficient assistant. I also want to thank Jeffrey Steele, Dennis Lord, Stephanie Cox, Sherrill Blackman, and Stanton Mott, who provided a great deal of new information about the Nashville music industry, and about the music industry in general. There have been many changes on Music Row since our last edition—even the geography has changed! The interviews with these talented and knowledgeable people will bring our readers up-to-date with the latest information—me included!

Introduction

Y ou may have heard that Nashville is a tight-knit clique completely closed to outside writers. Nothing could be further from the truth.

Nashville loves songs. Nashville loves songwriters. Nashville welcomes you with open arms.

On your first trip to Nashville you will learn what true Southern hospitality is all about. When someone asks, "How are you?" (as they frequently will), they really, truly want to know how you are, how your family is doing, how your life is going. An important part of doing business in Nashville is sharing personal concerns with each other.

This book reads like many how-to books. It's filled with lots of dos and don'ts. Please remember that these rules are simply general guidelines for you to work from. Your success is basically going to depend on a single factor—your own people skills. If you are positive, enthusiastic, and love the process of pitching your songs as much as you love writing them, you are bound to succeed—that is, *if* you are a *great* songwriter, artist, or musician.

The hardest thing for Nashville to deal with is someone who doesn't have the faintest idea how to write a good song; someone, in fact, who doesn't even know the difference between a good song and a bad song. An astounding number of people fall into this category. They have written what they believe is a good song, and they think that now all they need to do is get someone in the music business to listen to it. They think that once someone listens to it, that'll be it; the song will be recorded, become an instant hit, and they'll get rich! Consequently, Nashville is bombarded with amateur songwriters trying to get someone to listen to their CDs. Unsolicited CDs are almost always returned unopened.

The purpose of this book is to prevent you from falling into the category described above. Nashville *does* listen to zillions of CDs—demos of amateur, developing, and professional songwriters. By using the right approach, you can get your songs heard and you can start developing working relationships with music business professionals. Ultimately, you will be interacting with many different people who can help you get your song to the right artist. It's a long and difficult process, one that takes your continued effort and dedication.

This book will tell you more than you can possibly imagine about pitching songs, but my best advice is to try *not* to make pitching your very first priority. In Nashville, songs are usually discovered in the process of working with them, while co-writing, recording in the demo studio, or listening to them at a live performance. Relax and enjoy the creative atmosphere of Music City. Listen and learn how things are done, then slowly ease your way in.

You are truly welcome in Nashville, so I hope you'll come on down soon. Please stop by to see me when you do!

About the Author

SHERRY BOND has a B.A. in music from the University of California at Santa Barbara. After receiving her degree, she took over the copyright and royalty

Photo by Teddie West

administration for the music publishing companies of her father, artist/writer Johnny Bond (*I Wonder Where You Are Tonight*), and the legendary Tex Ritter (*High Noon*), both of whom are members of the prestigious Country Music Hall of Fame. The catalogs of Johnny Bond Publications include the works of the Delmore Brothers (*Blues, Stay Away From Me*), Tommy Duncan (*Stay All Night, Stay a Little Longer*), and Harlan Howard (*The Blizzard*). In 1983, Bond moved from Los Angeles to establish offices in Nashville. Since moving to Nashville, she has had songs recorded by Johnny Cash (*Going by the Book*), Marty Stuart (*Burn Me Down*), and Lyle Lovett (*There's More Pretty Girls than One*).

After writing the first edition of *The Songwriter's and Musician's Guide to Nashville* in 1991, Bond became the fourth executive director of the NASHVILLE *entertainment* ASSOCIATION (NeA), and during her tenure, she nurtured the organization into a nationally recognized trade organization for aspiring artists and musicians. NeA Extravaganza showcased over four hundred acts from all genres of music before top industry professionals from Los Angeles, New York, and London. NeA Music City Music, a country music showcase, was created and produced by Bond to assist the Nashville recording industry in its search for new talent. As a result of this showcase, several acts were signed to record deals, including Chad Brock (Warner/Reprise), Dean Miller (Capitol), and SHeDAISY (Lyric Street).

Bond left the NeA in 1998 to return to music publishing in the new climate of Americana and alternative country music. She is a graduate of Leadership Music and an active member of the Country Music Association, Academy of Country Music, Nashville Songwriters' Association International, National Academy of Recording Arts and Sciences, and SOURCE, a networking organization for top female industry executives.

1

An Overview of Nashville

Nashville!

The name evokes all kinds of images: A place where everyone walks around wearing cowboy boots, hats, and jeans adorned with big silver belt buckles, carrying guitars over their shoulders. A place where you can come to see your favorite country artists performing at the local bars around town where songs are written about drinkin' and cheatin' and the grittier side of life.

REALITY VERSUS MYTH

You will be really surprised when you arrive in Nashville. It is nothing like those fantasies mentioned above. The perception of Nashville, created by songs from a long-gone era, is quite different from the reality of Nashville today. In fact, this false perception has impeded the efforts of city government officials to attract new industries to Nashville. Fortunately, they have been able to overcome this obstacle and have led the city to remarkable growth and prosperity. New industries continue to relocate here, giving the city a next-to-zero unemployment rate for several years running. Nashville even has one of the nation's top arenas and a state-of-the-art football stadium, home of the Tennessee Titans (formerly the Houston Oilers).

The only "cowboys" you'll find in Nashville are the tourists or aspiring artists trying to look the part. You'll find them wandering around downtown, on Broadway and Second Avenue North, away from the country music industry district, where industry executives, and artists/musicians wear anything but boots, hats, and big belt buckles. Country artists are almost unrecognizable in their casual clothes.

The biggest surprise for tourists is the fact that there is very little country music performed here. The likelihood of hearing one of your favorite artists is very remote. True, Nashville's best-kept secret is that the city has a vibrant live music scene. Any night of the week you can go into any one of the many music venues and hear an awesome performance. But it's not country. Jazz, blues, rock, pop, swing, and alternative music thrives in Music City because the session musicians who record country music in the studios during the day go out and create their own original, non-country music at night in the clubs. Also, the city attracts outstanding musicians looking for studio gigs, and they are playing in the clubs as well. It is a wonderful opportunity to hear the greatest musicians ever, but most tourists don't take advantage of it because they came here expecting to find country music.

The music of Hank Williams, Patsy Cline, and Loretta Lynn is such an important part of our country-music heritage that it is difficult to break away from the stereotypes. While the Nashville Sound has progressed to contemporary themes, the legendary artists remain as popular as they ever were. This creates a huge problem for the country music industry: gaining recognition for a new, modern sound without diluting the past. Treading lightly through this tricky situation has caused the country music industry to remain stuck in time. Today's country music is much more modern and complex than it is perceived to be.

Although Nashville is located on the fringe of a loosely defined southern territory, it possesses all the charm and hospitality of a sophisticated southern city. Lush, rich greenery and spectacular blooming foliage frame stately brick mansions standing on their own acres of land. Many residential neighborhoods are divided by majestic stonewalls built by slaves for erstwhile plantations. They are protected today as important works of art. Many a building contractor has altered architectural plans to incorporate history into the landscape. No visit to Nashville would be complete without a drive through its residential areas.

THE LAYOUT OF THE CITY

Nestled in the center of Middle Tennessee (the state is divided into three sections: East, where Knoxville and the Great Smoky Mountains are located; Middle; and West, where Memphis is found), Nashville is Tennessee's second-largest city (after Memphis), with a population of over one million people, and is the state capital. Located in the heart of the Bible Belt, the city's main industry is printing, primarily Bibles and hymnals. Hospitals, many of them corporately based in Nashville, are also a major industry of the city. Because of the Grand Ole Opry, CMA Music Festival (formerly Fan Fair), the Country Music Hall of Fame, and other attractions associated with country music, tourism is a major source of income for Nashville.

There are two separate tourist areas: downtown and the Opryland Hotel Complex. Downtown Nashville thrives and bustles with activity almost every night. Weekends bring gridlock to the two main streets, Broadway and Second Avenue (North and South). The blue lights on patrol cars blaze away while the police try to keep the traffic moving along. There is a congenial mix of locals and tourists roaming the streets and enjoying the great variety of restaurants. Locals head to their favorite bars to play a game of pool and sample one of the numerous beers offered by micro-breweries. Later in the evening they will club-hop among the various dance clubs. Or, if they are in the mood for music, there is a lot going on in the live music venues downtown. During the summer, there are a lot of outdoor music festivals at Riverfront Park, a huge hillside facing a stage on the Cumberland River.

There are numerous tourist attractions downtown, including a host of interesting shops and street vendors. Hard Rock Cafe, Planet Hollywood, and the NASCAR Cafe each offer their own distinctive charm. Unique to Nashville are the Wildhorse Saloon, Tootsie's, and the Ryman Auditorium.

The Wildhorse Saloon is a tourist's best chance to see a rare perfor-mance by a country star. Only occasionally will country artists perform at one of Nashville's two larger venues, the Arena or the First American Music Center (an outdoor amphitheater).

Tootsie's is a small bar located in the middle of a honky-tonk area the locals named "Lower Broad," because it is at the end of Broadway, away from the river. Here you will find a dense population of aspiring country artists performing in the hopes of being discovered. Tourists and locals alike provide enthusiastic support for these hopefuls. Some have attracted record label attention, most notably recording act BR549. Tootsie's is the most famous of the honky-tonks because of its back entrance into the stage of the Ryman Auditorium. Opry performers used to sit in Tootsie's while waiting to go on stage. Their faded and tattered pictures adorn the walls today. In those days there was no live music performed in Tootsie's—it was added in recent years to keep pace with the surrounding clubs. Tootsie's also has the coldest beer in town.

The Ryman Auditorium was the original home of the Grand Ole Opry before it moved out to the Opryland Hotel Complex. Originally a church, it has been beautifully restored and houses an interesting museum on Opry's history. Today the Ryman hosts a variety of outstanding musical offerings. Extreme care is taken to ensure the highest quality of perfor-mances on the Ryman stage. No trip to Nashville would be complete without attending a concert or a musical event at the Ryman, just to enjoy the superb acoustics and historical significance. Also a must for your itinerary is the spectacular Country Music Hall of Fame, where you can have lunch or a snack in the majestic lobby. Be sure to check their Web site during your visit, as they often have music industry events you might want to attend (*www.countrymusichalloffame.com*).

The Opryland Hotel Complex is located northeast of the city, near the airport. It was at one time the largest convention hotel in the United States. The Opryland Theme Park was unique in its mix of fast rides, quality food courts, and many music stages throughout the beautifully landscaped park. Being one-of-a-kind is difficult, though, and competition with faster, scarier theme parks prompted Opryland decision makers to take a different course. They closed the park and replaced it with Opry Mills, a huge shopping mall and entertainment center. Disgruntled Nashvillians who miss their beloved theme park have dubbed Opry Mills "Shopry-land"!

For tourists and conventioneers, the Opryland Hotel has much to offer. The hotel itself is spectacular, especially during the Christmas holidays. Several huge arboretums grace the interior, along with waterfalls, clusters of little shopping and restaurant communities, and an indoor boat ride. Lots of live entertainment is offered. The General Jackson Showboat offers dinner cruises on the Cumberland River. The Springhouse Golf Club has one of the more popular eighteen-hole courses in the city. The award-winning country radio station WSM-AM/FM is part of the Opryland Complex and broadcasts live from the stage of the Grand Ole Opry.

The Grand Ole Opry is a unique show all its own, a very exclusive fraternity unlike any other. The Opry is presented every Friday and Saturday night, in half-hour segments, each segment hosted by a different celebrity. Performers wander on and off stage casually, as if it were a radio show only, and not the live performance that it really is. Family and friends of the performers sit on stage in a special section reserved for them. There are regulars on the show, and Opry members take turns performing throughout the year. Although membership in the Grand Ole Opry does not impel artists' careers, acceptance into the fraternity is still a very important milestone for them. While Nashville's tourism industry is perceived to be all about country music, the most interesting tourist attractions are far removed from the music industry. The Cheekwood Botanical Garden and Museum of Art, once the private estate of the Cheek family of the Maxwell House Coffee fortune, is now home to a valuable collection of eighteenth and nineteenth century paintings and decorative art, featuring prominent American artists. The many different gardens are breathtaking. Civil War enthusiasts will want to visit the Carnton House in nearby Franklin, where a family fought the battle in their own backyard. President Andrew Jackson's home, the Hermitage, is located in Nashville, as well as the elegant Belle Meade Mansion and Carriage House. In the summer you can enjoy a picnic while listening to jazz on the lawn of these two magnificent estates.

Residents of Nashville are very blessed indeed. Their graceful, attractive city provides an easygoing lifestyle, with lots to do evenings and weekends. Everyone is friendly and moves at a slow pace. It's easy to get around if you have a car, but one important warning: Street names change at random. For example, Wedgewood becomes Blakemore, which then becomes Thirty-first Avenue South—all in just a two-mile stretch. Broadway splinters off into West End, which eventually becomes Harding Road before it splits into two highways, 100 and 70. So do as the natives do—slow down your pace and stop to enjoy life. That's easy to do in Music City, U.S.A.

A BRIEF HISTORY OF MUSIC IN NASHVILLE

The Nashville music scene has changed drastically from the days when the Ryman Auditorium was the home of the Grand Ole Opry. Back then, in the 1930s, the Opry was an important part of the country music scene, and the Opry's live show on WSM was the most significant of many live radio broadcasts across the country. Performers would vie for a chance to appear on the Opry, as this was where record labels looked for new talent. Numerous country legends such as Hank Williams, Roy Acuff, and Ernest Tubb launched their remarkable careers from the Ryman stage.

Downtown Nashville was where the action was. Every Friday night performers and others in the music industry stood and chatted in the hallways of the Charleston Hotel (no longer there). Other artists, such as Dolly Parton and Country Music Hall of Famer Uncle Dave Macon, stayed at the Merchant's Hotel on Broadway, downtown's main street. (Merchant's is no longer a hotel, but an elegant restaurant.) Everyone, including dynamic Brenda Lee, fondly remembers hanging out at Linebaugh's sandwich shop (no longer there, a courtyard next to Merchant's marks the spot). John Hartford immortalized Linebaugh's and the changing times by writing the lament, "Nobody Eats at Linebaugh's Anymore," recorded by himself and the New Grass Revival. Hartford's song is a fitting tribute to the era many fondly remember, when the nearby Printers Alley was a one-block alley filled with bars featuring live country bands.

By the mid-1950s Nashville was well established as a leading music center and was dubbed "Music City, U.S.A." by a pop radio station disc jockey. Hank Williams' *Jambalaya* and *Your Cheatin' Heart*, Red Foley's *Chattanooga Shoe Shine Boy*, and many other country songs crossed over to the pop charts. Legendary producer Owen Bradley made the first record in Nashville (Zeke Clements' *Night Train to Memphis*) at a studio built in the WSM radio station on the top floor of the L&C Tower at Fourth and Union Streets. Then, in 1958, RCA Records asked Bradley to build a studio for the label in Nashville. They chose a site close to downtown, now known as Music Row. (Studio B, as it was called, is now part of the Country Music Hall of Fame Museum.) Bradley has a park on Music Row named after him in honor of the man who established Nashville as the center of country music.

Once RCA established offices in Nashville, others quickly followed suit. Visionary music publishers Jack Stamp (formerly of Tree Music Publishing, now Sony/ATV Tree) and Bill Hall (formerly of Welk Music Group, now Universal Music Group) situated their offices nearby. BMI, the first performing rights society to collect performance royalties for country music, opened a Nashville office. The Country Music Association was founded in 1958, and ground was broken for the Country Music Hall of Fame and Foundation in 1964.

But, while the tiny Music Row community continued to grow, the impact of rock 'n' roll took its toll on country radio. As Fats Domino, Chuck Berry, and Elvis Presley dominated the airwaves, the number of country music stations began to dwindle. The Grand Ole Opry and other live radio shows lost their importance in establishing country artists. As in many cities, Nashville's downtown district began to seriously deteriorate. The Ryman Auditorium was no longer the center of activity for country music throughout the nation or in Nashville. (In 1974, the Opry moved out to the newly built Opryland Complex of hotel, mall, and auditorium, preserving the Ryman as a museum.)

Still, Nashville continued to make great records, and somehow, the music got out there. The industry discovered that demand for music revolved in cycles, making pop/rock popular for a while, then shifting to country music. Then, it cycles back to pop/rock or rap or Latino, then back to country. Now the market is changing drastically. With the deregulation of the airwaves, smaller radio stations are being bought at a frightening pace. Radio programmers who once determined the playlists for forty stations now program five hundred stations. The Internet, with the innovation of the mp3 format and file sharing, has changed the way music is marketed and sold.

There will always be changes in the country music industry. But one thing is constant: A great song, a great singer, a great musician all stand the test of time. And Nashville will always be on the lookout for great new talent.

ABOUT MUSIC ROW

The Nashville music industry is tucked into a quiet residential district just southwest of downtown, on Sixteenth, Seventeenth, Eighteenth, and Nineteenth Avenues, between Blakemore/Wedgewood, Broadway and Division Street, two miles deep and less than a mile wide. Ninety-nine percent of everything to do with the country music recording industry takes place within this small area. A few recording studios are located outside these boundaries but, for the most part, the business of music takes place here.

Once upon a time, not too long ago, the bulk of the music industry was located in beautiful old houses along Music Row. They were not recognizable as publishing companies, artist management companies, and other music-related businesses. Then along came Garth. The country music boom began. Major record companies built big new buildings and others followed suit. The landscape of Music Row changed drastically. Whereas ten years ago you could stand in the middle of Music Row and feel like you were in a residential area, today there is no mistaking the presence of successful music businesses.

It is impossible to calculate what portion of income the city derives from the country music recording industry, since much of the income it generates is collected and reported in other states, through main corporate offices. There are no statistics available on how many people travel to Nashville, work in the city's service occupations, and patronize its hotels, condos, restaurants, and stores because of the country music industry. But you don't need statistics to tell you that the impact of country music on Nashville is astounding. You will be amazed at the number of people you meet in service capacities who are aspiring songwriters or artists. You will especially be astounded at the remarkable talent everywhere you turn—not only performers featured in special showcases, but even those just "sitting in" at a corner bar. The competition is incredible and the city is saturated with talent. How you interact with this competition and present your own special gifts is very important.

That's what this book is all about. You will learn how to display your own particular talent in the best possible light and how to time your approach to give yourself the very best advantage. Most important of all, you will learn how the Nashville music industry thinks. The purpose of making a trip to Nashville is not to learn about the music industry. It is assumed that you already know the difference between a manager and a booking agent, between a producer and an engineer; the function of a performing rights society (and can name all three), of an A&R executive, and of a publisher; what a publisher can do for you; and a little bit about copyright protection.

If you are a country music singer and/or musician or if you are a songwriter of almost any kind of music, frequent visits to Nashville are a must. It may not be the best place for you to perform or showcase your talent, because sometimes it is best to be discovered outside of Nashville, in your own setting, but the business end of country music is centered on

(continued on page 10)

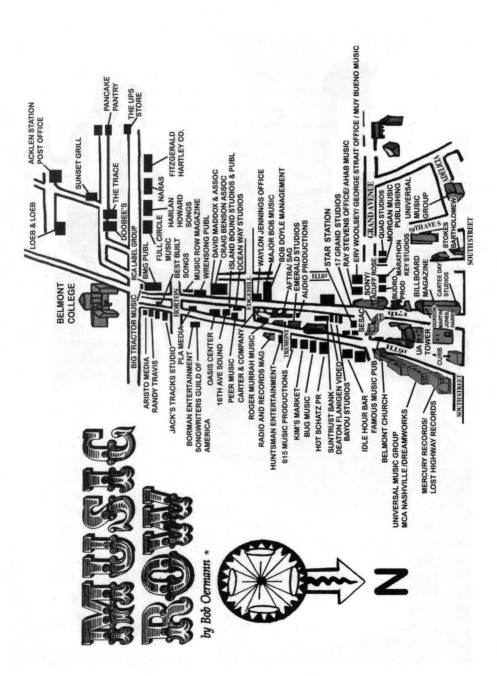

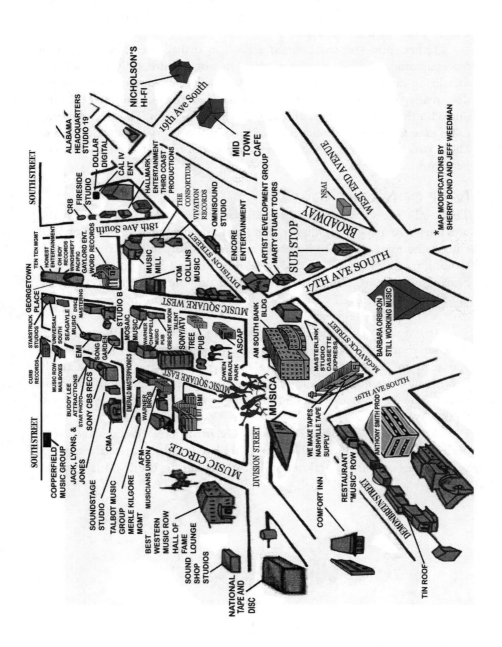

Music Row. All major record labels have divisions in Nashville, independent of their New York or Los Angeles offices. The signing of country acts, A&R representation, promotion, and marketing are run by these divisions. The same is true for publishing companies. Most country music publishers are located in Nashville because the people they are trying to reach on a daily basis work in Nashville.

Other music-related businesses, such as management, booking, legal representation, and other matters that do not require daily contact and socializing can be located just about anywhere; it really doesn't matter. What does matter is that you go to Nashville and meet the decision makers. Find out who they are, how they think, and what they want. They are the ones calling the shots. They are the ones who control country music. You need to know what their needs are and whether you can fill that need. If not now, perhaps in the future.

MAP OF MUSIC ROW

This bird's-eye view of the heart of Nashville's music industry (on the previous two pages) highlights the major companies on the Row. Of course, there isn't room to list every single company, and the ones you are looking for might not be listed here, but this will help you to get your bearings. If you are able to do nothing else on your first trip to Nashville but familiarize yourself with a few of the businesses on this map, you will have accomplished a great deal.

It would be a good idea to take one morning or afternoon just walking around the Row with this map, making notes of the companies you plan to visit as you go. Note that Music Square West is actually Seventeenth Avenue South, and Music Square East is Sixteenth Avenue South. The street names and numbering system change once you pass Grand Avenue.

Music Row celebrity Robert K. Oermann created the artist's rendering of Music Row in 1990. It was updated with additional drawings and a little computer tweaking by Jeff Weedman for the 2004 landscape.

2

A Crash Course on the Music Industry (As It Pertains to Nashville)

Copyright protection is one of the biggest concerns of a songwriter making his first trip to Nashville. What if someone hears his great idea, takes the hook, changes the lyrics, and thereby steals his song? It's a catch-22 for writer and publisher alike. Everyone has to be careful and wary. You have to find your comfort zone.

COPYRIGHT PROTECTION

A song is protected from the moment of creation. The problem is proof of creation. If you have unlimited funds, register every song with the Copyright Office of the Library of Congress, which almost always has the final say.

However, most Nashville publishers do not register a song with the Copyright Office until there has been some strong interest in it. Only if they are certain that a song will be recorded will they go ahead and register it. If every demo in Nashville were registered the Library of Congress would need a new building just to hold all the CDs! Waiting until you are further along in the process is a good idea, because your songs are probably going to go through some changes before they are finally recorded with the Copyright Office.

What you can do, whenever you put any of your songs in print, is protect them with a copyright notice: © 2005 John Doe, all rights reserved, is best; but just © 2004 will do. ALWAYS put this copyright notice on every CD and lyric sheet you create, even for home use—no exceptions. If your song is what you consider to be a finished creation, make a copy, put it in an envelope, and mail it to yourself. Do not open the envelope, and put it in storage. This is what is known as a "poor man's copyright." It won't hold up in court, and you shouldn't rely on it to protect your song, but it is a good first step until your song has actually been placed "on hold" by an artist.

If you are really worried about your songs falling into unscrupulous hands, go ahead and spend the money to register them legally. Do whatever you deem necessary to protect them, and when you get to Nashville, stop worrying about it. It will be essential for you to share your songs with as many people as you possibly can. Sing them, give them to songwriters, give them to publishers, give out as many copies as possible. Give away all you brought with you.

If you are an independent artist with your own finished CD project that you plan to promote to radio, it is very important for you to copyright your entire CD as a *sound recording*. This method of copyright is being used more often by independent artists to protect their album project. Once registered, send proof of registration to the artists's performance rights organization, SoundExchange, at *www.soundexchange.com*. They will collect royalties for every digital use of your album on satellite radio, Web casts, and cable TV (but not terrestrial radio). This is an important new change in the copyright law. (See more about this on page 17 under "About Digital Watermarking and Fingerprinting.")

THE ROLE OF A MUSIC PUBLISHER

Under copyright law, every song has to be published, and the publisher keeps 50 percent of the total earnings of the song for a minimum of thirty-five years, depending on what he can negotiate. So even if you write a song and your best friend Garth Brooks records it, you still have to have a publisher for your song. Have you heard that you should probably try to keep your own publishing? Don't even think about it. Nashville publishers are your best contact in Nashville. You can meet with producers and A&R execs directly; you can pitch directly to artists. But you are still going to need a publisher. Every song must have a publisher, and even if you've legally set up your own publishing company, it doesn't carry much weight in Nashville.

It's the publisher's job to demo songs (with his own money, not yours!), pitch the song to the right artists, and register the song with the Copyright Office. (The publishing company holds the copyright to the song, not the writer. If the songwriter previously registered the song, the publisher re-registers it in the company's name and gets an assignment of copyright from the writer.) The publisher registers the song with the proper collection agencies (there are lots of them), collects royalties, negotiates synchronization licenses (TV and film), markets the song to film companies, TV and cable shows, etc., and gives 50 percent of all earnings to you, the writer.

Nashville publishers do a lot more: They encourage developing writers and artists to build relationships with other artists in order to better understand what types of songs they relate to, set up co-writing opportunities, and generally help their writers network in the community. Nashville publishers are worth their weight in gold!

THE ROLE OF THE PROS

Performing Rights Organizations (PROs) collect money every time a song is played on the air. Mostly, collections come from radio airplay, but they also come from large and small music venues, TV, movies, restaurants, jukeboxes, and the Internet. They come from any place that uses music to attract business. PRO income is *more than half* of a songwriter's royalty income on a hit song single, the other half collected by publishers for mechanical and print royalty income.

ASCAP, BMI, and SESAC use very different systems for discerning who gets paid what, but their age-old methods are rapidly changing with the advent of fingerprinting technology. They will wear you out trying to convince you that their method is the best! Currently in Nashville, the importance of the PROs lies more in networking opportunities, since it's hard to determine who pays the most royalties. But that may change as the use of technology makes monitoring more accurate. Study each PRO thoroughly, talk to other writers, and take your time before you sign on with one company. Publishers belong to all three PROs, but a writer can only join one of them.

Each PRO office in Nashville is actively involved in finding hit songwriters, artists, and musicians and directing them to the best publisher, artist manager, or booking agent. Therefore, all three of the PROs should be an important stop in Nashville.

THE ROLE OF AN A&R DEPARTMENT

A&R stands for "Artist and Repertoire". Each record company has an A&R department. Its job is to assist each artist with selecting songs for her next album project and to coordinate the various outside parties that are also involved in the song selection process. Besides the artists themselves, who will often make appointments with publishers to go into their offices and listen to songs, other people who are looking for songs include record producers (usually not part of the record company) and artist managers. Also, most artists write or co-write songs for their album, so they have their own publishing company which is connected with one of Nashville's major publishing companies. That publisher may help the artist look for songs from other companies as well as their own catalogs, a very common practice in Nashville. The artist's A&R rep has to coordinate all the songs collected from these different sources.

Once the A&R rep has determined that a good number of songs are under consideration, he will call a meeting of all those concerned: artist, producer, and maybe the artist manager as well. They will decide which songs they are serious about, and then the A&R rep will call the publishers of the songs and put the songs "on hold." The "hold" policies of record companies and producers often come under fire from Nashville's music publishers. Once a song is put "on hold" for an artist, the publisher is prohibited from pitching it to another artist, tying-up a great copyright. Publishers object to this practice when the A&R rep puts too many songs "on hold" (more than can be recorded) and the recording session date is a long way off. The danger is that when they finally get in the studio they change their minds and don't record the song after all. In the meantime, the publisher has lost an important opportunity to pitch the song to another artist. An opportunity to pitch a great song to the right artist doesn't come along very often, considering that an artist may only record one album a year.

Usually, an A&R rep helps the artist decide on a direction for an album project. A ten-song album should have a common theme, some balance in tempo that includes a mix of up-tempo, mid-tempo, and ballads, and it should be consistent with the image of the artist.

The A&R department also helps coordinate all the different internal departments of the record company that affect an album project—marketing, promotion, and publicity. Each of these separate departments work closely together to "sell" an artist—and the songs are a very important part of that "sales pitch." It's the responsibility of the A&R reps to make sure the selected songs fit into the total picture of an artist's entire career, a big job when you consider how many different individuals are working separately to find songs for the artist.

THE DIFFERENCE BETWEEN AN ARTIST MANAGER AND A BOOKING AGENT

Although an artist manager and a booking agent have clearly defined roles, their jobs are intricately intertwined, making it essential for the two to cooperate. An artist manager has creative control over an artist's image: what songs to record, what clothes to wear, what clubs to play, what interviews to grant, what TV shows or films to do, what products to endorse, and all other issues which affect an artist's career.

The booking agent books all dates for the artist, which may sound simple on the surface, but is really a complicated process. An agent must handle moving an artist and his entourage across the country from city to city, booking the best clubs and state/county fairs, spacing performances so that the artist isn't overbooked or facing too much downtime, and must execute all of this in the best, most cost-effective manner. The booking agent books the dates, but the artist manager works with the artist's road manager, who makes sure all the stage equipment arrives and gets set up in time for the show, supervises concessions, and performs endless other tasks.

OTHER IMPORTANT PROFESSIONALS

It doesn't stop here. Artists need several more people on their payroll.

An Entertainment Attorney

Entertainment attorneys are needed to negotiate those very complicated recording contracts. They cover not only the percentage points an artist will make on the sale of each album, but controlled compositions (a kickback to the record company on songs the artist writes), video costs, special markets like record clubs, and many more factors that cut into the potential earnings for the artist. In the music industry, and in Nashville particularly, an entertainment attorney is an integral part of an artist's career. In fact, if you are an artist or musician looking for a record deal, a great entertainment attorney may be a good place to start.

A Business Manager

There are so many people on an artist's payroll, and so many different sources of income, it's a full-time job just keeping track of it all. Most artists turn this big job over to a business manager. It's not unusual for an artist to be put on "an allowance," with the business manager deciding how much can be spent on a house, on clothes, and even on dinner Friday night!

An Accountant

A business manager doesn't file the complicated tax returns required for an artist. He'll need an accountant to do that, and manage long-term investment planning.

A Publicist

The record company handles most of the publicity needs for the artist, but an outside publicist can make a big difference in an artist's career. Again, for the artist or musician looking for a record deal, a great publicist can be just the place to start.

There are so many people on the artist's payroll—so many taking a piece of the pie—that it takes a rather long time for the artist to start realizing any substantial income. From the record company expense-side alone, an artist who sells 500,000 albums will just break even. Artists selling under that amount are usually dropped from the label after two, or even one album release.

THE COUNTRY CHART SYSTEM

The Nashville major record labels use one predominant method of marketing their product: They heavily promote a single song chosen from an artist's current album to be played on targeted country radio stations across the country. They work closely with the station program directors that sometimes control the programming for as many as five hundred stations. In the early 1980s, when record labels were told that new technology could monitor exactly how many times a single had been played, the record companies rejected that system and went with one that was more easily manipulated. Technology won. Today, record companies use "fingerprinting" to trace the use of their product.

Record companies use *Billboard's Country Airplay Monitor* to chart the progress of their country singles. *Billboard* in turn uses Broadcast Data Systems (BDS) to monitor which songs are being played, and how many times per day. The Top 10 songs get 37 percent of the airplay; the Top 20 get 26 percent. That's over 50 percent of total airplay for those twenty songs. Combined, the Top 25 songs get 74 percent of airplay; songs that chart from fifty-one through one hundred get only 3 percent of airplay. If you just get a chart position of fifty or so, you're not really in the game. Those levels are not going to pay much at all. These figures pertain to mainstream country radio.

Americana radio stations and other small niche stations are not monitored by BDS or *Billboard*. There was a trade publication, *Gavin*, which had an Americana chart, but they are no longer in business. So the Americana Music Association started their own chart system, which tracks the amount of airplay Americana and non-mainstream country artists receive. This chart is more of a marketing tool for an artist to attract the attention of a major record label or to help sell CDs. Very little money, if any, is collected for performance rights. This is why an independent artist should be very careful about marketing his own CD to radio; a lot of money can be spent, with no possibility of a return on his investment.

ABOUT DIGITAL WATERMARKING
AND FINGERPRINTING

A digital watermark is a non-audio code that is embedded into sound and video recordings. The term comes from the watermarking system that already exists for high-quality stationery and currency. In those industries, a watermark serves as a code of excellence and authenticity. Audio watermarks are more specific. They contain information about copyright ownership and can include as much information as desired: date, copyright registration numbers, publisher, writer, and so on. This code becomes an integral part of the music itself as it travels through any transmission media, including radio, television, cable, satellite, Internet, CD, DVD, and cassette tape. There are many different companies creating their own watermarking systems.

Fingerprinting is a system used to log a song into a database that can detect whenever that song is played on radio. The largest and most recognized audio database system is Broadcast Data Systems, or BDS. All major record companies, and most independent record companies, use BDS to monitor the airplay of their songs. They do this by sending BDS a fifty-nine-second version of their song. BDS then logs this fifty-nine-second song into their database, thereby making a "fingerprint" of the song. BDS then monitors selected radio stations to determine when this fingerprint of the song is played. At the end of the day BDS provides a report to *Billboard Country Airplay Monitor* and the performing rights organizations, which also are interested in radio airplay. There are approximately 2,500 stations that play country music in all, and BDS monitors more than half of all country radio. Over the years BDS has logged millions and millions of songs, claiming to log 100 million songs a year for all music genres combined.

The technology is rapidly changing, and there are many new companies that excel in fingerprinting methods. One new company can monitor a song with a ten-second version of a song. But the fact that BDS already has a huge database of songs helps keep them in front of the competition. SESAC was the first to use BDS to monitor airplay for their affiliates and still uses this system. ASCAP and BMI each have their own fingerprinting systems, and use a combination of their system and BDS to calculate airplay for their members.

This may all have changed by the time this book is in print. One very new technology that came about because of the ability to monitor digital audio is SoundExchange. CEO John Simpson, the former manager for Mary Chapin Carpenter, created this new nonprofit performing rights organization for artists and record companies. SoundExchange licenses, collects and distributes revenues for the use of sound recordings on cable, satellite and webcast services. Prior to 1995, sound recording copyright owners (SRCOs) did not have a performance right. This meant that, unlike their counterparts in most of Europe and other nation around the world, recording companies and artists were not entitled to receive payment for the public performance of their works.

The Digital Performance in Sound Recordings Act of 1995 and the Digital Millennium Copyright Act of 1998 changed all that by granting a performance right in sound recordings. As a result, copyright law now requires that users of music pay the copyright owner of the sound recording for the public performance of that music via certain digital transmissions. This is still a small amount of collections for the use of record company product, but it is the beginning of a whole new way of looking at our industry.

Who knows what is next? Stay tuned!

DIFFERENT SOURCES OF INCOME AND HOW IT IS COLLECTED

For a songwriter, there are two primary sources of income: performance and mechanical. Performance money is collected by one of the PROs and paid directly to the writer. The publisher will share in 50 percent of the performance earnings, but the PRO will pay the writer and publisher separately.

Mechanical earnings come from the sale of CDs and cassettes. There is a statutory rate for all mechanicals, so everyone is paid the same for each three minutes of recorded music. The record companies issue a royalty statement four times a year, one each quarter; and they categorize their mechanical earnings according to publishers, including songs from several different CDs and cassettes on one royalty statement. Because this can get very confusing, the National Association of Music Publishers set up a clearinghouse for publishers called the Harry Fox Agency. Most publishers belong to this agency. The record company sends their royalty statement to the Harry Fox Agency, which reviews the statement, keeps 4.5 percent for the effort, and then sends the money and statement to the publisher.

The publisher then creates its own royalty statement, which lists all of the writer's songs and all of the different record companies who have paid mechanicals on these songs. The publisher keeps 50 percent of the earnings and sends the other 50 percent to the writer. It would be unethical for the publisher to deduct any fees or services—demo costs, for example—from the writer's 50 percent share. All costs incurred in the marketing of a song are the publishers responsibility. It is a generally accepted practice to deduct the Harry Fox fees off the top, with the publisher and the writer absorbing 2.25 percent each. Although the publisher collects from Harry Fox four times a year, the writer gets paid only twice a year: on February 15 for the collection period of July through December, and on August 15 for the period of January through June.

The terminology of publishing income is very confusing. If a song earns $100, the publisher and writer each receive $50. However, the 50 percent share of the publisher is referred to as 100 percent of the publishing. So if a publisher says he has 100 percent of a song, he means he will get fifty percent of the earnings from the song. Usually, there is more than one publisher for a song, and two publishers will generally split the earnings

50/50. Splits for other than equal shares are very rare. The same applies for co-writers. If you decide to share your ideas with another writer and you end up writing most of the song, be prepared to give away 50 percent of the song anyway. It's just the way it's done, and if you aren't willing to share 50/50, your co-writer will feel like she's been treated unfairly.

Artists have lots of different sources of income: They are paid a certain number of percentage "points" for each CD sold (this can vary widely depending on what an artist is able to negotiate; that's why you need that great lawyer!). The sad thing is that almost everything a record company spends on an artist—the master recording, videos, costs associated with TV appearances, and advances to help the artist get by until he starts establishing an income—are taken out of the artist's royalties. So an artist really won't make anything unless he sells over 500,000 units; that's usually the break-even point. A record company is almost like a lending company, putting up the money to launch an artist's career. Other income for an artist comes from concerts, merchandise sales, songwriting, and some publishing revenue if he's lucky enough to establish his own publishing company.

Here is the most startling thing about this industry: an artist does not get paid for radio airplay! Only the writer and the publisher are paid for all that wonderful music we hear on the radio. That's why artists want to write and publish their own music if they can. What they usually wind up doing is co-writing with a hit songwriter. The hit writer may bring the most expertise to the table, but he is almost assured of getting his song on the album in return.

Musicians don't earn any royalties at all. They get a flat fee and that's it. There is a set union scale, and session musicians earn double, triple, or more. Once the record is cut, that's it. It doesn't make any difference whether it sells fifty or 500,000. But down the line, if the master session they played on is used in a film or some other source, musicians are paid the same fee again.

In Nashville, most of the live music clubs are considered "writers" clubs—so the club owners get away with not paying anything at all for the great music performed in their clubs night after night. Clubs vary greatly in the way they book and "pay" bands. For the clubs that allow a cover charge, the band usually gets to charge at the door and has some kind of agreement to share the earnings with the club owner. Other clubs don't allow bands to charge a cover, so those bands have to rely on a "tip jar" set up at the front of the stage. Another famous Bradley, Harold Bradley, brother of Owen, is president of the local musicians' union, the AFM. Since taking on presidential duties, he has worked hard to try to help musicians get paid in Nashville clubs. There is a reasonable club rate set by the union that can be used as a negotiating tool, but the chances of getting paid to play are still slim.

I hope that this chapter has given you a quick overview of the music industry, so that you have an idea of how things work when you come to Nashville to pitch your songs. However, a more comprehensive understanding of the music field—applicable law, possible careers, technological advances, etc.—is always desirable and useful. For information about these and other aspects of the music business (see "Recommended Reading" on pages 232–235).

3

How to Know If Your Talent Measures Up to Nashville Standards

OK, we know. Your mom (or spouse, or kid) loves your songs. There is an intrinsic special quality to your songs, because they are part of you. It is wonderful that you have a gift to share your thoughts, feelings, and emotions through songs. However, they may not be commercial.

LITMUS TEST FOR SONGWRITERS

You need an objective opinion in order to evaluate your song's commercial potential, and here is how to get one:

1. **Have your song evaluated by the Nashville Songwriters Association International** (NSAI). Their Web address is *www.nashvillesongwriters.com.* You will probably have to join in order to take advantage of their song critique service, but it will be worth it. Joining NSAI is the most important step you can take in the advancement of your Nashville songwriting career.

2. **Have your song evaluated by a songwriters' organization in or near your hometown.** Join every songwriters' organization in your vicinity. Start going to as many meetings as you possibly can, performing or playing your songs for members, critique sessions,

anything that can get you some feedback from other writers or publishers. If you don't know of any organizations near you, then call NSAI at (800) 321-6008 and ask them for the one closest to you. NSAI has chapters all across the country. Come to think of it, information about the chapters is also posted on their Web site.

3. **Attend songwriting seminars, workshops, and conferences.** There are many of these held all across the country every month. Start seeking them out and attending as many as you possibly can. You will learn a lot and meet some very important people who may influence your songwriting or artistic career. How can you find them? Try songwriter magazines, music magazines, the Web, and the PROs.

4. **Get professional advice from the PROs.** ASCAP and BMI have offices in New York, Los Angeles, Chicago, Atlanta, Miami, London, Puerto Rico, and Nashville; SESAC in New York, London, and Nashville. If you are close enough to any one of these cities to visit their offices, then do so and ask for an *honest* evaluation of your songs. You want to know if they would be willing to invest time in the advancement of your career. If they think you are talented, they will want to help you as much as they can, because they make money when you are successful. If they don't see any potential in your music, then you have to ask yourself why. They are an excellent barometer for your songs.

5. **Call and ask permission to send a song for evaluation to the Nashville PRO offices.** You have to ask for a writers' representative by name, so it will take a little research on your part to learn who writers' representatives are. BMI has a policy to give an evaluation if asked. ASCAP and SESAC might be a little tougher to get someone to agree to listen, but they are both worth a try.

6. **Enter a song contest.** Again, you will have to track them down through songwriter magazines, music magazines, the Web, and the PROs.

7. **Contact recording studios in your immediate area and ask for their feedback.** They are in the song business—what do they think of your songs?

8. **Try to get a local band to perform or record your songs.** Who are you writing for? People who love your music! They don't have to be just the top recording artists. Your songs could shine with an unknown artist. Which bands and artists are the most popular in your area? What do they think of your songs?

LITMUS TEST FOR ASPIRING ARTISTS AND MUSICIANS

In order to attract the attention of Nashville record labels, you are going to need a pretty awesome track record as a performing artist. They will be looking for experience—it helps if you've played in bands for years, and maybe won some awards (local contests). If you are packing them in at the local watering hole on weekends, it won't be difficult to get someone from Nashville to come and see your act. Aim for the top. What label do you think you'll fit in the best? Call that company and let it know what's going on in your hometown. What producer do you want to work with? What publisher? What artist manager? What booking agent? Call these people if you really have a strong following in your local club and can count on a good enthusiastic crowd.

They are looking for a unique quality. It is very, very important that you have a strong self-image. Contrary to what you might have heard, the record labels will not shape you into what they want you to be. You have to decide who you are and stick to it. That is harder than it sounds, because you probably can and have sung and played all styles of music. But they are listening to what you are trying to tell them—your own personal message.

You must perform original music for the music industry. You probably have a great repertoire of country favorites that you perform regularly in a local club; fans like to hear the hits. But the industry wants to hear new songs. If you don't write your own material, then you will have to find some great writers who will let you perform their songs. If you can find some writers who can't perform their songs themselves, then you have a perfect situation. You will be helping each other.

How much time have you spent in a recording studio? It is much harder than you might think to get your message across in a studio. There is a lot going on that has nothing to do with you, but it will distract you and interfere with your performance. Just picking the right microphone for your voice is a major challenge. The more experience you have had in this area, the better. You might want to hang around local studios and offer your services for free if you need more studio time under your belt.

4

A Basic Understanding of Music Row

Probably the one thing that is going to surprise you most about Nashville is how helpful everyone is. The main topic of conversation for just about everybody is, "Who's looking for songs right now?" Not only will your peers share this information with you, they will actually tell you how to get a song to whoever is looking. Although it is a highly competitive field, everyone on Music Row will go out of their way to help you succeed. It is a true fellowship, a camaraderie not found in any other highly competitive field.

The reason for this is that *the best song wins.* When it comes right down to it, it really doesn't matter who you are, who you know, or whether you've had songs recorded before. All that counts is that your song says what a particular artist wants to say, in the way she wants to say it.

THE WRITING ENVIRONMENT

The biggest mistake most songwriters make when they go to Nashville is to spend all their time trying to get appointments to play their songs for someone. As hard as this may be to understand, appointments with publishers or producers should not be your highest priority. Spending as much time as possible in the writing environment should be your primary goal.

You will find yourself in the writing environment as soon as you step off the plane, hop off the bus, or pull your car up beside the motel door. Everyone in Nashville is a songwriter, or knows someone who is. Be open, be friendly to everyone you meet—they are going to be exceptionally friendly to you. And it's not just lip service—they mean it. Your Nashville experience starts the minute you arrive. The person you meet in the airport terminal might turn out to be the most valuable contact you make on your entire trip. Don't allow yourself to miss an opportunity by having certain expectations; be open to just about anything. Of course, there are places where songwriters "hang out," and you will want to spend as much time in these spots as possible. They are:

- Writers' nights and open mic nights (page 30)
- Publishing companies (chapter 5)
- Music Row area restaurants (chapter 10)
- The Acklen Station post office (chapter 10)
- Golfing, fishing, playing tennis (chapter 10)

Surprisingly enough, you are not likely to find songwriters in Nashville's tourist areas. All the places you've just read about—the Wildhorse Saloon, Tootsie's, the Grand Ole Opry—don't attract aspiring songwriters, artists, and musicians, unless there is a specific industry showcase taking place. This book will tell you how to figure out where to go to hang out with the industry, and how to tell the difference between an industry gathering and a tourist gathering.

THE IMPORTANCE OF COLLABORATION

Ninety percent of the songs recorded in Nashville are co-written and copublished. This is one more demonstration of the strong emphasis that Music Row places on networking and working together. The first question a publisher will ask a writer is, "who do you write with?" Co-written songs are taken more seriously in Nashville. There are many reasons for this phenomenon:

- Co-writing provides expanded opportunities for pitching the song
- Co-writers challenge each other to do their best writing
- Co-writers bring different skills to the songwriting project
- Co-writing is a learning experience that can't be duplicated in the classroom
- A well-known co-writer provides name recognition for an unknown writer
- Co-writing is motivational
- Co-writing provides opportunities to write with someone closely connected to an album project, such as the producer or artist

INDUSTRY INTERVIEW WITH JEFFREY STEELE

"I always tell songwriters the secret of success is 'Go there' . . . go to Nashville! A lot of songwriters outside of Nashville think like I did at one time, 'if I go there, I'll have to give up everything I stand for!' No, that's not true. But you do have to prove yourself. Al Anderson, longtime member of the influential band N.R.B.Q., is the one co-writer who really, really made me see not to doubt myself, and not to try to be anything else.

"It was the California earthquake that helped me make the decision to move to Nashville. My house was practically demolished. I decided if I was ever going to make the move, now was the time to do it. About this same time my band, Boy Howdy, broke up. We had released three albums on Curb Records, and had five hit songs, but fate intervened. Boy Howdy's drummer was in a bad car wreck, and although he recovered, he never had the energy required to keep up with this dynamic, rockin' band.

"I moved to Nashville, holed up in a room and started writing songs, making a commitment to myself to be as good as I could get. I set goals for myself and put blinders on to keep focused. I started making lists of things I wanted to accomplish, and in 1997 I wrote, 'I want to be Songwriter of the Year'. I accomplished that goal in 2003, because I wrote it down, focused on it, and made it happen.

"The move to Nashville also gave me the opportunity to meet great writers. Al Anderson, Craig Wiseman, Bob DiPiero and Kent Blazy were four of the first hit writers I met who gave me a chance to write with them and still let me express myself. Al and I wrote *Unbelievable* (Diamond Rio) and *Big Deal* (LeAnn Rimes). They became hit singles in 2000, and that was the year I wrote 250 songs in a one-year period! After that, people started coming to me for more songs.

"My dad always set the example. I learned from him that it is a lot more exciting to listen to someone else's story instead of telling your own over and over. So I started watching and listening at a very early age. As the youngest of five—two older brothers and two older sisters—there was a lot to see. I soaked it all in, getting a lot of perspective. They talked about Vietnam, and my father talked about his experiences in World War II—my sisters would take sides, creating dynamics between family members. I'm interested in the people I meet, where they live, where they are from; maybe some pretty lyric will come to me through their story.

"California had a great live country music scene back in the 1980s—the Palomino, Crazy Horse, and Silver Bullet. I started playing the clubs when I was seventeen, and hooked up with Boy Howdy in 1987. We became the number one L.A. club band, but the country music industry said we were 'too rock 'n' roll for country radio.' When the Gulf War broke out, I wrote a song called *When Johnny Comes Marching Home Again*. It was an up-tempo, John Cougar-ish type song. A lot of the clubs we played were near the El Toro Marine Base. The Marines flocked in to hear that song, and it became a big hit in L.A. All of a sudden, record labels were coming to see us! Everyone was interested in what we were doing.

"I was in the men's room at the Silver Bullet, and Dick Whitehouse of Curb Records was standing next to me. He said, 'I hate your band, but I love your songs!' I retorted, 'We don't think your record label is that great either!' 'Will you take a meeting with us next Monday?' Whitehouse said. 'Yes,' I replied. We played Curb a bunch of songs, including '*A Cowboy's Born with A Broken Heart*,' the band's first hit single. The war went away and so did our war song—it was never released as a single.

"One of the times I was writing my list of goals, I made a list of all my favorite songs. There are so many great songs throughout time—I thought they deserved recognition. So I wrote *Tip Your Hat to the Teacher*. This song I wrote without a co-writer, it was so personal to me. Music my dad listened to had a great influence on me . . . songs by Willie Nelson, Roger Miller, Johnny Bond's *Hot Rod Lincoln*, and so many more. I put them all in a song and included it in my solo album for Sony Music. They told me it was 'too rock 'n' roll' for country, but Marty Stuart recorded it and went on to have a hit with it.

"As a songwriter you will hear 'you can't do this, you can't do that!' My most important advice to all songwriters is, put the music first. Stay true to your heart. So many of my friends ask me, what did I do to change? Nothing's different—I never changed anything I did. Maybe I've gotten a little smarter, but it's just me going out, wanting to write stuff that people respond to. I feel I have a responsibility to touch nerves, so when people hear these songs, they mean something. When I first heard Montgomery Gentry sing *My Town* on stage; that was powerful. I love to write stories about life."

JEFFREY STEELE excels at songwriting, performing both as a lead singer and as a session player on bass, and in between 200 club dates a year, produces Montgomery Gentry (Sony) and Julie Edwards (Warner Bros). He was named BMI and NSAI's 2003 Songwriter of the Year, and BMI awarded Jeffrey for over twenty million airplays. Steele played bass on the title track for Steve Wariner's album *No More Mr. Nice Guy*. He started his own record label, 3 Ring Circus, with Lofton Creek Records, and their first album is titled *Outlaw*, released in July 2004. Jeffrey is also an avid weight lifter and mountain biker.

ABOUT THE AMERICANA FORMAT

Most of the writers you will run into in the Nashville clubs will be performing Americana music instead of Nashville's "formula" songs. Writers who hang out in the clubs and share their songs tend to write down-to-earth songs from the bottom of their heart. Until recently, these songs were hardly noticed by the Nashville music industry. But as record sales continue to fall, and the country fan base continues to diminish, the executives on Music Row have started to take notice of Americana writers and artists. As much as this book is about following the Nashville way of doing things, it is also about staying true to yourself. The Americana music format just may be where your music belongs.

As described by the Americana Music Association, Americana is American roots music based on the traditions of country. While the musical model can be traced back to the Elvis Presley marriage of hillbilly and R&B that birthed rock 'n' roll, Americana as a radio format developed during the 1990s as a reaction to the highly polished sound that defined the mainstream music of that decade. By also including influences ranging from folk to bluegrass to blues and beyond, Americana handily bridges the gap between Triple A radio and mainstream country.

One reason Americana has been squeezed out of the mainstream country radio format is because of the deregulation of the airways, and the change in law that allows one company to own multiple radio stations. Prior to deregulation, one company could own approximately fifty radio stations. Now Clear Channel Communications owns over five hundred radio stations—and the same person who was programming fifty stations now programs five hundred stations. The wide range of music choices narrowed down to just a few big artists, making it impossible for fresh new artists to get any radio play at all.

It was obvious to everyone, however, that there was a lot of great music that wasn't getting on the radio. In 1999, a loosely affiliated group of music industry leaders organized a "town meeting" during that year's SXSW convention to discuss the possibility of creating an Americana trade association. The fifty or more professionals in attendance overwhelmingly endorsed the idea of coordinating, sharing, and developing resources to expand the audience for Americana. Accordingly, and after much e-mail discussion, a formal event was convened during October 1999. At the conclusion of that professionally facilitated two-day conference, the Americana Music Association (AMA) was born.

One of the association's main purposes was to get more radio airplay for Americana artists. Even tried-and-true Americana artists like Johnny Cash and Willie Nelson were not played on Clear Channel Stations. So the AMA commissioned a study on Americana radio, and found the demographic profile of the listener to be predominantly male between the ages of twenty-five to forty-four, having four or more years of college education, making over $40,000 a year, and very active in purchasing CDs and attending live concerts. This study gave the AMA a target audience for radio advertisers.

The AMA also started its own charting system, so artists can see how they are doing in relation to other artists. For this chart, and more information on Americana artists and their association, go to *www.americanamusic.org*.

The writing environment in Nashville is rich with many different styles of music, filled with the kindest, most dedicated, sincere people, who wish as much success for you as they do for themselves. They will become your brothers and sisters, your mentors and students as you travel through the wonderful world of writers' nights in Nashville.

ABOUT WRITERS' NIGHTS AND OPEN MIC NIGHTS

In June of 1982, an entrepreneur by the name of Amy Kurland opened a little restaurant in Green Hills (south of downtown), featuring musical entertainment on weekends. She decided that, in a songwriting town of great stature, only original music would be played in her establishment. It became apparent rather quickly that the Bluebird Cafe was a room that was meant for acoustic music. She found as well that songwriters needed a place to share their songs with each other, so she set aside Sunday nights as "Writers' Night." The small restaurant, which has a capacity of only a hundred people, soon became standing room only on Sundays. It became necessary to hold auditions, and soon, Sunday nights were booked months in advance.

Within a short time, the Bluebird became a full-time music club with live music seven nights a week, from 6:00 P.M. until the wee hours of the morning. Today, the Bluebird Cafe is world-renowned. Much of the footage for the major motion picture about a songwriter in Nashville, *The Thing Called Love*, was shot inside the Bluebird. Those scenes captured the true essence of the magic that takes place in this unique setting. Also, many songwriters have gone on from their performances at the Bluebird to sign record deals, the most famous being Garth Brooks. Brooks had been seriously shopping for a record deal, had a great master recording that he had played for all the A&R reps and producers in Nashville, and was turned down by every label. He took the stage at the Bluebird to sing three of his songs at a writers' showcase. A representative from Capitol Records was in the audience, and the rest is history.

Amy has a strict policy concerning bookings at the club. All songs must be original material (no cover bands allowed), and songwriters must audition in advance either live or by tape (or now, CD) submission. And when you are in the club either listening to the performers or waiting for your turn to go on, don't be surprised if you get "shushed." There is no talking allowed during performances.

Another very important writers' club is Douglas Corner, on Eighth Avenue South. This club is always filled with writers, most of whom have had several songs cut by major artists. Writers have a very strong bond with their songwriting friends, and the majority of their time is spent playing their hits and their favorite songs (that may never get cut) with their buddies. All of the shows on the Douglas Corner stage are put on by full-time songwriters who actively co-write, pitch, and play their songs. Just the people you want to meet.

You can't go wrong if you spend your evenings in Nashville in one of these two clubs, but there are many, many others to consider. Since one of your goals should be to perform your songs on a writers' night showcase, one of the lesser-known forums might be easier to get a slot on the show. There are lots of different formats, as well. Here's what to look for:

Writers' Nights

Writers' nights are generally a one or two-hour rehearsed show. They vary greatly in format, but the common thread is that the shows consist of songwriters performing their own original material, usually by acoustic guitar. Songwriters audition live or by CD submission. It is especially interesting to be able to hear a well-known hit performed on an acoustic guitar by the person who wrote it. This has to be, without a doubt, the best classroom available for a developing songwriter.

Performing Rights Organizations' Writers' Nights

ASCAP, BMI, and SESAC all produce their own writers' nights, featuring their own writers (or writers they are hoping to sign soon). There is no predicting when they will hold a writers' night, so you might want to give them a call to see if they have one scheduled. If they do, make sure you don't miss it! The writers are guaranteed to be top-rate.

Publishers' Writers' Nights

Similarly to performing rights organizations' writers' nights, publishers showcase their writers to the industry from time to time. Not only will the writers be some of the best in Nashville, but the audience will most likely be filled with industry executives, A&R, producers, other writers, and other publishers—another don't-miss-under-any-circumstance event. This kind of showcase will not be easy to find—this is where your networking skills will be put to the test. You will find hints about how to hone those skills later in the book.

Hit Songwriter Nights

Big-hit songwriters will put on a show from time to time, usually to raise money for charity, but sometimes just because they want to. They might sing a lot of their hits, or songs they just wrote. Either way, it's really interesting to see them perform. You'll find a lot of industry folks in the audience as well.

Writers in the Round

Whoever first started this format at the Bluebird Cafe really started something. Now it's the most popular format used. Four songwriters sit in a circle in the middle of the room and take turns singing their own songs and backing each other up. There's lots of ad lib chatter and joking around, and more than a tad of competition between the four of them.

Musicians' Showcase

Many studio musicians who enjoy playing together perform with various bands they have assembled. It's almost always *not* country music! And again, it's hard to find out about these showcases unless you are really familiar with the individuals who are playing. One rule of thumb: If musicians are playing a non-country, non-songwriter showcase at the Bluebird, they are probably popular studio musicians. Almost everyone who performs at the Bluebird has some industry connection.

Writer/Artist Showcase

Hit songwriters who are looking for an artist deal put on live shows—these are well-rehearsed, polished, full-band showcases. Some serious money is put into the show to make it as perfect as possible. Studio musicians are normally used; a publicist is hired to make sure the industry attends; and there is most likely a publisher or an artist manager involved as well. An aspiring artist needs to make sure all the bases have been covered before attempting a writer/artist showcase for the industry (see chapter 18).

These various types of showcases are featured every night in Nashville. The best nights to find industry types in the audience are Tuesday, Wednesday, and Thursday. The industry usually doesn't come out on a weekend night unless it's for something very special, or for an event planned by one of the several professional organizations. A serious songwriter, aspiring artist, and musician should plan to spend as much time as possible in these clubs, for a variety of reasons:

- It is a firsthand look at the competition
- It is a great opportunity to meet other writers and set up possible co-writing appointments

- It is not unusual for publishers, producers and/or record executives to be in the audience
- It is your opportunity, and the best opportunity Nashville has available, to pitch your songs

Think of writers' nights as your first priority. Plan to be out in the clubs every night. The cover charge at most clubs is under $10. At most writers' nights the audience mainly drinks water or coffee. In fact, it's hard for a club owner to make money on writers' nights, because the audience is in a work mode instead of a party mode. So you can have a few beers or not drink at all and be perfectly comfortable in the writers' night environment. Nothing is expected, except that you are courteous to the performers and listen quietly, applaud generously, and try to laugh at their jokes.

Open Mic Nights

Open mic nights are the best opportunity for songwriters and aspiring artists to perform on stage. Open mic nights operate on a first-come, first-serve basis. Writers show up about an hour before the showtime, sign up, and then wait for their turn to go onstage. The format is a two- or three-song acoustic guitar set, depending on the number of people that sign up. A piano is generally not available but there may be one or two extra mics set up if you want to have another guitar player, bass player, or vocalist for harmony. These songwriter forums are for original material only; no cover material is performed at open mic nights.

Open mics are usually scheduled at 6:00, 10:30, or 11:00 P.M. If you get there for the early open mic time and don't get on, you can stick around for the writers night, or leave and come back for the late time slots. Don't be worried about the neighborhood surroundings; although a lot of these clubs are in the "poorer districts," they are very safe areas and are welcomed to the neighborhood. East Nashville especially has become quite an important little place.

INDUSTRY INTERVIEW WITH STANTON MOTT

Stanton Mott is a deeply passionate person who moved his family from San Francisco to Nashville in 1984 to pursue his love of songwriting. He has had several singles and album cuts, including the single and album track, *Country Music Never Let Me Down* by Larry Jackson, which was a Top 10 chart single in Europe. In the two decades he has lived in Nashville, there have been highs and lows. Once he even considered moving back to San Francisco. Those feelings passed, his family put down roots, and they are now an integral part of Nashville community. His loving wife, Millie, has a successful career at Vanderbilt University where his son, Jonathan, is a student. Stanton has become a veteran player in Nashville's songwriting community. He took us

on an intimate guided tour of Nashville's writers' hangouts, and shared some of his secrets with our readers.

"A true songwriter just can't give up, and when you are out in the clubs, you will see the really dedicated songwriters. 'By their fruits you will know them'. Committed songwriters are always risking the high-wire act, performing their fresh new songs instead of the same ones their friends and fans come to expect. After awhile, it's discouraging to hear a writer perform the same three songs over and over.

"A true songwriter would write songs for nothing. He has to write songs forever, whatever the consequences. I've taken several different day jobs in Nashville, but I try not to do something that gets in the way of my songwriting. I didn't come to Music City to sell another end table! Perhaps my true calling will be to help show the new kids how to get out of their ruts! For the songwriter in a rut, I would advise you to expand your harmony studies—this will open up a whole new world! Improve your skills on your main instrument, and buy a metronome and learn to use it. I like the triangle-shaped, wind-up Taktell brand that sells for under fifty bucks.

"When a writer comes to Nashville, there are a lot of distractions that get in the way. Whatever moves forward I've made have been because I have worked on reducing those distractions. I've renamed anything that gets in the way of my songwriting as a distraction; something to be removed. The space created by the removal of these things is filled up with music. Most of us lack either the desire or the willpower to bring them under control and so working on doing that is as important as scales or a rhyming dictionary.

"A songwriter has to write about life. Even though there are only eight notes in the diatonic scale and four more in the chromatic, the songwriting possibilities are infinite. We've all seen what eight bits in a byte are capable of. Music is infinite in a way that we can never control and completely master. In some ways, there is nothing new. We recycle the same ideas, but humans forget! This may explain sitcom TV!

"Nashville has taught me a great lesson. It's not the writing of the song, it's the re-writing of the song! No matter how wonderful our original idea may be, it can always be better, clearer, and made easier for another artist to sing. I mean that, both the text of the lyric and the way they fall on the beats, affects the physical act of singing words and sounds.

"I run into so many songwriters that are worried that someone will steal their songs if they perform at writers' nights. They can look at it two ways—with scarcity or abundance! Jesse James probably got robbed by somebody! If it happens, you can say 'I've got something worth stealing!' The truth is that the chances that a new writer's work will be stolen are very small. It's just a fact that you can't copyright titles. The other side of the coin is to hide out and never take your songs out to test your ideas in the arena with other committed people. You'll miss getting their insights, experience, and companionship. Playing clubs is how you network in places like Nashville, whether you've been here for a while or just arrived. Songs are the children of your soul. Don't hide them in a closet. Take 'em out. Sure, they're going to get knocked around, but the water in the well gets sweeter and cooler.

"When I first came to town, two of my friends that I knew in San Francisco put a floor under me in Nashville. Mike Brown became my first co-writer and was responsible for tuning up my writing so that the first cuts could happen. He had a successful country band in San Francisco before moving here, and I was quite excited that he was willing to work with me. Art Sparer was a hellacious country guitar picker who is, unfortunately, no longer with us. He was at home on both acoustic and electric instruments. He played and jammed with such notables as Richard Leigh and Linda Ronstadt, and did some road band playing with Johnny Cash. Art took me over to the legendary Jack Clement's house and introduced me to the man who wrote the song that was the first piece of sheet music I ever bought, *Guess Things Happen That Way*. Arty introduced me to Tony Brown, Bob Oermann, and one of my favorite folks, Argyle Bell. Argyle started the popular and successful annual Gram Parsons tribute night until the man upstairs needed another player.

"A writer's life is practicing, studying (music theory), writing and re-writing your songs, and rehearsing them. Many young writers that play the clubs seem to be less effective for lack of rehearsal of their songs. They could all take Bob Dylan's advice, 'I'll know my song well before I start singing!' You need to rehearse if for no other reason than to show respect for yourself and the audience's time, money, and attention. If a writer lacks singing or instrumental skills, they should consider using other musicians to help them, especially when they play out.

Sometimes, writers' night hosts ask the writer to 'put a round together'—two or three other writers that will come in with you to do the night. Generally, one writer is asked to create the round and then is given an approximate time slot. This writers' round frequently shows up in *The Tennessean* and *Nashville Scene*, giving you free publicity!

"The major cause of failure in Nashville is not being authentic. This is a business of creativity—a person of genuine creativity has the best chance of making it to the top! When I came to Nashville in '84, it was the beginning of the full-tilt commercialization of mainstream country. Now "country music" seems to be struggling to define itself. Interestingly enough, I believe that I see the beginnings of a new scene emerging. In East Nashville, we are seeing a new Greenwich Village. Clubs and restaurants are springing up across the river with people playing music for the love of it, and enjoying each other while doing it. Rednecks are welcome, hippies are welcome, there are some very talented African-American writers, such as Sabrina, who are livening everything up. There's room for everyone!

"The last word of advice I'd like to give is that writers should carry around a little notepad to write down ideas as they present themselves. Keep it intact. Don't tear out pages! I hope to meet you all at one of the clubs listed below! Just remember, writers' nights are like a box of chocolates . . . you never know what you are going to get! Enjoy!"

NASHVILLE CLUBS THAT FEATURE WRITERS' NIGHTS AND OPEN MIC NIGHTS

Boardwalk Cafe
4114 Nolensville Pike
Tel: (615) 832-5104
    A legendary showcase club. The ownership has changed, but it's still important to the locals. A good venue to put on your resume. Jeff Lindsey has a new Monday night writers' night, and Jack Scott books a writers' night for the Boardwalk & the French Quarter. You can contact Jack at *www.writerartist.com* or (615) 826–9550.

Commodore Lounge (Holiday Inn)
2613 West End Avenue
Tel: (615) 327-4707
    Debi Champion is the queen of writers' nights! You can reach her at *championdebi@hotmail.com* or *www.mymusicguide.org/news*.

Douglas Corner
2106A 8th Avenue South
Tel: (615) 298-1688
    Douglas Corner has the reputation of being the club where the hit writers hang-out. It's the place to go to meet the top songwriters in town. Chet O'Keefe runs the Tuesday night writers' night.

The French Quarter Cafe
823 Woodland Street
Tel: (615) 227-3100

A great room with three different hosts: Contact Jack Scott (info on previous page under "Boardwalk Cafe"); Barbara Cloyd can be reached at *www. barbaracloyd.com;* and Terri Lynn, a blues-oriented singer, hosts a chart night. Practice your Nashville Number System skills and play with a hot band! You can reach her at *terrilynn1blues@aol.com.*

Hair of the Dog
1831 12th Avenue South
Tel: (615) 386-3311

You don't have to be Irish to enter! Don't let the neighborhood scare you away, it's in the resurgent 12 South neighborhood.

Hobo Joe's
918 Main Street
Tel: (615) 262-0096

The hip, cool place to be on any night in Nashville.

It's All Good Cafe
414 51st Avenue North
Tel: (615) 383-3881

A wonderful little club hosted by David Lee Slate.

Nashville Crossroads
419 Broadway

Lower Broad's newest addition, hosted by Lee (tacos and chili, man!) Rascone. It's located next door to Ernest Tubb's Record Shop—another place you want to be sure to check out!

NASHVILLE CLUB HOPPING: A NIGHT ON THE TOWN WITH STANTON MOTT

First Stop: East Nashville. "East Nashville is growing very rapidly," says Mott. "It's becoming a very important writers' area. It's really not that far from downtown—going East to the end of Broadway (West End) until you come to the Cumberland River, passing all the Lower Broad clubs like Tootsie's and Robert's Western World, turn left on First Avenue North. It will take you right over the river to East Nashville. You'll have to jog left to get to Main Street, then right on Main. Hobo Joe's will be on the right-hand side. In fact, we just passed Hobo Joe's, so let's make a right onto Woodland Street and stop in the French Quarter Cafe first, also on our right."

Jack Scott is behind the console. The French Quarter Cafe used to be a recording studio, so it has one big room with a stage at the far end. It has lots of room for a large band. We arrived just as a writers' round was getting onstage—a vocalist sitting on a tall stool, keyboardist front and center, and a rhythm guitarist. They took turns doing one of their songs, backing each other up with harmonies and instruments. As we were listening, a writer in a white shirt came in, checked in with Jack, and set his guitar in front of the console.

The French Quarter Cafe has lots of little rooms where you can sit and talk and eat, if you don't want to listen to music at the moment. It also has a pool table and great Cajun food! Yum! It all was very inviting.

We stayed to chat with Jack and listen to each writer do one song, then it was on to Hobo Joe's Songwriters Cafe. "This is the happening new place in Nashville," says Stan. "I especially love the writers' room, right here off the entry way." It has a desk, sofa and chairs—all a writer would need. Stan adds, "Writers can hang out here and tune their guitar for the next set, or write a song with friends, or just jot down some ideas. They usually have writing utensils as well, but they wind up walking off as souvenirs . . . I can't find anything to write with!" The main room has tables, sofas, a little wicker chair, with the bar and console along the back. It's not a large room, well lit so you feel like you are in someone's living room (almost!). Very comfortable.

At Hobo Joe's we ran into several writers' who have gained a nice reputation for themselves. Moke Cameron and Craig Lackey came over to say hello. Moke Cameron's song, *Getting Close* co-written with Craig Lackey and Larry Vail was signed to a publishing contract with RPM Music in Nashville, Tim McGraw's publishing company. It was the first song Moke ever demoed. Larry Vail's songs, *The Gift*, co-written with Craig Lackey, and *The Difference is Love*, co-written with Nicky Berns, were picked up by Noel Nutt at Horipro Publishing in Nashville. Craig Lackey's song, *Even the Angels Knew*, co-written with Cathy Carlson and Marty Axelrod, was placed in the NBC TV show *Passions*.

These are all major milestones in a writers' career, even if this first step doesn't wind up as a money jackpot! One thing that may have helped all of them along the way is that they are active members of the NSAI Los Angeles Area Workshop. NSAI has over a hundred workshops around the United States, and hit writers from Nashville and around the country interact with these workshops to help new writers. You can checkout the NSAI L.A. area Workshop at *www.mindspring.com/~hitmeister*. Actually, we found it by just typing in "Moke Cameron" on the MSN search engine.

Americana artist and writers' night guru Mark Wehner took a break from running the console to come over and chat with us. Mark played the famous writers' nights at the Douglas Corner for many years. He still appears there as a booked artist and helps put Tuesday night writers' rounds together, but he also spends his time at Hobo Joe's. He just finished promoting his latest CD to Americana radio, *That's The Way That It Goes*. We asked him about that experience.

"The way I look at Americana," Mark explained, "is that it has changed over the last three years. Since Americana has gotten more attention, the major Americana record labels like Sugar Hill and Rounder have gotten actively involved. They are squeezing out the independents again—just the kind of problem that we had on country radio. It's harder to break into the Top 40 album chart.

"The nice thing for Americana artists is that you've still got enough radio stations that make their own decisions about what to play. You still have to talk to individual DJs at the station (as opposed to the program director), so you might have to take two or three CDs to the same radio station," Mark observes. "Unfortunately, there still isn't a strong connection between Internet sales and radio or satellite radio airplay to help sell your independent album.

"I hired the best for my project—Al Moss for promotion, Bill Wench for publicity, and a distribution company—we worked hard to get the album out there! I'm writing more songs so I can do it all over again. Americana is such a catchall, and I don't think that's all bad. But I want to hear stuff that still feels and sounds fresh. Americana lets me say what I want to say. People tell me I'm good at reading other people, and that means a lot to me!" You can learn more about Mark Wehner at *http://members.aol.com/tnsongguy*.

It was time to head on to West Nashville. We listened to one more song from each writer onstage, and then quietly headed for the door. When I looked back at the crowd, I saw the writer in the white shirt who had come into the French Quarter Cafe earlier, sitting in the little wicker chair. Maybe we will get to hear him sing next time.

West Nashville is another nice little neighborhood stretched along Charlotte Avenue. Driving west from East Nashville along Charlotte, we passed noted sculptor Alan LeQuire's studio (Alan sculpted "Athena" in Nashville's reproduction of the Parthenon and most recently, "Musica," the dancing musician's in the middle of the Music Row roundabout). We also passed the Darkhorse Theatre (Nashville is also a thriving community for aspiring actors!), and just off Charlotte we turned into the It's All Good Cafe.

This little club is getting a lot of buzz in Nashville, and for several different reasons—it's a writers' club, an art gallery, and it has awesome barbeque! Just the smells from the grill alone will entice you into the club. But don't forget, we're here for the music. You can meet some of Nashville's top hit writers: Wood Newton (*Twenty Years Ago*), Chuck Cannon (*How Do You Like Me Now?*) and a veteran Nashville songwriter and performer,

Marc-Allen Barnette. Marc-Allen puts on a rockin' southern music show that you don't want to miss if he is performing in Nashville when you are in town. Marc-Allen also spends a lot of his volunteer time helping aspiring songwriters at NSAI workshops. He has also written a book on songwriting tips, which you will want to pick up when you stop by NSAI.

Well, it's 11:30 P.M. We could go on down to Lower Broad. Those clubs will be rockin' (sorry, honky-tonkin') until 2:00 A.M.! But hanging out in Nashville's writers' clubs is hard work, not just fun . . . I'm bushed! Thanks, Stan, for a great songwriter's tour!

THE BLUEBIRD CAFE: WHAT TO EXPECT, BY AMY KURLAND

Country music may be in a little bit of a slump these days, but the phone at the Bluebird just keeps ringing. Songwriters and artists want their chance on stage. And we continue to try to find a way for them to play. Open mic on Monday provides a place for any writer, no matter their skills or credentials, to play. Each week, forty or more writers arrive at the Bluebird before 5:00 P.M. to put their names in a hat, for the chance to play two songs. As long as the songs are original, and you can accompany yourself (no backing tracks) you are eligible. Will the open mic show be your ticket to wealth and fame? Probably not. But it is the place where an important door to the music business opens.

Open mic is good for three things:

1. A chance to try out your material on a friendly audience
2. A chance to work on your performing skills (and, please, learn to tune your guitar and remember your lyrics)
3. A chance to make friends, meet potential co-writers, and find your place in the music community.

My rule is, if you don't get out to play when you are in Nashville, you are wasting one of the greatest opportunities the city has to offer.

Sunday writers' nights are different. For these shows you must pass an audition, and those are only held once every four months. What is the key to passing the audition? A good song. I have heard thousands of songs over the years, and my standards are pretty high. We are already booked months ahead on Sunday nights, so I want to pass only the best. So take the time to write a lot, try out your material at open mics, and take classes and workshops from the Nashville Songwriters Association International.

One other thing about the audition: Follow the rules. We ask you not to play introductions to the songs, or explain them, so don't do it.

We've had songwriters from as far away as Australia play at the Bluebird, and many, many people come from all over the country to play their three songs. I guess people want to play here because of our reputation. The songwriters' nights are really the first rung on the Nashville ladder to success. Another rung is our early set, which can function as a mini-showcase. The writers invite the publishers, and often a few show up. Our feature late-evening shows are very difficult to get on, even as an opener, but it's truly just a matter of working hard, writing extraordinary songs, and having the patience of a saint. Some of the success stories we claim are Garth Brooks, Vince Gill, Radney Foster, Hal Ketchum, T. Graham Brown, Sweethearts of the Rodeo, Kathy Mattea, Jill Sobule, Steve Earle, Michael Johnson, Kelly Willis, Kevin Welch, Pam Tillis, Ashley Cleveland, and many, many others.

Our songwriting successes are exciting also. My personal favorite, Mark Irwin, moved here from New Jersey and started washing dishes in the Bluebird's kitchen the third night he was in town. He had a number one hit with Alan Jackson's *Here in the Real World*. More and more writers that I know from the Sunday writers' nights are turning up with their names on the *Billboard* charts. Our former waitress Liz Hengber is now a very successful songwriter with multiple hit songs for Reba McEntire, including *And Still* and *For My Broken Heart*. And Kim Richey, a former Bluebird cook, is now a marvelous recording artist.

Somewhere in Nashville there is at least one songwriters' night every night of the week. And so the wise newcomer makes the tour: Bluebird on Monday, Douglas Corner on Tuesday, and so on. Writers have the opportunity to play for each other, improve their performance, test out their songs with an audience, meet other writers for co-writing and performing, enjoy a social life, and pray that there is a publisher or an A&R person in the audience. During their time off they make demos and go to appointments with publishers.

Is there an average "new songwriter" in Nashville? The age range is very broad, the majority are between twenty-five and thirty-five, but many are younger or older. Male and female are equally mixed, and there are some couples. Most are pretty well-educated, with some college, but they are ready to wait on tables, do carpentry, and work in sales to get by. I would estimate that there are at least a *billion* songwriters in Nashville, which has an overall population of about 500,000! Every housepainter, window washer, cook, dishwasher, temp, cab driver, and street person is a songwriter. Many of the lawyers, doctors, and stockbrokers are writing also. In fact, many of the staff at the Bluebird are aspiring music professionals—one bartender, three out of five waitresses, and one cook. How does this thing work? How do you move to Nashville and strike it rich as a songwriter? Forget about striking it rich. Like any other creative job, if you don't do it for the joy of the work, if you wouldn't go on with it even if it didn't pay, then you are in the wrong business. Love and commitment show, to everyone—to audiences, to publishers, to other writers.

Leave your ego at the city limits. Yes, back where you came from you probably did write songs that were miles better than anyone else's. But not here. Here you have a chance to share music, to learn from the others. It has been my observation that the newcomer is welcomed warmly by the writer who got here last month. This is probably because that guy is so glad to have someone around who knows less than he does. And the established writers will be friendly too, because they remember what it was like. But don't ask to write with them, don't give them CDs; you will only get a reputation as a pest. Your time will come, and the more patient you are the more quickly it will happen.

Write and play, write and play, write and play. It's like homework. The more songs you write, the better you'll get. Don't think that you need to keep playing your one masterpiece over and over; it's not the only good song you'll ever write. If you aren't going to go out and play your new songs for someone, you might as well have stayed at home. People tell me that the Bluebird is the difference between Nashville being a good or a bad experience for new writers in town, so come on down and play.

I love Nashville and recommend it as a swell place to live. The people are friendly, rents are not too bad, and it has a small-town atmosphere. But don't come here thinking that songwriting is like winning the Publisher's Clearinghouse Sweepstakes. It takes a long, long time before you will feel like you've had any success. But there is success in following your dream. I believe it is better to fail in doing something than to succeed in doing nothing.

AMY KURLAND, a Nashville native, received a B.A. in American literature from the George Washington University in Washington, D.C., and returned to Nashville to open a small restaurant and nightclub in 1982. She recognized a need for a place where songwriters could meet and share their songs and ideas with each other. Writers' Night at the Bluebird grew to such proportions that she decided to take the focus away from the restaurant and devote the club to music. Since she started the Writers' Night in 1983, others have cropped up in clubs all over town and have become an invaluable way for publishers, producers and record executives to find new talent. The Bluebird has traveled with shows from New York to Los Angeles and taken songwriters to perform at Robert Redford's Sundance Resort, and can be seen in a weekly TV show, *Live From the Bluebird Cafe* on the Turner South network.

HOW TO PLAY THE BLUEBIRD CAFÉ
(These instructions are handed out at your first visit to the Bluebird.)

Open Mic
For writers who haven't played at the Bluebird and writers from out-of-town, Open Mic is the place to start. It gives songwriters a chance to play two of their own original songs, solo, or accompanied by no more than two others on stage. Drums and backing tracks are not allowed. Open Mic is a great place to try out new material, meet other writers, become a part of the songwriting community, and practice your performing skills. We recommend that all new writers play Open Mic here at the Bluebird as well as at the many other writers' clubs in Nashville, on a regular basis. Often, we have more writers come to Open Mic than we have time and space for. In this case, we offer writers a "play next time" ticket, so that if the writer doesn't get to play the first time he tries, he will definitely get to play the next time. Sign up starts on Monday nights at 5:30. You must be signed up by 5:45. The lineup is announced at 6:00, and the show runs from 6:00 to 9:00.

Sunday Writers' Nights
These shows are scheduled by audition, and through this screening process, writers know that they have been selected to play along with other writers who show growing talent and maturity in their songwriting and performance skills. These shows feature between nine and twelve songwriters playing three songs each. Each show is hosted and ends with a special guest performance by a hit-writing songwriter from the Nashville music industry. Sunday nights are always well attended, which gives the writer a chance to perform for a full room. This is a good chance to develop a following and collect names for a mailing list. The writers' performances are rated and filed for use by the Bluebird to determine when a writer might be eligible to perform during the week on our early shows and spotlight shows. All performances must be acoustic: no drums, backing tracks, and no more than three people on stage. Auditions are held quarterly, and are only open to Nashville residents, people residing within a hundred-mile radius of Nashville and active members of an NSAI regional chapter. They are judged by Bluebird staff and professionals from the music industry. Call (615) 383-1461 to get the date of the next audition.

Early Shows: Tuesday through Saturday, the Bluebird Cafe features the best up-and-coming songwriters from our Sunday writers' nights in no-cover-charge shows at 6:30 P.M. These shows are always acoustic: bands, drums, and large groups are not part of our early shows. Writers who have played Sundays at least four times and at least one "Picks" night (the first Sunday of the month), and have high scores from our judges, are eligible to play on Early Shows. If you don't already have a following (a number of people who will come out especially to hear you perform), you should continue to play Sunday nights and Open Mics. Other writers who are eligible to play are staff writers from established Nashville publishing companies and touring artists with product and good press from out-of-town newspapers. We only book touring songwriters who we believe are as good or better than the best local early show writers. If your package does not include professional product and press, it will not be considered. To submit material for Early Shows, send to: the Bluebird Cafe, Early Shows, 4104 Hillsboro Road, Nashville, TN 37215. If you have played four Sundays and at least one "Picks" night, call (615) 383-1461 to see if your scores make you eligible for an Early Show.

Sunday Spotlights

The Bluebird Cafe does not offer many opportunities for bands to play. The exception is our Sunday Spotlight, a no-cover show each Sunday from 6:30 to 7:15 P.M. The same criterion applies as for our early shows—writers who have played Sundays at least four times, and have high scores from our judges are eligible to play on Sunday Spotlights. Other eligible writers are staff writers from established Nashville publishing companies and touring artists with product and good press from out-of-town newspapers—but this slot is for bands up to six pieces including drums. The solo writer must have played an Early Show to be eligible to bring her band to play a Sunday Spotlight. To submit material for Sunday Spotlights, send to: the Bluebird Cafe, Sunday Spotlight, 4104 Hillsboro Road, Nashville, TN 37215.

Frequently Asked Questions

- *I am a singer and I don't write my own songs. How can I play the Bluebird?*
  Unfortunately, Nashville and the Bluebird Cafe offer very few showcases for singers. You may perform at an Open Mic with songs by local writers, as long as the songs have not been released by a major label or aired on the radio. You should see this as an opportunity to help a writer present his or her songs, this is not a show for the singers as much as it is for the songwriters.

- *What if I don't play an instrument?*
  We do not allow backing tracks at any shows. Some choose to sing a cappella, but it is probably to your advantage to find a guitar player to back you onstage. That is one of the benefits of Open Mics and Writers' Nights; you will meet many people there who would be happy to help out on a show. The songwriting community is very supportive in this way.

- *Does the Bluebird provide instruments for the shows?*
  No, sorry. You will need to bring your own guitar or keyboard. We do provide a good sound system and someone to operate it for you.

- *How are the late shows booked?*
  Late show time slots are reserved for local or national acts with a large following. Openers for these shows are sometimes selected from the best early show performers, although these opportunities are extremely limited.

- *What is a showcase, and how do I get one?*
  A showcase is an early evening show to which the performer invites members of the industry in the hopes of getting a recording deal. Many venues charge a substantial fee/rent for this. It is the Bluebird's policy not to rent our room for showcases unless the request comes directly from a major label representative, established manager, or publishing company.

- *What other resources do you recommend for songwriters?*
  The NSAI and SGA are great organizations that offer many services to writers including seminars and classes, office and writing rooms, song screenings, and solid information and advice. Also, the bookstores are full of good material on songwriting; keep working and educating yourself all the time.

5

A Basic Understanding of Nashville's Music Publishers

I f you look at the listing of publishers on the *Billboard* country chart, you will find hundreds of companies listed there. In reality, there are only a very few publishing companies that are getting cuts in Nashville. Every large publisher has three companies: an ASCAP, BMI, and SESAC company. The songwriter is the one that determines into which company the publisher will put a song. If the writer is signed with ASCAP, the song goes into the publisher's ASCAP company, and so forth.

For example, the letterhead on my publishing companies's stationery reads: "Red River BMI/Crimson Creek ASCAP." When I publish the work of a writer who belongs to ASCAP, his song is published by Crimson Creek, but if he belongs to BMI, the publisher is Red River. I don't have a SESAC company, but if I discovered a great new writer whose affiliation was with SESAC and I wanted to work with him, I would start a SESAC company as well. When people refer to publishing companies, it is not uncommon for them to identify them as, for example, "AMR/New Haven." People automatically know that refers to an ASCAP and a BMI company even if they rarely mention it.

ABOUT NASHVILLE PUBLISHERS

Over the years, the large publishers have purchased valuable publishing companies, and although a song may now be owned by a new publishing company, the old company's name might still be used. For example, Cross

Keys is the same company as Sony/ATV Music Publishing, as well as many, many others owned by Sony. So many of the publishing companies listed on the charts may be owned by larger companies.

Once songwriters have consistent chart success (most of the writers on the *Billboard* charts), they are then in the enviable position of being able to keep a portion of their own publishing. So their publisher will enter into a copublishing deal with them. The writer will now earn 75 percent of his song royalties, instead of the usual 50 percent, with 25 percent of the earnings going to the writers' publishing company. It's just a way of giving the writer a larger portion of his own creation; in most instances, the writer isn't really running a publishing company. In fact, his publisher most likely administers his publishing company for him. The majority of publishing companies listed on the charts, especially those with really imaginative names, are songwriters' companies.

There are three different levels of publishing companies in Nashville that you should be aware of. On your first trip to Nashville, make it your goal to try to get an appointment with one company from each of these three categories.

NASHVILLE'S MAJOR MUSIC PUBLISHERS

BMG Music Publishing (BMG/RCA Records, BNA Records, aka RCA Label Group)
1400 18th Avenue South
Nashville, TN 37212
Tel: (615) 858-1300
Web site: *www.bmgmusicsearch.com*

Curb Music Publishing (Curb Records)
47 Music Square East
Nashville, TN 37203
Tel: (615) 321-5080
Fax: (615) 321-9532

EMI Music Publishing (Capitol Records)
35 Music Square East
Nashville, TN 37203
Tel: (615) 742-8081
Fax: (615) 726-2394
Web site: *www.eminashville.com*

Sony/ATV Music Publishing (Sony Music, CBS, Columbia, Epic, Lucky Dog, Monument Records)
8 Music Square West
Nashville, TN 37203
Tel: (615) 726-8300
Fax: (615) 244-6387
Web site: *www.sonyatv.com*

Universal Music Publishing Group (MCA Records, Mercury Records)
12 Music Circle South
Nashville, TN 37203
Tel: (615) 248-4800
Fax: (615) 248-9300
Web site: *www.umpgnashville.com*

Warner/Chappell Music (Warner Bros. Records)
21 Music Square East
Nashville, TN 37203
Tel: (615) 748-1880
Fax: (615) 733-1885
Web site: *www.warnerchappell.com*

These publishing companies are owned by huge corporations and are linked to record companies owned by the same corporations. They account for more than half of all songs recorded in Nashville, but not necessarily on their own record label. Artists will go to all the big publishers in Nashville looking for songs, not just their own company. These publishers have big budgets, a highly respected general manager (usually someone who has been around Nashville for a long, long time), a creative manager, lots of song pluggers, a big staff of writers, a recording studio, and a production company.

There isn't any need to try to get to the top executive in this company; try to get a meeting with one of the song pluggers. Song pluggers can be found in the *Music Row* publications, in both the "In Charge" edition and the "Publisher Special" edition. They are more accessible, and work with songs on a daily basis. And they are constantly focused on getting a great song to the right artist. Yours might be the one they are looking for.

NASHVILLE'S HOT INDEPENDENT MUSIC PUBLISHERS

When editing this section, I was pretty shocked to see how many "hot" independent music publishers had closed their doors! SIX! Out of TEN! Wow! Acuff-Rose Music Publishing, one of Nashville's oldest and most respected companies founded by Roy Acuff and Fred Rose, was sold to Sony/ATV Music Publishing. Almo/Irving Music was sold to Universal Music Group. ZZ Top's manager Bill Ham closed his Nashville office (Hamstein Publishing), and Madonna did the same (Maverick Music). Reba McEntire closed her publishing/production/management company, Starstruck Writers Group, and rented out the extraordinarily beautiful office building to Universal South record company.

Here are the ones that are still going strong, plus a few more we'll designate as "hot" independents!

Big Tractor Music
1503 17th Avenue South
Nashville, TN 37212
Tel: (615) 292-5100
Fax: (615) 292-2934
E-mail: *info@bigtractormusic.com*
Home to hit writers Kenny Beard, John Bettis, and Trey Bruce.

Famous Music Corporation
65 Music Square East
Nashville, TN 37203
Tel: (615) 329-0500
Fax: (615) 321-4121
Music Row is often musical chairs! Respected Music Row songman Glenn Middleworth came to Famous Music from the head job at EMI Music Publishing.

Major Bob Music Co., Inc.
1111 17th Avenue South
Nashville, TN 37212
Tel: (615) 329-4150
Fax: (615) 329-1021
Web site: *www.majorbob.com*
Bob Doyle's publishing company. Bob discovered Garth Brooks.

Ten Ten Music Group
33 Music Square West, #110
Nashville, TN 37203
Tel: (615) 255-9955
Web site: *www.tentenmusic.com*
Publishing company of the respected artist manager Barry Coburn, credited with launching Alan Jackson's career.

Windswept Pacific Entertainment
33 Music Square West, #104B
Nashville, TN 37203
Tel: (615) 313-7676
Web site: *www.windsweptpacific.com*
> Please see the Jeffrey Steele interview, pages 27–28.

Wrensong Publishing
1229 17th Avenue South
Nashville, TN 37212
Tel: (615) 321-4487
Fax: (615) 327-7917
Web site: *www.wrensong.com*
> Publisher of the Oak Ridge Boys' *Little Things*, and many others.

These independent music publishers carry a lot of weight in Nashville. You would almost think they were one of the majors, considering how many cuts they get. They probably account for more than 20 percent of the songs cut in Nashville. They too have a large staff of writers, one or two song pluggers, a demo studio, and production company. If you can get an appointment with *anyone* in any one of these companies while in Nashville, you will have accomplished a great deal.

INDUSTRY INTERVIEW WITH STEPHANIE COX, CO-OWNER, LARGA VISTA MUSIC, ASCAP/ VISTA LARGA MUSIC, BMI

"I know this is hard to believe, but I don't have an extensive background in music. In fact, I don't ever recall my family playing a lot of music around the house. My aunt did have one of those huge consoles that had a turntable and an eight-track player— they listened to a lot of Eagles and Kenny Rogers. My favorite country singer, when I was a little girl growing up, was Barbara Mandrell. When I tell people I'm from Texas, they immediately think that the music scene there might have influenced my music. But I'm not a hip, cool Texan, I'm a Barbara Mandrell Texan!

"*I Was Country When Country Wasn't Cool* is all about me! I would beg my friends to go to a country music concert, and I would drive for any length of time to go and see the Judds perform. It was almost stalker-ish! I saw so many Judd concerts Wynonna finally said, 'Hey girl, move to Nashville and get a job!' So I did.

"My dad knew someone whose niece lived in Nashville, so my friend and I grabbed a tent and headed for Nashville. We camped at the KOA Campground at Opryland, and called this perfect stranger. She said 'Any friend of Aunt JoAnn is a friend of mine, so come on over.' We were invited for dinner and she was so sweet and nice. Turned out she knew someone at Sony/ATV/Tree and introduced me. It also turned out that she had some major connections in Nashville—she was none other than Linda Davis, an awesome country/pop artist!

"I had a hard time trying to decide between going to Belmont University or Middle Tennessee State University, but finally decided on MTSU. I was going to school, working at a bank twenty hours a week, and interning for two companies—Little Big Town Music and Ken Stilts, the Judds's management company. I quickly learned that I *didn't want* to be an artist manager—and I did have an interest in music publishing. So when I graduated, I set two goals for myself before I reached thirty: One, obtain my dream salary; and two, own my own publishing company!"

Stephanie Cox achieved both of her goals, while at the same time learning several different aspects of the music business, surviving different management styles, and even "getting fired." "My publishing internship was with Woody Bomar at Little Big Town Music, and he would take me with him to pitch songs. One of our first meetings was with my idol, Barbara Mandrell! 'Do you think you can handle it?' Woody asked, knowing my love for Barbara. We were standing in the room with Barbara's producer, Jerry Crutchfield, when Barbara walked in. She walked right past Woody as if he wasn't there, and came over to me to look at my hair! 'This is the most beautiful hair I have ever seen,' she said. So I considered that a very good first pitch meeting, even though I never even pitched a song!" (And Stephanie's head of thick, curly locks is truly beautiful!)

"I heard that Reba McEntire's company, Starstruck Writers Group, was hiring a new creative director and looking for a song plugger. Reba, and her husband/manager Narvel Blackstock, wanted to concentrate on publishing and building the catalog. It was an opportunity to be an instrumental part of the development of the company—I knew I would fly or fall flat on my face! It would also be an opportunity to work with two staff writers that I knew quite well, because they had co-written with writers at Little Big Town—Mark D. Sanders and Sunny Russ.

"Of all of my jobs, Starstruck was the most fun job I ever had! The greatest growth period of my career, the greatest diversity (sixteen writers) we had a great time together, got a ton of cuts—it was just great! And Narvel had the greatest management style. When Cliff Williamson hired me, Narvel met with me and said, 'We are going to put you in front of the basket; then we are going to give you a ladder to climb up to the basket; then we are going to put the ball right in your hand and help you drop it into the basket!' And they did.

"While we were at Starstruck, Mark D. Sanders and I made a strategic plan. His personal career goal was to be ASCAP Songwriter of the Year. So we mapped out a strategy and worked together to make it happen. We worked hard for two and a half years, and Sanders received his ASCAP award in 1997.

"Nobody could have offered me a another publishing job to leave Starstruck. Actually, Scott Hendricks was starting Big Tractor Music and he wanted me to head it up. I was scared to death to run a big company, but I had to at least think about it. And I talked to Narvel about it. He asked me how much Scott was offering, and met his offer the very next day with a raise in my salary. But not too long after that, Scott came back with another offer that I couldn't refuse—senior director of A&R at Capitol Records. Again I went to Narvel, and this time he asked me what my long-term goals were. When I told him honestly that I wanted to own my own publishing company someday, he gave me his blessing to leave Starstruck.

"I left Capitol one year later, almost to the day. I gained some very valuable insights, which have been helpful in my career. One, I was exposed to the politics that exist inside a record label; two, I got to work with yet another management style; and three, I got to witness every aspect of making a record—I got to sit in on marketing talk, publicity talk, and promotion talk. It was fabulous to witness the incredible minds at the record label at that time. I can't say enough about how brilliant they are. I concentrated on the careers of Deanna Carter and Trace Adkins, and I'm proud that I brought two hit songs for John Berry, *Change My Mind* and *She's Taken a Shine*. Deanna Carter had the monster hit *Strawberry Wine* during the time I was there.

"But when Jody Williams was going over to MCA Music Publishing and asked me to join him, I couldn't turn him down. I went to Scott to discuss it, and he let me out of my contract with Capitol. He wrote the sweetest letter to the Capitol staff, saying, 'Stephanie's heart is in publishing and she should follow her heart.'

"One of the first things Jody and I did was to sign Mark D. Sanders (*I Hope You Dance*) and Chely Wright (*Single White Female*) to MCA Music. I was excited about signing Mark and Chely, but I was really blown away when Kye Fleming came into my office and said, 'I've been thinking about signing with a publisher ... you!' I had met Kye back when I was interning at Little Big Town—I was in awe of her. After all, she had written my favorite country song (*I Was Country When Country Wasn't Cool*) for my favorite country singer (Barbara Mandrell)! It was great to be able to finally work with Kye. And then something unexpected happened . . . I got fired!"

Actually Stephanie wasn't fired. MCA Music Publishing purchased PolyGram Records and Publishing, and the two merged into the Universal Music Group, replacing the entire staff. "I like to refer to this experience as being fired, because it fires me up!" Stephanie says. "I had been keeping in touch with California folk writer Steve Seskin (*Grown Men Don't Cry*, number one hit by Tim McGraw), who I met when I was at Little Big Town Music, and about this time we were having breakfast in Hillsboro Village and I told him what was going on at MCA. We had become big buddies when I was an intern, because he would come to town often and want to hang out, so we would go to the Bluebird Cafe together. I told him I was glad I went to MCA for the corporate experience, and he said, 'I'm not a big company guy—do you want to start a small company together?' He wrote some things on a napkin, and our company was started.

"I wanted to name the company after my hometown, Longview. But the name was already taken by polka king, Frank Yankovic. So a friend suggested I use the Spanish name for Longview, and I named my ASCAP company Larga Vista Music. Then, when I was traveling out West I saw a sign for Longview that read 'Vista Larga.' So I named my BMI company Vista Larga!"

Larga Vista Music is recognized as one of the most promising young companies on the scene. In just a few years, the company has been gaining success with hits such as Trace Adkins' *Then They Do*; George Strait's history making fiftieth number one of his career, *She'll Leave You with a Smile*; and Tim McGraw's rendition of Steve Seskin's song, *Grown Men Don't Cry*. Staff writers include Sunny Russ, Brandy Clark, Jon McElroy, Stephanie Urbina Jones, Scott Bomar, and Tom Damphier . . . and of course, Mark D. Sanders.

"There are a million different deals you can make with songwriters—I have so many different contracts my attorney jokingly said to me, 'Hey, it's not a bad thing to do a normal deal!' But I try to work with the writer's needs. I don't often meet with developing writers, but I do try to meet with ASCAP, BMI, and SESAC references and writers whom I've known for a long time.

"My advice for developing songwriters is to join NSAI and their local songwriting organization, and don't try to see publishers too soon! Get lots of feedback first. I think a songwriter's biggest mistake, even the established writers, is overlooking the fact that they should be interviewing the publisher. Just because a publisher wants to sign a writer or a song doesn't mean it is the right thing to do. A bad deal can really put a funk in a writer's career—I've seen some great writers unable to write hit songs when they are in a bad deal.

"The industry is changing rapidly, and I think that we have to get the notion out of our head that one big thing is going to save the industry—independent record labels, or satellite radio, or whatever. We need a new business model—find every outlet we can—and take a broader approach to the industry.

"There are lots of rewards in this business, and this one was very unexpected: I was sitting in my office one day when Kye Fleming called. She said she didn't give birthday or Christmas presents, but she had a gift for me—could she come over? Kye has been presented with forty-two BMI Awards for all of her hit songs, and never framed or displayed any of them. But she did frame one of her awards, and brought it to me for my office. It is for her song *I Was Country When Country Wasn't Cool.*"

STEPHANIE COX grew up in the Texas panhandle and was a diehard country music fan at a time when "country wasn't cool!" She took a trip to Nashville to see what it was like, and decided it would be a great place to go to college. While attending Middle Tennessee State University, Stephanie worked as an intern for Ken Stilts Management and Sony/ATV/Tree Music Publishing, and also worked a paying gig part-time at a bank. Upon graduation, she was hired to work at Little Big Town Music, where she met several people who were to become lifelong friends and business associates; Kye Fleming, Steve Seskin, Mark D. Sanders, and Sunny Russ. She left Little Big Town Music to become the creative manager for Reba McEntire's company, Starstruck Writers Group. She detoured into A&R for Capitol (Liberty) Records, and then turned back to publishing again as vice president of creative services at MCA Music. She started her own publishing company, Larga Vista Music, in 1999 with hit songwriter Steve Seskin. Due to her passion for songs and ability to build a valuable catalog in just five years, Larga Vista has scored numerous cuts with singles including hits by Tim McGraw, George Strait, and Trace Adkins. To continue on the road with Stephanie and her friends, visit them at *www.songjourney.com.*

OTHER IMPORTANT INDEPENDENT MUSIC PUBLISHERS

There are zillions of music publishers in Nashville—almost as many as there are songwriters, but not quite. The majority of independent music publishers are struggling hard to get their songs heard, and they know that a great song will make its way through to the top. There are many more great publishers than the ones listed here, and just because they are not included here does not mean that you should omit them from your own list of publishers. Hopefully, you have created your own target list of publishers by reading the label copy on CDs, reading the *Billboard Country Airplay Monitor*, and by information you have obtained from *Music Row* magazine, especially the "Publisher Special" edition. These are all very different companies, with varying styles of music and a completely different approach to the industry. You should learn as much as possible about each company, the songs in their catalog, and their team of writers; then match the companies to your own catalog.

A word of caution! Nearly half of the independent publishers listed in the revised edition of, *Songwriter's and Musician's Guide to Nashville* (2000) have gone out of business for this edition! In this rapidly changing climate for the music industry, it is advisable to add a clause to your songwriter's contract that spells out what happens in the event the publishing company is closed or sold.

Here is a list of recommended independent music publishers, with a few notes about each one.

Affiliated Publishers, Inc.
1009 16th Avenue South
Nashville, TN 37212
Tel: (615) 327-9050
E-mail: *apiimage@mindspring.com*

Instrumental in the development of Joe Diffie's career. Run by publishers/producers Johnny Slate and Wyatt Easterling, the company also offers artist management.

Air Deluxe Music Group
23 Music Square East, #301
Nashville, TN 37203
Tel: (615) 726-1204
E-mail: *bob@airdeluxemusic.com*

Bob Berg, owner and song plugger, has run Air Deluxe Music Group for several decades.

Allisongs, Inc.
127 Academy Square
Nashville, TN 37210
Tel: (615) 313-8764
E-mail: *jim@allisongs.com*
Web site: *www.allisongs.com*

Songwriter and producer Jim Allison has been influential in the careers of Linda Davis and Billy Ray Cyrus.

Americana Entertainment Publishing, LLC
903 18th Avenue South
Nashville, TN 37212
Tel: (615) 341-0060
Web site: *www.americana-music.com*

Founder Jon Grimson was the force behind the new Americana radio format, which is now an accepted genre of music, representing today's most progressive songwriters and artists. Hit songwriter Larry Shell (*Highway 40 Blues*) runs the publishing arm of the full-service company.

Ash Street Music
1508 16th Avenue South
Nashville, TN 37212
Tel: (615) 383-8775
Web site: *www.ashstreetmusic.com*
New publishing company on Music Row, with offices in Nashville, Los Angeles, and Denver.

Best Built Songs
1317 16th Avenue South
Nashville, TN 37212
Tel: (615) 385-4466
Web site: *http://bestbuiltsongs.com*
Proof positive that if you work hard and just keep at it, you will succeed. Larry Sheridan started out with nothing but drive, and has done very well.

Big Ears Music
33 Music Square West, #102B
Nashville, TN 37203
Tel: (615) 742-1250
Web site: *www.ohboy.com*
Publishing company of John Prine.

Big Fish Entertainment
704 18th Avenue South
Nashville, TN 37203
Tel: (615) 327-3004
E-mail: *bernardporter@aol.com*
Publishing company of Bernard Porter.

Big Picture Entertainment
2820 Erica Place
Nashville, TN 37204
Tel: (615) 292-7440
E-mail: *alan.kates@bpemusic.com*

Alan Kates is the managing partner and has led the company for five years. Writers include Keith Stegall.

Big Yellow Dog Music
803 18th Avenue South
Nashville, TN 37203
Tel: (615) 329-9583
Web site: *www.bigyellowdogmusic.com*
   Publishing company represents John Scott Sherrill and Shawn Camp.

Blacktop Music Group
1222 16th Avenue South, Floor 3
Nashville, TN 37212
Tel: (615) 695-2587
Fax: (615) 321-2773
E-mail: *msebastian@blacktopmusicgroup.com*
   Publishing company of super songman Mic Sebastian and financial guru Charles Sussman.

Bluewater Music Corporation
1218 17th Avenue South
Nashville, TN 37212
Tel: (615) 327-0808
Web site: *www.bluewatermusic.com*
   Bluewater specializes in the international market. They provide full copyright collection, bypassing the massive Harry Fox Agency.

BME (Brewman Music and Entertainment)
56 Music Square West
Nashville, TN 37203
Tel: (615) 320-0007
E-mail: *info@bmemusic.com*
Web site: *www.bmemusic.com*
   Offices in Nashville, and represented in Los Angeles by super song plugger Mason Cooper.

Brentwood-Benson Music Publishing, Inc.
741 Cool Springs Boulevard East
Franklin, TN 37067
Tel: (615) 261-3300
Web site: *www.providentmusic.com*

Brentwood–Benson Music is the publishing arm of Christian music label Benson Records and Provident Music Group.

Brumley Music Group
209 10th Avenue South, #433
Nashville, TN 37203
Tel: (615) 646-7178
Web site: *www.brumleymusic.com*

Publishing company of the Gospel Music Hall of Fame member Albert E. Brumley, and run by musician/songwriter/publisher Mic Porter, a twenty-year music business veteran.

Bug Music
1026 16th Avenue South
Nashville, TN 37212
Tel: (615) 726-0782
Web site: *www.bugmusic.com*

Another innovative company, Bug Music administers writers' catalogs. Highly respected for managing the publishing rights of major self-contained acts, they have adapted to the Nashville climate by pitching artists' and writers' catalogs to other artists. Offices in Nashville, Hollywood, New York, and London.

Cal IV Entertainment
808 19th Avenue South
Nashville, TN 37203
Tel: (615) 321-2700
Web site: *www.cal4.com*

Cal Turner is a highly successful businessman and entrepreneur of Dollar General stores. His son, Cal Turner III, has done an excellent job starting a new music publishing company by putting together a stellar staff with Music Row veterans Daniel Hill and Billy Lynn.

CDB Music
1217 16th Avenue South
Nashville, TN 37212
Tel: (615) 327-5474
E-mail: *charliecdb@aol.com*

The sons of Charlie Daniels and Alabama lead singer Randy Owen run this new company on Music Row.

CDP Music Group
3610 Mayflower Place
Nashville, TN 37204
Tel: (615) 292-9904
Fax: (615) 292-9904

If you are looking for a woman who knows the ropes and has a great song sense, C. Dianne Petty is the one. She was in charge of writer/publisher relations at SESAC for many years.

Channel/Cordial Music Companies
123 Walton Ferry Road
Hendersonville, TN 37075
Tel: (615) 824-1947
E-mail: *dotwool@bellsouth.net*

Publishing companies of the late, great Sheb Wooley.

Collins Music
21 Music Square West
Nashville, TN 37203
Tel: (615) 255-5550
Fax: (615) 256-6467

Publishing company of Barbara Mandrell's producer, Tom Collins.

Combustion Music
1609 17th Avenue South
Nashville, TN 37212
Tel: (615) 515-5490
Fax: (615) 269-6883

Award-winning producer/songwriter Chris Farren started this music publishing company with artist manager Ken Levitan. Worked on the *We Were Soldiers* soundtrack.

Copperfield Music Group
1400 South Street
Nashville, TN 37212
Tel: (615) 726-3100
Fax: (615) 726-3172
Web site: *www.copperfieldmusic.com*

Publishing company of Kin Biddy, husband of the first female record company label head Sheila Shipley-Biddy (she was head of Decca, a now-defunct subsidiary of MCA/Universal Music Group).

Corlew Music Group, LLC
50 Music Square West, #300
Nashville, TN 37203
Tel: (615) 321-5767
E-mail: *jnewtonkbm@aol.com*
    Publishing company of businessman Tom O'Grady and David Corlew,
Charlie Daniels' business manager.

Crutchfield Music
1106 17th Avenue South
Nashville, TN 37212
Tel: (615) 321-5558
Fax: (615) 321-5598
    Publishing company of Tanya Tucker's longtime producer Jerry
Crutchfield.

EMI Christian Music Publishing
101 Winners Circle
Brentwood, TN 37024
Tel: (615) 371-4400
Fax: (615) 371-6897
Web site: *www.emicmg.com*
    Leading Christian music publisher operates within the EMI Christian
Music Group, which also contains Sparrow Records, Forefront Records,
and Chordant Records.

Extreme Writers Group Publishing and Productions
40 Music Square West
Nashville, TN 37203
Tel: (615) 259-5320
Web site: *www.extremewritersgroup.com*
    Publishing company of Universal South label head Tim DuBois.
Represents artists Shannon Lawson, Matthew West, Sixwire, and Debutante.

Fame Publishing
1500 17th Avenue South
Nashville, TN 37212
Tel: (615) 383-0350
Fax: (615) 383-0576
Web site: *www.fame2.com*
    Muscle Shoals comes to Nashville.

Forerunner Music Group

1308 16th Avenue South
Nashville, TN 37212
Tel: (615) 298-5499
Fax: (615) 385-2611
E-mail: *Fore.runner@nashville.com*

Publishing company of Garth Brooks' producer Allen Reynolds.

Fretboard Publishing Company

2824 Dogwood Place
Nashville, TN 37204
Tel: (615) 292-2047
Web site: *www.soundcontrolstudio.com*

Publishing company of producers Mark and Andy Moseley, who designed and crafted the rockabilly double-neck guitar, made famous by legendary guitarists Joe Maphis and Larry Collins.

Frizzell House

118 16th Avenue South, Suite 250B
Nashville, TN 37203
Tel: (615) 244-8082
Web site: *www.musiccityinformation.com*

Publishing company of recording artist Allen Frizzell, son of Lefty Frizzell.

Froehlig Palmer Music

812 19th Avenue South, #A
Nashville, TN 37203
Tel: (615) 329-4687
E-mail: *fpmusic@aol.com*

Celia Froehlig ran Famous Music for many years. She has an awe-inspiring Rolodex.

Full Circle Music

1900 Wedgewood Avenue
Nashville, TN 37212
Tel: (615) 321-8686
E-mail: *Michael@fullcirclemusicpublishing.com*

Music Row veteran Mic Hollandsworth runs this new Music Row company.

Gary Nicholson Music, LLC
9 Music Square South, #410
Nashville, TN 37203
Tel: (615) 473-3639
Web site: *www.garynicholson.com*
    Gary Nicholson has a long line of credits as a songwriter in several different genres of music, a record producer, a touring guitarist, and as a solo performer. His own CD release features Bonnie Raitt, Vince Gill, Steve Cropper, and Ivan Neville.

Goodland Group
1620 16th Avenue South
Nashville, TN 37212
Tel: (615) 269-7073
Web site: *www.aristomedia.com*
    Publishing companies of Music Row video promotion guru and publicist Jeff Walker.

Harlan Howard Songs
1902 Wedgewood
Nashville, TN 37212
Tel: (615) 321-9098
Fax: (615) 327-1748
Web site: *www.harlanhoward.com*
    Harlan's wife, Melanie Smith-Howard, has done a great job representing the contemporary catalog of this legendary songwriter (*I Fall to Pieces, Heartaches by the Number,* etc.)

Horipro Entertainment Group
1819 Broadway
Nashville, TN 37203
Tel: (615) 329-0890
Fax: (615) 329-1874
    Once upon a time, every record produced in Nashville included a song published by Bob Beckham. Beckham is honored by his peers as a man who helped create the Nashville sound.

Island Bound Music, Inc.
1204 17th Avenue South
Nashville, TN 37212
Tel: (615) 320-5440
E-mail: *studio@islandboundmusic.com*

The dynamic duo of Brad and Julie Daniel have shown that they really know how to pitch songs, celebrating one decade of success.

iv music publishing
1701 Church Street
Nashville, TN 37203
Tel: (615) 320-1444
Web site: *www.ivgroup.cc*

The iv group includes artist management, a record company, and marketing, with clients Coca-Cola, Budweiser, ABC, AT&T, and Warner Bros. Pictures, just to name a few.

J. Aaron Brown & Associates
1508 16th Avenue South
Nashville, TN 37212
Tel: (615) 385-0022
Fax: (615) 386-9988
Web site: *www.lullabyes.com*

The king of lullabies.

Jody Williams Music
1602 17th Avenue South
Nashville, TN 37212
Tel: (615) 329-3500
Web site: *www.jodywilliamsmusic.com*

Jody Williams is a Music Row veteran who started his own company four years ago.

Johnny Bond Publications
P. O. Box 158029
Nashville, TN 37215
Tel: (615) 297-7320
Web site: *www.johnnybond.com*

Publishing companies of the author.

KMG/Criterion Music
30 Music Square West, #206
Nashville, TN 37203
Tel: (615) 242-2424
Web site: *www.chriskeatonproductions.com*

Chris Keaton served as vice president of publishing for the Roy Orbison catalog. He currently represents the catalogs of Rodney Crowell, Lyle Lovett, Barry Mann, and Cynthia Weil, among others.

Larga Vista Music
P. O. Box 41164
Nashville, TN 37204
Tel: (615) 467-7065
E-mail: *lrgvista@bellsouth.net*
　　　Run by Stephanie Cox; writers include Los Angeles writer Steve Seskin (*Don't Laugh at Me* by Mark Wills).

Life Music Group
P. O. Box 128288
Nashville, TN 37212
Tel: (615) 292-6363
E-mail: *lifemusic@earthlink.net*
　　　Specializes in Christian music.

Little Shop of Morgansongs
1800 Grand Avenue
Nashville, TN 37212
Tel: (615) 321-9029
Fax: (615) 321-3640
　　　Hit songwriter Dennis Morgan's publishing company.

Love Monkey Music
1313 16th Avenue South
Nashville, TN 37212
Tel: (615) 292-8444
Web site: *www.bobdipiero.com*
　　　Publishing company of hit songwriter Bob DiPiero (*American Made, That Rock Won't Roll*).

Magnet Music Group
P.O. Box 120725
Nashville, TN 37212
Tel: (615) 467-3860
E-mail: *tdchoate@aol.com*
　　　Publishing company of former Capitol Records A&R head Terri Choate and artist Larry Gatlin.

Malaco Music Group
33 Music Square West, #110
Nashville, TN 37203
Tel: (615) 327-0440
E-mail: *malaconashville@prodigy.net*
Publishing company of the blues/gospel label Malaco Records in Jackson, Mississippi. Their Nashville office sticks to country songs only.

Marathon Key Music
1708 Grand Avenue
Nashville, TN 37212
Tel: (615) 329-4244
E-mail: *www.marathonkeypub@aol.com*
Publishing companies of super-picker and in-demand session player Billy Joe Walker, Jr., run by his wife, Ginny Johnson.

Matt Lindsey Music
P. O. Box 128573
Nashville, TN 37212
Tel: (615) 321-1184
Web site: *www.mattlindseymusic.com*
Over twenty years on Music Row, with cuts by Garth Brooks and the Dixie Chicks.

Mighty Isis Music
1019 17th Avenue South, #201
Nashville, TN 37212
Tel: (615) 320-5355
E-mail: *isomighty@aol.com*
Songwoman Whitney Daane jokingly calls herself the "Empress of the Southern Kingdom," and that's about right!

Monk Family Music Group
P. O. Box 150768
Nashville, TN 37215
Tel: (615) 292-6811
Fax: (615) 292-7266
E-mail: *monkfamily@aol.com*
Publishing company of the honorary mayor of Music Row, Charlie Monk.

Moraine Music Group
2803 Bransford Avenue
Nashville, TN 37204
Tel: (615) 383-0400
Web site: *www.morainemusic.com*
    Publishing company of the Judds' producer, Brent Maher.

Mosaic Music Publishing
1305 16th Avenue South
Nashville, TN 37212
Tel: (615) 320-9971
Web site: *lconway@mosaicla.com*
    A new publishing company on Music Row, run by Lionel Conway, who most recently opened an office in Nashville for Madonna's Maverick Music. Conway signed U2, Tom Waits, and Robert Palmer to Island Music.

Murrah Music Corporation
1109 16th Avenue South
Nashville, TN 37212
Tel: (615) 329-4236
Web site: *www.murrahmusic.com*
    Legendary songwriter Roger Murrah has hits spanning three decades, receiving dozens of airplay and achievement awards.

Muy Bueno Music Group
1000 18th Avenue South
Nashville, TN 37212
Tel: (615) 327-9229
Fax: (615) 327-9234
    Publishing company of George Strait's manager, Erv Woolsey.

New Company Song Group
20 Music Square East
Nashville, TN 37203
Tel: (615) 733-1861
    Publishing company of Music Row veteran Chuck Neese.

Noble Vision Music Group
920 19th Avenue South
Nashville, TN 37212
Tel: (615) 327-0461
Web site: *www.noblevisionmusic.com*

Publishing companies of publishing veteran Hal Oven. Current cuts by Clay Walker, Buddy Jewell, and Sherrie Austin.

Of Music
204 Burgundy Hill Road
Nashville, TN 37211
Tel: (615) 333-2872
Fax: (615) 834-3660
Company with the most imaginative songs on the Row! President Tom Oteri is the father of former *Saturday Night Live* member Cheri Oteri.

On the Mantel Music
P. O. Box 111401
Nashville, TN 37222
Tel: (615) 776-5059
Web site: *www.jamesdeanhicks.com*
Publishing company of hit songwriter James Dean Hicks.

Paden Place Music
3803 Bedford Avenue
Nashville, TN 37215
Tel: (615) 292-5848
E-mail: *tpaden2002@comcast.net*
Another company that proves staying power pays off!

Paradise Cove/Prissy Girl Music
2 Music Circle South
Nashville, TN 37203
Tel: (615) 329-2810
Web site: *www.merlekilgore.com*
Publisher Merle Kilgore wrote *Ring of Fire*; he also manages Hank Williams, Jr. (if he can be managed, that is!).

Peermusic
1207 16th Avenue South
Nashville, TN 37212
Tel: (615) 329-0603
Web site: *www.peermusic.com*
One of the most successful independent music publishers, with copyrights dating back to the 1940s. Offices worldwide.

Randy Scruggs Music
2828 Azalea Place
Nashville, TN 37204
Tel: (615) 298-1238
Fax: (615) 279-9444
　　Publishing company of producer, writer, and artist Randy Scruggs, son of the legendary Earl Scruggs.

RPM Music Group
209 10th Avenue South, #229
Nashville, TN 37203
Tel: (615) 345-2525
Web site: *www.rpmweb.com*
　　Publishing company of artist manager Scott Siman, whose clients include Tim McGraw, Jessica Andrews, and Billy Gilman.

SDB Music Group
P. O. Box 158507
Nashville, TN 37215-8507
Tel: (615) 758-2447
Fax: (615) 758-2447
　　Publishing company of Sherrill Blackman (see interview, page 72), who was the office manager for NSAI under the direction of the much-loved Maggie Cavender.

Sea Gayle Music
35 Music Square East
Nashville, TN 37203
Tel: (615) 259-9460
Fax: (615) 259-3470
　　Staff writers include Brad Paisley and Chris Dubois, son of Universal South's Tim DuBois.

Shell Point Music, Inc.
816 18th Avenue South
Nashville, TN 37203
Tel: (615) 782-8200
Web site: *www.shellpointrecords.com*
　　Catalog contains the 2001 CMA Song of the Year, *Murder on Music Row*, by Grammy nominee Larry Cordle.

Singing Roadie Music Group
P. O. Box 120672
Nashville, TN 37212
Tel: (615) 780-2997
Web site: *www.roadierecords.com/srmg*
    Los Angeles transplant Garth Shaw, doing great in Nashville.

Southern Writers Group USA
2804 Azalea Place
Nashville, TN 37204
Tel: (615) 383-8682
Web site: *www.musicnashville.com*
    Publishing company of the Music Row veteran Buzz Cason.

Still Working Music Group
1625 Broadway, #600
Nashville, TN 37203
Tel: (615) 242-4201
Web site: *www.orbison.com*
    Publishing company of the late, great, legendary Roy Orbison.

Street Singer Music
1303 16th Avenue South
Nashville, TN 37212
Tel: (615) 327-4425
E-mail: *streetsing@aol.com*
    Hays, Kansas, transplant Mark Meckel doing great also!

Sunset Ranch Music/Norman Productions
204 Heady Drive
Nashville, TN 37205
Tel: (615) 352-5353
Web site: *www.sunsetranchmusic.com*
    Publishing veteran Norman DeVasure started his own company recently.

Talbot Music Group
2 Music Circle South, #202
Nashville, TN 37203
Tel: (615) 244-6200
E-mail: *TalbotMusic@aol.com*

Publishing company of Music Row veteran Joe Talbot, honored by his peers as a man who helped create the Nashville Sound.

Western Beat Music
P. O. Box 128105
Nashville, TN 37212
Tel: (615) 248-5026
Web site: *www.westernbeat.com*

If your songs are Americana or very traditional country music, this is the company for you. Billy Block also produces a weekly artist showcase and radio show for Americana and alternative country music.

Zamalama Music Group
P. O. Box 120907
Nashville, TN 37212
Tel: (615) 321-0033
E-mail: *zamalama8@aol.com*

Another company that signs songs with character, outside-the-norm type material. Company of the writer and artist Kacey Jones.

ABOUT SONG PLUGGERS

There are people on Music Row who do nothing but pitch songs all day long to artists, producers, and A&R reps. They are called "song pluggers." The major publishing companies have several song pluggers and the smaller independents have one or two; every Nashville publisher has a song plugger or is a song plugger herself. This creates a highly competitive environment for publishers trying to get their songs heard by the right people.

All of the song pluggers know each other and, sometimes, even hang out together. Sometimes they even share inside information with each other. It's not uncommon for producers or A&R reps to call a special meeting with all of the song pluggers at one time, to play them some sides they recorded on a new artist in order to give the pluggers an idea of what they are looking for. Believe it or not, it is extremely difficult for artists to find great songs for an album project. Every time they go into the studio, artists listen to thousands of songs. The songs may have been written by big hit writers and they may be great songs—but they are not necessarily exactly what the artist is looking for. Artists and record companies work closely with Nashville's top song pluggers to help speed up the process of looking for songs.

From time to time, song pluggers will organize themselves and form a song-plugging group. They hold monthly meetings and invite artists, producers, and A&R reps to come and listen to their songs. Or the industry folks will tell them about the current project they are working on and what they are looking for. Two very successful song-plugging groups (which may or may not be in existence anymore) are the Young Turks and Chicks with Hits. By working together, they give themselves an extra opportunity to pitch a song.

The fast track to getting your songs recorded is by signing a publishing contract with a publisher who has a great song plugger, or who is a great song plugger himself. This information needs to be researched before you talk to publishers about your songs. Without a great song plugger, the chance of getting the right exposure for your songs is very slim.

INDUSTRY INTERVIEW WITH SUPER SONG PLUGGER SHERRILL BLACKMAN

"I grew up playing sports and knew I didn't have what it took to become a professional ballplayer, so I naturally looked for a career that was highly competitive. I can't think of anything more competitive than the country music business!

"Things have just seemed to fall into place for me ever since I started my own company," says the soft-spoken Blackman. "Several writers came to me and asked me to pitch their songs; I've been making a living doing that for ten years now.

"The first thing I did was to put a catalog together that was like a spice rack! I like to have access to all types of songs, and make sure the songs in my catalog don't compete with each other. When I agree to represent a writer's songs, I only sign songs that fill a niche of what I don't already have. I only represent writers who are successful, and know how to write great songs. And they have sufficient income to pay a monthly retainer. In addition to a monthly fee, I receive bonuses on the back end when a song starts bringing in income.

"More and more artists are being encouraged to write their own songs, so there are less and less slots available on each album. There are approximately three or four slots, where there used to be ten. A plugger needs to pitch the hit single, or a song that is uniquely different and stands out from the others.

"Most song pluggers today belong to pitch groups. Indie pluggers and in-house pluggers join together and pitch songs with each other. The two pitch groups I belong to are IPA (Independent Pluggers Association) and TAP (Ten Angry Publishers). We get together fairly often to pitch songs to the top artists and producers. You won't find these groups listed in the phone book and you can't just join without being invited. I also belong to NPN, the Nashville Publisher's Network, which doesn't pitch songs, but does discuss topics related to music publishers. All of these groups are very important to my business.

"I represent some of the top songwriters in town, so I don't have trouble getting in to see anyone. In fact, A&R execs, managers, and producers usually call me to tell me what they are looking for, or to invite me to sit in on special song meetings. When I do make an appointment with an artist or producer, I go in with a specific idea of what I want to play. But I also take in a CD book with all the songs I represent; so if the producer or artist says that's not what he's looking for, I can easily change directions.

"I like to put my CDs in a thin plastic case. I got this idea from Sam Ramage, when I was pitching songs to him at RCA Records. He was loading up his briefcase with CDs to listen to over the weekend, and he mentioned that he liked the thin-style cases, (as opposed to the thick commercial kind), so he could get more CDs in his briefcase. Ever since then I have used the thin plastic case. I also use blank CDs that don't have any writing on them, so when I put my label on the CD, the manufacturing logo doesn't show through.

"I try to see everyone on a rotating basis, and drop off songs in between appointments. I may not call some people more than once a year, others I see once a month or more. It depends on the situation. I look at a big part of what I do as trying to eliminate the various opinions by getting as close to the artist as I can. First I try to get directly to the artist, then manager, then producer, and my last option for a pitch is to the A&R executive—because the A&R departments are bombarded with too many people and songs.

"I love what I do—it's all about great songs! Good songs are a dime a thousand; the bar is so high! When I pitch a song, I feel that I have to take in a 'Song of the Year' type song. Of course, everyone wants that type of song, in an up-tempo format!

"Sometimes songs are ahead of our time. I pitched *Three Wooden Crosses* to everyone in Nashville! They all passed on it. I knew I had a hit song, and I was so frustrated because I really believed in it. But I couldn't get it recorded. It finally found its way to Michael Peterson, who took it to producer Kyle Lehning, who played it for Randy Travis. Even Randy was hesitant to record it because of the 'hooker' line in the lyrics. But I'm sure he is glad he took his producer's advice!

"There is a strong peer group, a circle of close friends, and the industry always stays true to their friends when they can, without going outside of that circle. So it makes it even harder to get a song cut. I'm not afraid to pitch to new artists, or great artists that have been dropped by the major labels and are now signed to the independent record companies, like Chad Brock (Broken Bow) or Mark Chesnutt (Vivaton) or Neal McCoy (SEA).

"I truly believe that the independents are going to be the salvation of our industry. Artists are being given a second chance by people who really believe in them. And the emphasis is on great songs, not a big budget. The listener can't tell the difference between an album produced for $40,000 and one produced for $250,000! The independent labels spend less and have to recoup less, so everyone can make a profit.

"A lot of people try to put a time limit on success, but I don't do that. My approach to success goes back to having that athlete's mentality! I am not going to win every day, but I am going to give it my all every day, and find a way to win as much as I can."

SHERRILL BLACKMAN moved to Nashville from North Carolina in 1980 for two reasons: to get a music business degree from Belmont University, and to pursue a career in the music industry. To support himself, Blackman worked every conceivable part-time job before landing a position with American Image Productions, a jingle company that produced radio and TV ads. He kept sending out his resume, and that finally paid off when Maggie Cavender, then executive director of NSAI, found him while looking for an assistant. Blackman worked at NSAI for six years, meeting everyone on Music Row, including over 30,000 aspiring songwriters, artists, and musicians. During his very last week at NSAI, renowned music publisher Marijohn Wilkin called to ask if he knew of anyone looking for a job. So, on the next Monday after leaving NSAI, he started working with Buckhorn Music. There he learned the music publishing business from A to Z from the publisher of *For the Good Times, Little GTO,* and *One Day at a Time.*

When Blackman left Buckhorn Music four years later he really didn't know what he was going to do. But several hit songwriters approached him and asked him to pitch their songs—thus, began a new career in independent song plugging and publishing that has lasted a decade. He has placed songs with many artists, including Don Williams, LeAnn Rimes, John Michael Montgomery, George Jones, Blackhawk, Trace Adkins, Steve Holy, and Jerry Springer (no kidding!).

Sherrill also did write several notable songs; one gospel/wedding song published in six songbooks, and a song he co-wrote with NSAI co-worker Richard Helm that was "inducted" into the Baseball Hall of Fame. In May 2004, *Music Row* magazine named him Songplugger of the Year.

ABOUT STAFF WRITERS

All major Nashville publishers have a staff of songwriters under contract to write exclusively for their company. During the term of a contract, every song that a writer creates belongs to that publisher and remains with that publisher even when the writer leaves the company, even if the song was never recorded.

Staff writers are paid a nominal fee. The fee is based on anticipated earnings for one year, and with hit songwriters it is very easy to calculate a fee based on past earnings. Generally, the major publishers pay $12,000 to $24,000 per year for a development deal, and $25,000 to $50,000 per year in mid-range.

If the writer has a proven track record with several songs recorded (cuts) and great contacts with artists, A&R, and producers, he or she may receive top level—over $50,000 plus copublishing.

These are the top-name writers, often an artist or a very close friend of one or more artists. These writers consistently produce chart-topping songs, and can open any door.

It is expected that the staff writer will be available full time to write for the company and will be able to live on his advance. Contracts require ten to twelve whole copyrights turned in, which could mean twelve songs written only by the writer, or twenty-four co-written songs, or thirty-six songs with three writers.

Term of contract is usually one year with a publisher's option for the next four years. Of course, if the staff writer is unhappy with his situation and wants out of his contract when the year is up, the publisher will most likely not use his option.

Staff salaries are an advance on future royalties, and all monies paid will be deducted from future income. So a staff writer can have a big hit on the charts, but never see the resulting windfall of money because he will have spent it already. On the plus side, if he leaves the company without ever getting a song recorded, he doesn't have to pay the money back. Song publishing makes for some very creative financial statements and is one reason the banks in Nashville have offices that specialize in the music industry.

Advantages of a Staff Writing Position

- **Immediate access to a top publisher.** As a freelance writer, much of a writer's time is spent looking for a publisher for each song. With a staff position, a writer can eliminate that worry and concentrate on writing songs.
- **Immediate access to co-writers.** There are no guarantees that staff writers will be compatible, but generally there is someone on the staff who will make a good collaborator.

- **Introduction to other top songwriters outside the company**. A few publishers do not allow their writers to co-write with writers from other companies. If an outside co-writer is unpublished, he may be expected to sign his song over to the staff writer's publisher.
- **Access to fresh song ideas**, from artists and producers that have specific ideas about what they want to record.
- **Immediate feedback on completed songs**.
- **Access to a demo studio**.
- **A position "inside" the hub of activity**, with lots of support and encouragement.

A staff writing position is very attractive to the developing songwriter. It pays him a little money, which in all likelihood won't be recouped; it's like going to school on a scholarship. However, as wonderful as a staff writing position sounds, there are some major drawbacks.

Disadvantages of a Staff Writing Position
- **When a writer leaves the company, his songs stay behind**. If his best songs are signed to a company that no longer is interested in him, the chances of getting his songs recorded are very slim indeed.
- **Highly competitive writing environment**. The pressure is on in a staff-writing situation. The publisher can't possibly demo every song written, and has to make choices between songwriters on his staff.
- **The same goes for pitching songs**. The publisher will decide what songs to pitch and will expect his writers to check with him before pitching one of their own songs.

Although it may seem on the surface that a staff writing deal is a great way to go, there are many important factors that should be considered before signing on the dotted line. Make sure you have a lot of professional advice before entering into a staff writing commitment.

Getting a Staff Writing Position in Nashville
Staff writer is not a position you can apply for, so don't hurry to type up your resume. The best way to achieve a staff position is to keep a very close personal relationship with publishers. Plan to see them at least once a week, keep them informed of new songs you've written and new co-writers you are writing with, and invite them to any writers' nights in which you plan to participate. In other words, act like one of their staff writers anyway. When a position does open up you'll know about it—and the publisher will have a good feel for you and whether or not you'll fit on his staff.

WORKING WITH PUBLISHERS ON A SONG-BY-SONG BASIS

There are so few staff positions available in Nashville that a full-time job is not something you can step into right away. There are many advantages to working with a publisher on a song-by-song basis. Publishing contracts are as varied as music publishers. Throw away the books you've read and go with your instincts. If a publisher is interested in pitching your songs, then work with him.

Duration of Contract

Copyright reversion is a four-letter word to publishers, but it is something they've had to learn to live with. It takes a long time to get a song cut, even if the artist is interested from the day he hears it. A two-year reversion is the norm, but five years is not unreasonable. If he insists on no reversion (which will be the case with the majors), then look him in the eye and ask whom he intends to pitch it to tomorrow. It doesn't really take too long to get the song to the right artist if you have a firm idea about who should record the song.

Demo Costs

Publishers pay all demo costs. If you have already demoed the song and it's a great song demo that the publisher wants to pitch, then you should be able to keep half of the publishing or be reimbursed for your costs. If the publisher has to re-demo the song in order to pitch it, then he absorbs the cost and keeps 100 percent of the publishing. When you are looking for a Nashville publisher, it's not a good idea to get hung up on demo costs at the outset. Sign the song over 100 percent even if you've paid for the demo—but if it needs to be redone, the publisher pays. The Golden Rule is that the songwriter never pays costs that a publisher should absorb. But the reality is that a songwriter spends a lot of money just trying to get his song into the right hands. Walking a fine line, publishers sometimes take advantage of writers in regard to costs, but you can work together to get the job done.

Handshake agreements are not uncommon—the publisher likes your song, will pitch it for six months or so; if he gets a cut with a major artist, then he gets the publishing. This kind of agreement calls for a great deal of trust on both sides, but it focuses on what matters most—getting the song recorded. It's worth the risk, and the biggest risk lies with the publisher!

6

A Basic Understanding of Nashville's Record Companies

There are only six major record labels in Nashville and each of these is a very small division of a huge corporation, several owned by foreign companies. Although the Nashville labels have their own autonomy when it comes to marketing and promoting their artists, their budgets are subject to the financial health of their parent company. The threat of consolidation looms over the record industry, and the broadcast industry as well. The size of a label's artist roster will suffer the first impact of consolidation in either of these industries.

Nashville's Major Record Labels

In order to control a larger share of radio airtime and maintain a larger artist roster, some major record labels divide into smaller labels, each with their own A&R, marketing, and promotion staff. Most of these smaller companies share the same offices, but some have separate offices. It will be very important for aspiring artists to familiarize themselves with the artist roster of each label, and have some idea of where they would best fit in. Here is a listing of Nashville's major record labels and their biggest stars.

Capitol Records Nashville (EMI)
3222 West End Avenue, 11th Floor
Nashville, TN 37203

Tel: (615) 269-2000
Web site: *www.capitol-nashville.com*
    Garth Brooks, Chris Cagle, Dierks Bentley, Keith Urban

Lyric Street (Disney)
1100 Demonbreun Street, Suite 100
Nashville, TN 37203
Tel: (615) 963-4848
Web site: *www.lyricstreet.com*
    Aaron Tippin, SHeDAISY, Rascal Flatts, Sawyer Brown

RCA Label Group (BMG/RCA Records, BNA, Arista)
1400 18th Avenue South
Nashville, TN 37212
Tel: (615) 301-4300
Web site: *www.rcalabelgroup.com*
    RCA: Alabama, Tracy Byrd, Sara Evans, Martina McBride, Clay Walker; BNA: Kenny Chesney, Lonestar, The Warren Brothers; Arista: Brooks & Dunn, Diamond Rio, Alan Jackson, Brad Paisley

Sony Music Nashville (CBS, Columbia, Epic, Monument, Lucky Dog)
34 Music Square East
Nashville, TN 37203
Tel: (615) 742-4321
Web site: *www.sonynashville.com*
    Columbia: Mary Chapin Carpenter, Buddy Jewell, Montgomery Gentry, Travis Tritt; Epic: Rodney Crowell, Patty Loveless; Monument: Dixie Chicks with their own company, Open Wide Records; Lucky Dog: The Derailers

**Universal Music Group Nashville
(MCA, DreamWorks, Mercury, Lost Highway & Universal South)
MCA Nashville/DreamWorks Records**
60 Music Square East
Nashville, TN 37203
Tel: (615) 244-8944
Web sites: *www.mcanashville.com, www.DreamWorksRecords.com*
    MCA: Vince Gill, Reba McEntire, George Strait, Lee Ann Womack, Trisha Yearwood
    Dream Works: Toby Keith, Jessica Andrews, Darryl Worley

Mercury Records/Lost Highway
54 Music Square East, Suite 300
Nashville, TN 37203
Mercury: Tel: (615) 524-7500
Lost Highway: Tel: (615) 524-7800
Web site: *www.mercurynashville.com*
    Mercury: Terri Clark, Shania Twain, Mark Wills; Lost Highway: Willie Nelson, Lyle Lovett, Lucinda Williams

Universal South
40 Music Square West
Nashville, TN 37203
Tel: (615) 259-5300
Web site: *www.universal-south.com*
    Joe Nichols, Bering Strait, Dean Miller, Matthew West

Warner Bros. Records (Seagrams)
20 Music Square East
Nashville, TN 37203
Tel: (615) 748-8000
Web site: *www.wbrnashville.com*
    Warner Bros.: Faith Hill, Neal McCoy, John Michael Montgomery, Blake Shelton

NASHVILLE'S INDEPENDENT RECORD LABELS

The hottest topic on Music Row today is the impact that independent record labels are having on Nashville's music scene. If you look at the artist rosters of the independents, the names are household words, even more recognizable than the artists signed to major labels. And they are getting radio airplay and selling records in noticeable quantities. Because the smaller record labels spend less money to produce and market their product, an artist doesn't have to have a gold or platinum album just to break even.

    Not too long ago the independent record labels weren't taken very seriously, or were thought to be simply a niche market. Now, many people are saying the industry is headed in their direction. Some even say the independents will save the music industry. Certainly they are worth some serious consideration. Here are just a few.

Audium Records
1709 19th Avenue South
Nashville, TN 37212

Tel: (615) 269-4500
Web site: *www.audiumrecords.com*
  The Tractors, Dale Watson, Ray Benson, John Anderson, Dwight Yoakam

Bandit Records
635 West Iris Drive
Nashville, TN 37204
Tel: (615) 242-1234
Web site: *www.banditrecords.com*
  George Jones, El Cancionero de la Familia

Broken Bow Records
646 West Iris Drive
Nashville, TN 37204
Tel: (615) 244-8600
Web site: *www.brokenbowrecords.com*
  Chad Brock, Craig Morgan, Joe Diffie, Sherrie Austin, Lila McCann

Compass Records
117 30th Avenue South
Nashville, TN 37212
Tel: (615) 320-7672
Web site: *www.compassrecords.com*
  Alison Brown, Victor Wooten

Compendia Music Group
210 25th Avenue North, Suite 1200
Nashville, TN 37203
Tel: (615) 277-1800
Web site: *www.compendiamusic.com*
  Merle Haggard, T. Graham Brown, Crystal Gayle, Gene Watson, Don Williams

Curb Records
47 Music Square East
Nashville, TN 37203
Tel: (615) 321-5080
Web site: *www.curb.com*
  Tim McGraw, Jo Dee Messina, LeAnn Rimes, Hank Williams, Jr., Wynonna, Lyle Lovett

Door Knob Records
3950 North Mount Juliet Road
Mount Juliet, TN 37122
Tel: (615) 754-0417
Web site: *www.doorknob-rec.com*
    Don Sepulveda, Michael Martin, Billy Garland, Donna Parsons, Charlie Wayne

Dreamcatcher Records
2910 Poston Avenue
Nashville, TN 37203
Tel: (615) 329-2303
Web site: *www.dreamcatcherenter.com*
    Kenny Rogers

Dualtone Music Group
1614 17th Avenue South
Nashville, TN 37212
Tel: (615) 320-0620
Web site: *www.dualtone.com*
    Jim Lauderdale, Radney Foster, Jeff Black, John Arthur Martinez, David Ball

Equity Music Group
1222 16th Avenue South, Floor 2
Nashville, TN 37212
Tel: (615) 695-2350
Web site: *www.equitymusicgroup.com*
    Clint Black

Music City Records
2603 Westwood Drive
Nashville, TN 37204
Tel: (615) 269-3100
Web site: *www.musiccityrecords.com*
    Label run by respected promotion man Bob Heatherly. Charley Pride is on the label.

Nashville Underground
P. O. Box 120086
Nashville, TN 37212

Tel: (615) 673-7215
Web site: *www.nashville-underground.com*
    NU puts out a series of samplers on various artists. Great exposure for aspiring artists

Oh Boy Records
33 Music Square West, #102B
Nashville, TN 37203
Tel: (615) 742-1250
Web site: *www.ohboy.com*
    John Prine, Kris Kristofferson, Janis Ian, and Todd Snider

Sugar Hill Records (Nashville)
120 31st Avenue North
Nashville, TN 37203
Tel: (615) 297-6996
Web site: *www.sugarhillrecords.com*
    Respected independent label that recently opened a Nashville office. Represents Dolly Parton, Guy Clark, Jerry Douglas, Tim O'Brien, Maura O'Connell, and more.

Vanguard/Welk Music Group
120 31st Avenue North
Nashville, TN 37203
Tel: (615) 297-2588
Web site: *www.vanguardrecords.com*
    Lee Roy Parnell, Sinead O'Connor, Peter Case, Patty Larkin, and many others.

Vivaton Records
702 18th Avenue South
Nashville, TN 37203
Tel: (615) 255-9133
Web site: *www.vivatonrecords.com*
    Chely Wright, Curtis Lance

Western Beat Entertainment
P. O. Box 128105
Nashville, TN 37212
Tel: (615) 248-5026
Web site: *www.westernbeat.com*
    Represents Nashville's top Americana artists.

How to Approach Nashville's Record Companies

Most Nashville record labels, especially the majors, will not work with unknown writers or artists. They prefer to work with publishers, artist managers, or entertainment attorneys—business representatives of writers and artists. Whether you are a songwriter or an artist, you need someone to speak on your behalf.

If you've decided to start your own publishing company and pitch your own songs, then you will be approaching the record company as a publisher, not a songwriter. Each record company has its own policy regarding unsolicited material, but generally they will not accept songs unless they come from a publisher. Also, it must be stated very clearly on the CD itself to whose attention it is directed. There are a couple of "tip sheets" that will give you some specific information on who is currently looking for songs, and to whom you should get your CD.

Music Row Publication's Row Fax
1231 17th Avenue South
Nashville, TN 32132
Tel: (615) 321-3617
Fax: (615) 329-0852
E-mail: *news@musicrow.com*
Web site: *www.musicrow.com*

Comes to you via fax or e-mail, and includes the latest gossip on Music Row.

Tennessee Songwriters Association International
Monthly Newsletter
P. O. Box 2664
Hendersonville, TN 37077-2664
Tel: (615) 969-5967
E-mail: *ASKTSAI@aol.com*
Web site: *www.clubnashville.com/tsai.htm*

Has the latest in who's looking, as well as tips on how to approach them.

Both of these tip sheets are excellent, and will tell you about the artist, record label, producer, and recording date. You may have the greatest song in the world for Garth Brooks, but if he's not recording right now, it won't do any good to get it to him. Wait until he's looking for new songs. Your songs will have to be packaged just like all the other CDs on Music Row (see chapter 9). Again, you really shouldn't be pitching your songs directly to record companies and producers—country songs need a Nashville publisher.

If you are an aspiring artist and you've got it all together—lots of live performance experience, a great local following, terrific original songs, a great 8″ × 10″ glossy, and an awesome CD—then you are probably itching to get your artist package to one of the major record labels. STOP! Before you go any further, the best thing you can do for yourself is spend as much time in Nashville as possible before you tip your hand and reveal that you are looking for an artist's deal. Can you spend a week? A month? Move here for a year or so? Get a feel for the environment and observe your competition. They are the people you will be working with if you do get an artist's deal. You want to start building relationships as soon as you can.

Music Row is a very tight-knit community, and the artists have to feel comfortable here. Artists have to be familiar with publishers and other writers, because they will be relying on publishers and writers to supply them with great songs. Even if you plan to write your own material, you will still want to co-write with hit Nashville songwriters. So before you go marching into a record company office, get to know Nashville first.

Nashville record labels are interested in four specific things:

1. What is your unique quality?
2. How do you sound on tape?
3. Who is your support team?
4. How do you look and sound on stage?

#1—Your Unique Quality

What do you have that no one else has? A wispy sound? An extraordinary range? A booming bass? The labels will be looking for that something different from everyone else. What is the message you want to put across? You have to have a very strong sense of self—this is who I am and what I'm about. Are you a rebel? A strong woman? A kinder, gentler man? Contrary to what you may have heard, the labels will not shape you to fit their own mold. You have to let them know who you are and what you stand for. Stick to it!

#2—Your Artist's Demo

This is such an important part of your presentation to a record label that an entire chapter of this book is devoted to this topic (see chapter 11, "Packaging Your Product"). No matter how great a performer you might be, it is how you sound on tape that will make or break your artist's career.

#3—Your Support Team: Nashville's Top Managers and Entertainment Attorneys

Record labels will not only be interested in you, but will want to meet with everyone connected with your career. Who has helped you along the way?

Who do you work closely with to make important decisions about your career? Usually an aspiring artist has a family member or a close friend working as an artist manager—someone who "discovered" you and helped bring you along to where you are today. Even though you have an intense loyalty to your current team and they may be doing an excellent job, you should all be prepared to discuss other options with the label. The label will want to have a great deal of confidence in everyone connected with your career. Needless to say, the more people on your support team who are from Music Row, the stronger your presentation to the label will be.

There are three areas of representation you should consider before you go straight to a record label. They are publishers, artist managers, and entertainment attorneys. We have already discussed publishers in depth; here is a little info about Nashville's artist managers and entertainment attorneys.

Artist Managers

It is next to impossible to attract the attention of an artist manager before you are signed to a record label. It's another catch-22. Artist managers are paid a percentage of your live performance income, so you have to be able to demonstrate your ability to bring in enough income to make the time they spend on your career somewhat lucrative. The truth is, artist managers work for practically nothing in the formative stages of an artist's career, often putting up their own money to help get you started. It takes a lot of work over a long period of time before the money starts coming in. An artist manager has to really believe in you as much as you believe in yourself to get involved in your career. Many top artist managers don't even live in Nashville, so don't make that your criteria for picking a good one. Here are some of Nashville's top artist managers:

AS is Management
704 18th Avenue South
Nashville, TN 37203
Tel: (615) 327-3004
Web site: *www.asismanagement.com*
Al Schiltz manages Billy Ray Cyrus.

Bob Doyle & Associates
1111 17th Avenue South
Nashville, TN 37212
Tel: (615) 329-1040
E-mail: *gvoorhies@majorbob.com*
Instrumental in launching Garth Brooks; manager for Brooks and other artists.

Borman Entertainment
1222 16th Avenue South, Suite 23
Nashville, TN 37212
Tel: (615) 320-3000
E-mail: *borman@borman.cc*
    Prestigious Los Angeles–based firm with star client Faith Hill.

Carter & Co.
1114 17th Avenue South, Suite 103
Nashville, TN 37212
Tel: (615) 329-2145
Fax: (615) 329-0416
    Joe Carter moved to Nashville from Beaumont, Texas, where he discovered Tracy Byrd.

Creative Trust
2105 Elliston Place
Nashville, TN 37203
Tel: (615) 297-5010
E-mail: *info@creativetrust.com*
    Specializes in Christian artists, including Steven Curtis Chapman.

DS Management
2814 12th Avenue South, Suite 202
Nashville, TN 37204
Tel: (615) 385-3191
E-mail: *dsmngt@bellsouth.net*
    Denise Stiff manages Alison Krauss and others.

Erv Woolsey Company
1000 18th Avenue South
Nashville, TN 37212
Tel: (615) 329-2402
E-mail: *erv@ervwoolsey.com*
    Erv manages George Strait and Lee Ann Womack.

Falcon-Goodman Management
1103 17th Avenue South
Nashville, TN 37212
Tel: (615) 329-9220
E-mail: *falconmgt@earthlink.net*
    Gary Falcon and Jon Goodman manage Travis Tritt and others.

Fitzgerald Hartley Company
1908 Wedgewood Avenue
Nashville, TN 37212
Tel: (615) 322-9493
Fax: (615) 322-9582

Mark Hartley heads the Los Angeles office; Larry Fitzgerald is in Nashville. They manage numerous top country artists, including Vince Gill and Buddy Jewell.

FORCE
1505 16th Avenue South
Nashville, TN 37212
Tel: (615) 385-4646
Fax: (615) 385-5840

Nancy Russell manages Trisha Yearwood, Loretta Lynn, and Alan Jackson (with a Los Angeles firm).

Gold Mountain Entertainment
2 Music Circle South, #212
Nashville, TN 37203
Tel: (615) 255-9000
Fax: (615) 255-9001

Burt Stein manages Nanci Griffith, Ronnie Milsap, and Lorrie Morgan.

Hallmark Direction Company
15 Music Square West
Nashville, TN 37203
Tel: (615) 320-7714
Fax: (615) 320-5799

Music Row veteran John Dorris manages Montgomery Gentry, Blake Shelton, and many others.

International Artist Management
1105 16th Avenue South, Suite C
Nashville, TN 37212
Tel: (615) 329-9394
Fax: (615) 329-9397

Ted Hacker and Anita Hogin are responsible for Diamond Rio's career. They now manage Darryl Worley and Mark Wills.

JAG Management
41 Music Square East
Nashville, TN 37221

Tel: (615) 256-7154
E-mail: *jagbase@comcast.net*
    Publishing veteran Jimmy Gilmer started his own management firm. Represents Brad Paisley and Josh Turner.

Keith Case & Associates
1025 17th Avenue South, Floor 2
Nashville, TN 37212
Tel: (615) 327-4646
Web site: *www.keithcase.com*
    Manager and booking agent for America's top bluegrass and folk acts.

Lytle Management Group
1101 18th Avenue South
Nashville, TN 37212
Tel: (615) 329-3998
E-mail: *lytlemgt@bellsouth.net*
    John Lytle manages Gary Allan and Joe Nichols.

Merle Kilgore Management
2 Music Circle South
Nashville, TN 37203
Tel: (615) 742-3622
Web site: *www.merlekilgore.com*
    Manages Hank Williams, Jr., and wrote *Wolverton Mountain*; if you are looking for a manager with gusto, Merle's your man.

Mic Robertson Management
1227 17th Avenue South
Nashville, TN 37212
Tel: (615) 329-4199
E-mail: *assistant@microbertsonmgmt.com*
    Nashville manager for over twenty years; current clients include Patty Loveless and Carolyn Dawn Johnson.

Mission Management
1102 17th Avenue South
Nashville, TN 37212
Tel: (615) 340-9513
E-mail: *tracy@missionmgmt.net*
    Tracy McGlocklin's new company manages funnyman Cledus T. Judd.

Morris Management Group

818 19th Avenue South
Nashville, TN 37203
Tel: (615) 321–5025
Fax: (615) 327–0312

Responsible for the phenomenal success of Alabama, Kellie Coffey, and Louise Mandrell.

Refugee Management International

209 10th Avenue South, #347
Nashville, TN 37203
Tel: (615) 256–6615
Fax: (615) 256–6717

Stuart Dill manages Jo Dee Messina and *Nashville Star's* John Arthur Martinez.

Rendy Lovelady Management

1102 17th Avenue South, Suite 402
Nashville, TN 37212
Tel: (615) 340–9500
Web site: *www.rendyloveladymgmt.com*

Manages Marty Stuart, Little Big Town, and Jars of Clay.

rpm management

209 10th Avenue South, #229
Nashville, TN 37203
Tel: (615) 256–1980
Web site: *www.rpmweb.com*

Scott Siman manages Tim McGraw, Billy Gilman, and Jeffrey Steele.

TBA Entertainment Corporation

300 10th Avenue South
Nashville, TN 37203
Tel: (615) 742–9000
Web site: *www.tbaent.com*

Bob Titley and Clarence Spalding guide the careers of Brooks & Dunn, Terri Clark, and many others.

TKO Artist Management

1107 17th Avenue South
Nashville, TN 37212

Tel: (615) 383-5017
Web site: *www.tkoartistmanagement.com*
Manages Sawyer Brown, Chris LeDoux, and others.

Vector Management
1607 17th Avenue South
Nashville, TN 37212
Tel: (615) 269-6600
E-mail: *info@vectormgmt.com*
Ken Levitan manages Lyle Lovett, Patty Griffin, Emmylou Harris, and others.

Wunsch Management
1101 18th Avenue South
Nashville, TN 37212
Tel: (615) 329-3332
E-mail: *cwunsch@bellsouth.net*
Cindy Wunsch manages SHeDAISY.

Entertainment Attorneys

It will be a lot easier to find an entertainment attorney—they start at around $200 per hour. If you've got the money, honey, they've got the time. Actually that's not really true, because their reputation is on the line every time they take an aspiring artist to a record label. The more discerning about whom they represent, the better lawyers they are. So if you just walk in and they sign you up just like that, beware. It should be almost as difficult to convince an entertainment attorney to represent you as it will be to convince a record company to sign you.

Like an artist manager, the attorney you use doesn't have to be in Nashville. However, it is very, very important that your attorney is well versed in entertainment law and, even more important, has worked with Nashville record labels. Record contracts, songwriting and publishing contracts, and copyright law are all highly specialized fields that require expertise. The state of Tennessee doesn't really certify "specialists," but there are definitely specialists in the entertainment industry. Here are a few of the top firms:

Bass, Berry & Sims, PLC
29 Music Square East
Nashville, TN 37203
Tel: (615) 255-6161
Fax: (615) 254-4490

One of the oldest and most respected law offices in Nashville; recently opened a Music Row office with several of Music Row's top entertainment lawyers.

Craig Benson Law Offices
1207 17th Avenue South, #300
Nashville, TN 37212
Tel: (615) 320-0660
E-mail: *cbenson@maestrolaw.com*
In business twenty-six years, handles all aspects of entertainment law.

Gladstone, Doherty & Associates, PLLC
49 Music Square West, Suite 300
Nashville, TN 37203
Tel: (615) 329-0900
E-mail: *sgladstone@gladstone-doherty.com*
Steven Gladstone represents artists, songwriters, publishers, and managers.

Gordon, Martin, Jones & Harris, PA
49 Music Square West, #600
Nashville, TN 37203
Tel: (615) 321-5400
Fax: (615) 321-5469
Rusty Jones represents Nashville's most famous writer, Garth Brooks.

Hall, Booth, Smith & Slover, PC
611 Commerce Street, Suite 2925
Nashville, TN 37203
Tel: (615) 313-9911
Web site: *www.hbss.net*
Entertainment specialist Derek C. Crownover opened a Nashville office in 2002 for this Atlanta-based law firm.

Loeb & Loeb, LLP
1906 Acklen Avenue
Nashville, TN 37212
Tel: (615) 749-8300
Web site: *www.loeb.com*
International firm that represents music, film, television, trademark, and copyright.

David L. Maddox & Associates, PC
1207 17th Avenue South
Nashville, TN 37212
Tel: (615) 329-0086
> David Maddox is one of Music Row's top attorneys.

Stokes, Bartholomew, Evans & Petree, PA
901 18th Avenue South
Nashville, TN 37212
Tel: (615) 341-0068
Web site: *www.stokesbartholomew.com*
> Another established Nashville firm that hired top entertainment lawyers for their new Music Row office.

J. David Wykoff, Esq.
115 17th Avenue South
Nashville, TN 37203
Tel: (615) 242-6032
> Represents popular alternative rock and alternative country artists.

#4—About Live Auditions

Once the record label has heard your demo and met with you and your support team, it will probably request an artist showcase. Usually, if the company has requested a showcase, it will pay for it. However, you should still have a very thorough knowledge of the different types of showcases there are and the one that will work best for you (see chapter 17). That way, when the label asks you for a showcase you can tell them how you prefer to do it.

If you have several labels showing some interest, but no one seems ready to give you a commitment, it might be a good idea to go ahead and put on your own artist's showcase. It's OK to invite all the record labels; that is a very common practice in Nashville. If the label you are interested in knows that another label is interested in you, then most likely they will all show up! It puts you in the driver's seat. However, if you haven't been able to impress any of the labels, publishers, managers, or attorneys with your artist's package, better wait before putting on a show. First, get a buzz going, then have a showcase.

INDUSTRY INTERVIEW WITH ANTHONY SMITH

Successful producer and country/pop writer Anthony Smith has taken two new country acts to Nashville record labels and gotten them a deal. Here is how he did it:

SouthSixtyFive— Atlantic Records

"Delious Kennedy had discovered these five great young guys called SouthSixtyFive; nineteen-to twenty-two-year-olds—only one of them is over twenty-two. They have a great pop sound. He took them to Rick Blackburn and Al Cooley at Atlantic Records, and they were curious to see what SouthSixtyFive would sound like in the studio. Rick wanted a producer with a background in country and pop, so he called me in on the project. I liked the idea that the label was so excited about them, so I set up a time to meet with Delious. He was thinking

about giving it a month to produce some sides. I thought it would take at least six months, so we compromised and set aside three months to see what we came up with.

"They came into the studio and I asked them to sing a cappella. Several of them had never even been in the studio before. They had boundless energy at midnight! The wonderful thing was that they were so fun. It's great to get someone right at the beginning, with all of the fresh energy.

"We had a great project on tape, but I knew it was too pop to get played on country radio; so I asked Delious to give me some time and let me do the final mix. I cut the one side that got them their deal. They recently did Fan Fair, and the Oak Ridge Boys came and sang with them onstage. They all sang *Bobby Sue*—it was the old and the new together. It was so exciting."

Trini Triggs—Curb Records

"John Earl Roe and Herbert Graham of Graham Central Station (a popular five-story, multigenre dance club in several cities including Nashville) came to see me about Trini Triggs, a hot young singer that was getting a lot of attention in Louisiana. From the time they first came to talk to me about Trini and the time they finally talked me into working with him, a year and a half had passed.

"Charles Smith introduced me to Roe and Graham. Charles lives in Louisiana and made lots of trips to Nashville. I said I would meet Trini for breakfast. I had meant to spend one hour with him, but I liked him so much I spent the whole day with him! He had a demo tape he had done in Charles's Louisiana studio, but I wasn't able to shop it.

"He just kept at it. A year and a half later he came back with another tape that was produced by a well-known Nashville producer, but I still didn't hear anything I thought I could pitch. So we went into the studio. The secretaries started hanging around, hanging out in the studio; there was a buzz going. We knew something special was taking place. After a year and a half, all of a sudden, things happened really fast—three weeks, three hours, three labels! We were in the studio three weeks, and when we were through we started pitching the tape to labels. Within three hours we had three labels courting him—Decca, Asylum, and Curb. They were all blown away by the production.

"I was going through a Leadership Music class at the time (an in-depth study of all facets of the Nashville music industry for top industry executives), and Mark Wright of Decca Records kept following me around. 'I've gotta have him, man. You're going to give him to me, aren't you? We're Leadership Music buddies, right?' Mark kept goading. But I didn't want to have anything with the deal. I didn't expect a deal to come through anyway. You usually don't get that right away. Then Curb did a deal memo and that cinched it.

"How did I get started? I was finishing college, getting ready for grad school—I had a scholarship which covered half of my tuition, so I thought I'd go to Nashville and 'sell some songs' to get money for the other half. [*Anthony uses the amateur term 'sell songs' to reveal how green he was at that time.—S.B.*] I stopped by Muscle Shoals on my way, but the recording studios wouldn't see me. So I went to Fame Music Publishing, pushed the intercom on the door and said, 'I'm an arranger from the West Coast,' and they let me right in. They liked my songs, and a group called the Muscle Shoals Horns recorded one of them with Fred Foster producing.

"Fred brought me up to Nashville and introduced me to Bob Beckham; I became a staff writer for Combine Music. I started having more fun than I ever thought about having. I never intended to stay, thought I would just check it out. I was at Combine from 1982 to 1987. Then they sold the catalog. Nobody re-signed because we didn't know what was going on, so we all left. I had friends I was writing with over at Famous Music, so I went there until 1992.

"Susan Burns at Famous made writing appointments for me in Los Angeles and New York. When you live in Nashville and you go to Los Angeles or New York, you have priority time—studios that were booked will work around your schedule when you are from out of town. The same works in reverse. I would make as many as ten trips a year, writing songs and producing demos. When I would go out to places, they didn't know I was from Nashville. I've often heard, 'You don't look like you are from Nashville!' In 1989, I met Donna Summer. Famous could get you into places you just couldn't crack on your own.

"In Los Angeles, everyone has their own 'camp,' ten or twelve writers that they co-write with. They won't work with other writers and other studios. But being from Nashville, I can go from camp to camp. They can't do that or don't want to do that because, in their own camp, they are the general! Los Angeles writers are in and tied to major things; they can have as many people as they want around. They have their own little world.

"Nashville is such a songwriting center, everything revolves around the song. Los Angeles comes from a 'track' standpoint, it's a completely different process. They lay down tracks and get the whole thing rocking that way. Nashville is very structured; everyone works on a 10-2-6 schedule. Los Angeles works by the week, ten days, two weeks, in an unstructured manner. You sleep, then when you get up, no matter what time it is, you just resume working on the same project. In Nashville, you go to one project at 10:00, another at 2:00, another at 6:00! My favorite two things about Nashville are one, leaving; and two, coming back!

"So many of my friends started moving here, Nashville became 'Big Business.' Prior to that it wasn't perceived as 'Big Business' at all. But with all the consolidations it has really changed. For awhile Music Row did not embrace people coming here—it's gotten a lot better in the last five to seven years.

"Relationships are crucial in getting your songs cut. If you are writing really good songs, and they are getting heard, you will get some cuts. A great song goes right past the brain straight to the heart—you are just reacting to it. A smash is something different, it really stands out. Everybody hits the floor. What you have in Nashville is a lot of excellent songs—lots of outstanding songs to choose from. You just have to narrow down the ones that fit that artist.

"Anything that you do and get done requires a lot of work, and while we support the project in theory, we might not want to do the work. For example, I'm working with an aspiring artist right now. She was introduced to me by EMI Music Publishing. She had met people at different places, and they really liked her, but nothing was happening. It always takes longer than you initially think. I'll be working for six months at least. You need to put a lot of time into a project.

"For me, what I figured out is, a record tells it all—it answers all the questions. It becomes a product the record companies can sell. When it comes right down to it, that's what they do, they sell records. This is the record business—you've got to have a record. I can make a record—I don't need to put on a showcase for someone to see my act. The producer and the record label need to work together. If you make something they can 'sell,' then you've got a deal. I hate that word, but basically, it comes right down to that. You don't ever want to compromise, but you can use techniques that suit the label best—there is a lot of room in there. When you are trying to make your project the best it can be, it will be a lot better.

"I also don't put on showcases, or even go to see an artist's showcase. If the label wants a showcase, they will fund it. After you have something in your hand, then you can showcase. But if you are not well-funded, you can get substandard product that way.

"Just because someone says 'I want you on this label' doesn't mean you have a record deal. Even labels that I have relationships with might not be the right labels for an artist. You have to ask yourself, who gets the most excited about this artist? No artist is right for every label.

"I've always produced my own song demos, and that's how I got started. You have to be careful not to try to reinvent the wheel, and then bring it through this little bitty gate of industry standards; but you'll try that in the beginning. I'm either writing or in the studio for one reason or the other. There are also lots of meetings to do with production, endless business things that take a lot of your time.

"I like to do community work. I'm going to Memphis next week to sit on an ASCAP panel for NSAI along with Ralph Murphy and Roger Cook. The title of the panel is 'So You Think You're Something!' Everyone thinks they are going to take the town by storm. It just doesn't happen that way. So you give your time to helping educate people and give something of yourself back to the community. I used to have the 'save the world' mentality and tried to help people; but then you discover they don't want to be helped. They will go ahead and do exactly what you tell them not to do. Now I just give them the information they need and hope for the best for them.

"You don't do anything in this town without friends. Energy, drive, hard work are not enough—you can't do it without friends."

ANTHONY SMITH, a versatile songwriter, producer, and arranger, has achieved success in country music, pop, R&B, and jazz. Some of the artists who have recorded Anthony's songs include Lonestar, Clay Walker, Donna Summer, Regina Belle, Reba McEntire, Vince Gill, Jo Dee Messina, Neal McCoy, The Wilkinsons, Kirk Whalum, Suzy Bogguss, Kenny Rogers, John and Audrey Wiggins, Julie Reeves and Anita Cochran.

His hits include, *When Love Cries* (Donna Summer), *Watch This*, (Clay Walker), *What About Now*, (Lonestar, which is being used in the new Toyota campaign), *Love Happens Like That* (Neal McCoy), *Too Late to Worry* (Jo Dee Messina), and *Jimmy's Got A Girlfriend* (The Wilkinsons). His film credits include *Almost An Angel*, *Earth Force*, and *Graveyard Shift.*

As a producer, he produced the debut album for Atlantic recording artist, SouthSixtyFive, as well as the debut album for Curb artist Trini Triggs. Other production contributions may be found on the Kirk Whalum album *In This Life.* He also produced and co-wrote the *Titans on 2* jingle for News Channel 2, WKRN in Nashville. Lately, he has been busy developing new acts for H2E Entertainment.

He is a graduate of Leadership Music and has his own publishing companies: Works to Music (ASCAP), Notes to Music (ASCAP) copublished with Warner Chappell Music, and Words to Music (BMI) copublished with Notewrite Music. He is currently serving as a board member of NSAI and the Nashville Film Festival.

7

A Basic Understanding of Working as a Musician in Nashville

Amusician's life in Nashville is much different from that of a song-writer or an aspiring artist. There are no doors to knock on, no materials to prepare, and no one to help represent you. It's just you and your instrument.

NASHVILLE'S MUSICIANS

For the aspiring musician, all there is to do is network, hang out, network, hang out. There are lots and lots of live music venues of every size in Nashville, but they don't hire musicians. The people who play in the clubs put together their own bands. These are the people you need to network with.

To start out, you will have to volunteer your services. Offer to do demo sessions for free, offer to sit in if someone doesn't show up, offer to do just about anything to get the opportunity to be heard. Most of the people performing in clubs are songwriters trying out their songs on an audience. Usually songwriters are not the greatest instrumentalists. Offer to back them up and help them out.

Many musicians put bands together and spend a lot of time rehearsing in someone's garage. That's OK, too, if the band starts playing live sometime soon. But you don't want to spend too much time in that garage! You want to be in the clubs playing as much as you can, even if it's not your band and even if it's not a cool gig. Just get up onstage and play as soon and as much as you possibly can.

There are two very important things you need to know about being a musician in Nashville:

1. Nashville is on a 10-2-6 schedule.
2. All musicians are expected to be experts at the Nashville Number System.

10-2-6

All recording sessions in every recording studio are booked from 10:00 A.M. to 2:00 P.M.; from 2:00 P.M. to 6:00 P.M.; and from 6:00 P.M. to 10:00 P.M.; no exceptions. That's just the way it's done. Not only do the recording studios operate that way, but everybody else including songwriters and publishers are loosely on that schedule as well. That doesn't mean you can't get an appointment on Music Row at 9:00 or 11:00 A.M., but if you have a 10:00 A.M. writing appointment, don't be surprised if your co-writer has to leave for a 2:00 P.M. appointment with another writer. It's best to think in terms of 10-2-6, because there is a lot of activity going on in town that is on that time schedule, and everybody else works around it.

THE NASHVILLE NUMBER SYSTEM

The Nashville Number System is a method of transcribing music to paper so a song can be understood on the basis of chord relationships rather than notations in a fixed key. Nashville musicians do not think or write A-B-C-D-E-F-G. They think and write 1-2-3-4-5-6-7. This method works really well when someone wants to change key. The chart doesn't have to be rewritten, because it's still 1-2-3-4-5-6-7 no matter what key you are in. If you want to succeed as a musician in Nashville, you *must* learn the Nashville Number System. The best way to learn is to buy Chas Williams' book, *The Nashville Number System*, at *www.nashvillenumbersystem.com*. Here are some excerpts from the book:

> Nashville charts substitute numbers for the chord letter symbols found in traditional music notation. Rhythmic and dynamic notations, as well as chord voicing symbols from formal music, are used with the chord numbers. Since the Middle Ages, musicians have substituted Roman numerals for chord letters. However, around 1957, Neal Matthews, a member of the Jordanaires, originated the idea of substituting numbers for notes. Neal was familiar with the system of shape notes used by gospel quartets in the '30s and '40s, which used a different shape for each

note of the major scale. He began writing vocal charts substituting numbers for the shape notes and developed his own system of writing music with numbers.

In the early '60s, Harold Bradley (the music industry's most recorded musician), Charlie McCoy, Wayne Moss, and David Briggs noticed the unique approach that Neal and the Jordanaires used to map out a song on paper. Each of them began to devise his own number system, and the idea quickly spread among other session players in Nashville.

Musicians use the number system to chart out an entire song on paper while hearing a demo of the tune for the first time. This innovative system has become the standard method of music notation in Nashville and will remain so as long as records are produced in this town. One of the benefits of a number chart is that it can be played in any key, without transposing or rewriting the chart into a different key. The numbers represent the same relationship for a song's chord changes, regardless of the key.

Oddly enough, there is no one definitive version of the Nashville Number System. Many musicians use different symbols and notations to express the same musical idea. Everyone seems to have a system of notation that works best for him. Of course, a lot depends on whether you are writing a chart for your own purposes or for a band that has never heard your material or read your charts before. There are a wide variety of notational symbols acceptable in Nashville, so use the ones that work best for you.

The number system is the common language for communicating music in Nashville. If you are a songwriter it is a valuable tool to help you express your ideas so other musicians can understand and translate them effectively. If you are paying for a demo of your song, a well-prepared chart of the tune will save time and communicate your musical ideas precisely.

If you are a musician looking for work in Nashville, you will be presented with the task of reading or composing a number chart almost immediately. You'll be glad you had the opportunity to prepare ahead of time. The Nashville Number System is a musical shorthand that is simple, logical, and magical. If you learn it now, you'll be one step ahead of the game.

How the System Works

Numbers assigned to each note of the major scale represent chords as well as single notes. In the key of A, we have the major scale, A, B, C#, D, E, F# and G#. These become chords 1 through 7 in the key of A. It may seem too simple, but this is the method of assigning numbers to chords, which is the basis of the Nashville Number System. In the key of B, B becomes 1, etc. In the key of C, C is 1, etc. And so on for other keys.

A Sneak Peek at Harold Bradley's Notebook

Here are some basic rules, taken from the lecture notes of legendary session guitarist Harold Bradley.

1. All chords are major chords unless otherwise indicated, such as:
   Minor (−); Major 7th (s); Diminished (0); Augmented (+)

2. Use common time signatures. A number will hold for all beats within a section unless otherwise indicated. In 4/4 time, with each set of parentheses representing one measure:

$$(1 \quad), (1 \; 4 \quad), (1 \quad 4)$$

Add notations if you wish to indicate which beat corresponds to the chord change:

$$(14 \quad), (1 \quad 4)$$

3. If desired, you can use numbers for each beat or note:

$$(1444), (1114)$$

4. Bass notes can be indicated under the chords as follows:

$$1 \; \frac{54}{76} \; 5$$

5. Some prefer to write the number groupings down the page, others across the page:

```
1144
5511  or  1144 5511 1144 1515
1144
1515
```

There are many other symbols that can help you notate important areas of interpretation on your charts. A little study will add special notation for pickup notes, modulation, walkups and walkdowns, dynamics, feel and style, etc. Whether you are a songwriter or serious musician, a quick review of the Nashville Number System is well worth your time.

A Typical Nashville Session

Although there are no hard-and-fast rules, basic rhythm tracks are normally put down first, then, at different times, the vocals are done and various instruments are overdubbed. The basic rhythm tracks consist of drums (the most important to lay the foundation), rhythm guitar, lead guitar, bass, and usually keyboards. One of the musicians is named leader, which means many times he is responsible for hiring the other musicians, either choosing the musicians himself or helping the producer choose the musicians. He also helps with musical interpretations and files the paperwork for the rest of the musicians. He is paid double scale for his duties.

The producer starts by playing a demo of the song to be recorded, and the musicians write their number charts from the demo. Once in awhile the songwriter is asked to come in and perform his song live, instead of using a demo tape. This allows for more interpretation on the part of the musicians. Often a master session will turn out exactly like the demo, especially if the demo was done by Nashville's top session players.

Once the number charts are finished, the musicians will run through the song a few times, each working out his own contribution to the song. It is not unusual for Nashville's experienced session musicians to get a great basic rhythm track on just a few takes.

It is not difficult to get to know Nashville's top session players. They are often found sitting in at one of the showcases around town. Study the label credits on country albums; you'll see the same names on many different record labels. Then check the *Tennessean* and *Nashville Scene* for the clubs around town. There's a good chance some of the session players will be performing live, especially if there is a showcase for a major label artist or songwriter. Part of being successful in Nashville is getting to know the people who are already at the top.

Don't feel as though you have to get into the top recording studios to see what's going on in Nashville. Much of the activity is taking place in all of the various studios around town. Everyone is working on a project of some sort—a song, an artist project, a new studio. Get involved! You'll be surprised at how receptive others are to your fresh ideas.

Excerpted from *The Nashville Number System* © 1988, 1997 by Chas Williams. Available from the Nashville Number System, 1424 Robert E. Lee Lane, Dept. B, Brentwood, TN 37027 ($16.95 plus $6.00 UPS postage and handling—or check your local music store)

FOR MUSICIANS ONLY

June is Musician's Month in Nashville in honor of the city's ultimate guitar picker, Chet Atkins. Chet traveled to France one summer and discovered the most wonderful tribute to musicians. For one full month, the streets of France are filled with musicians of every craft and style, playing and entertaining the passersby. Restaurants and merchants join in the festival by making their wares available on the streets as well. Chet was deeply moved by the experience and felt that since Nashville housed the best and greatest musicians, the ultimate tribute to musicians should take place in Music City. He met with various organizations over several years, hoping to make his dream a reality.

Then, an enterprising businessman by the name of Tom Morales of TomKats Catering and Special Events, who was not afraid of a massive undertaking, took the challenge. He established the Chet Atkins' Musician Days, and for one week in June filled the city with outdoor stages free to the public, offered a guitar clinic, and a star-studded concert to benefit music education.

The festival was produced two years' running in June—you can visit a realistic bronze statue of Chet in front of the Bank of America building on Union and 5th Avenue North in downtown Nashville.

There are a few great references for musicians in Nashville. They are:

Music Row Publications—Annual Music Row Awards Edition

Published in May, this edition of *Music Row* magazine honors the best of the best. *Music Row* takes the top 50 albums that appeared in the top 10 of the *Billboard* Top Country Albums chart for a one-year period, and then they analyze the label copy of each album. Then they simply make a list of the musicians who played on these albums; categories are keyboards, engineer, bass guitar, guitar, drums, fiddle, steel guitar, and background vocals. These musicians are known as the "A" players. The survey came up with a list of less than forty musicians who played on the top 50 albums produced in Nashville! All of their names are listed in the May publication, and if you are an aspiring musician, your first priority should be to meet and play with as many of these Top 40 "A" players as possible.

All of these guys—no gals are listed except in the background vocal category—know each other really well, work together very well, and are used mainly because of the remarkable way they seem to read each others' minds. If you have hopes of one day becoming a studio musician in Nashville, then you will have to find a way to get to know these people. Some of them play out in the clubs at night. You might get lucky and find their name listed in the club listing in the *Tennessean* or *Nashville Scene*.

Dick McVey's Musician's Referral Service

"Serving the working musician since 1986–starting our 18th year!" If you need a gig or if you're looking for a musician, Dick McVey can help. In 1986, Dick founded the Musician's Referral Service in Nashville, with the goal of helping Nashville musicians find work. The service has been used by such artists and shows as Randy Travis, Alan Jackson, Chely Wright, David Lee Murphy, George Ducas, Holly Dunn, Tracy Lawrence, George Jones, Billy Dean, Tanya Tucker, Opryland, Disney World, Euro-Disney and several Branson and Myrtle Beach Theaters. You can reach McVey at *www.dickmcvey.com*, where his Musician's Referral Service is listed.

Terri Lynn's Chart Writer/Artist Showcase and Open Mic

Blues singer Terri Lynn hosts a showcase and open mic night at the French Quarter Cafe every other Tuesday at 7:00 P.M. If you are an aspiring musician, this showcase is a must for you! For information regarding the showcase, you can call (615) 889-0154 or contact Terri at *terrilynn1blues@aol.com*. You will find some information about Terri on the Internet, but it is out of date. Check to see if it has been updated by putting "Terri Lynn" in your favorite search engine.

INDUSTRY INTERVIEW WITH DAVE DUNSEATH, DRUMMER FOR DAN SEALS, T. GRAHAM BROWN, BILLY DEAN, AND LEE ANN WOMACK

"I've been interested in drumming ever since I can remember—got my first drum kit when I was eight years old. It was the 'Ringo' kit; a Black Diamond Pearl just like Ringo's—boy, what a beautiful set! I wish I still had it! I didn't really start playing in earnest until I graduated from college. I loved music, but I didn't want to teach music for a living so I majored in marketing and advertising at the University of Arkansas. Once I had my degree I decided just to go ahead and jump out and learn about the music business by playing. I played Top 40 and rock for about three years, going from St. Louis to Atlanta and surrounding areas. Then I picked up and moved to Nashville on one phone call.

"My former minister had moved to Nashville and was managing his sons. He told me they were getting out of gospel music and moving into secular music, and asked me if I could live on $1,000 per week! 'Gotta have you in three days,' he said. I was working with a band in Florida at the time, and I left the band in a lurch to hurry to Nashville for what I thought would be the opportunity of a lifetime!

"We wound up working at a Holiday Inn in Minnesota, playing for a lot less than a grand a week. It was all a sham. Nashville is full of dreams; if it weren't, none of this would be going on anyway! I wound up staying in Nashville, and decided to make my home here—just get down in the dirt and get to work.

"Musicians have a series of jobs; there's no such thing as a career—no retirement plan! I started doing small demo work. Everyone has a demo studio in his basement in Nashville. I did as much networking as I could, hanging out, sitting in occasionally for friends. Then I started being recommended for jobs.

"I heard about this great group of players who were looking for a drummer for the Starlight Lounge on Dickerson Road. I thought, 'Audition in a dive? Oh no!' But the players were Bob Regan (hit song-writer and session player) and two members of Reba's band. Here in this little dive bar were these great players! Actually, everyone should at least stop in once at the Starlight—it's a Nashville landmark.

"I got the gig but little did I know that these guys were going to leave the band. They all left, and there I was, on Dickerson Road. That led to another gig that turned out to be a great job working at 'Dad's Place' (a popular dance club for the over-forty jet set) at the Ramada Inn. I played there six nights a week for two years—tequila and beer helped me through it. The customers became like family, sending drinks to the band and showing lots of enthusiasm for our music—they were great.

"You can count on one hand the number of house bands there are in Nashville. There are pluses and minuses to paid work—it was the consistent paying job I was so hungry for, but it was also very hard work. Within three months of getting this job I also started doing carded (union) sessions. Other players recommended me. Even though I was working late nights, I never turned down a daytime session—I played for anyone who needed any help. You never know who's going to be on that session. You should want to take everything that comes along—hence the phrase 'paying your dues.'

"If you want to succeed in the arts at all, what are you willing to put up with? Rejection, low pay, bad treatment, not being paid at all—these are all part of the picture. If you can stay the course, you'll make it. Perseverance is the key!

"Dan Seals was putting a band together, and a friend that I met in one of these sessions recommended me for the drumming slot. The audition was the performance. I didn't even meet Dan until thirty minutes before we went onstage. I got that gig and subbed-out the Ramada Inn job when we went on the road. So I was working two jobs for two years. I learned an amazing thing about people's point of view outside of the music business. I made twice the money with Dan Seals and the gig was closer to my career goals, but when I went to buy a house they were more impressed with the Ramada Inn job.

"The best comments I've heard about drummers were from non-drummers. Duke Ellington said, 'Drummers are in the driver's seat . . . we are just along for the ride.' Being a musician is all about people skills. Being a good player, that's just expected. How do you get along with folks? That's the question. The artist, the way we travel together, the personality of the band—it all kind of plays in. Most players are just as nice as they can be; don't have a chip on their shoulder, don't have an attitude—the ones that tend to are not successful.

"I like to compare music to acting. Great actors don't necessarily succeed. John Wayne and Clint Eastwood are not the greatest actors in the world, but we love them! There are tremendous vocalists out there that only receive demo work—they don't make it to the top.

"Dan Seals started doing an acoustic unplugged set, went down to a trio, and didn't need a drummer. About the same time T. Graham Brown was looking for a drummer. He's one of the truly great singers in the industry. Every time a slot comes open in Nashville, everyone in the band has at least one friend to recommend. A friend of mine called to tell me about the gig and said it was mine if I wanted it. When I got there, there were at least ten other drummers auditioning for the gig. Actually, I prefer that, because the artist has a better disposition when he can compare you to others. They gave me a tape of T. Graham songs and had me work up two or three. The audition is just as important as a jam. I was hired, but, truthfully, I think it comes down to personal taste. A handful of drummers could do any one of these jobs. There is just a little something the artist is looking for. I've been to auditions with some great drummers, but they didn't always get the job.

"I left the Ramada Inn and went on tour with T. Graham for a year—then I got a call from a company that was putting together auditions for a band for Billy Dean. I said 'no' at the time, and they auditioned fifteen guys but didn't hire one. Then I got another call. They said Billy would be opening for Reba on her tour. I knew this was a golden opportunity, but I just didn't want to leave T. Graham. I went to the audition, and as I pulled up, the drummer for Jefferson Starship was just getting out of a cab. We both auditioned and I got the gig . . . it just goes to show you—he is a tremendous drummer!

"T. Graham is a drummer's dream job—funk, R&B—a blue-eyed soul boy and a great guy. I didn't know what to do. I called Lyle Lovett's drummer, a great friend, and told him I felt like I was losing all innocence—all the love of drumming I was trading in for money. He said that I knew in my heart I would have to make this career move, and he was right. I was three years with Billy, until he went unplugged.

"There is no such thing as a career as a sideman. It's just a job after another job after another job. There are no parting gifts; no going away party. It's just pretty much good-bye, don't come back. Billy's road manager said, 'Boys, you've all seen the schedule.' It's just 10-2-6, everyday.

"I hope I've helped some musicians figure out Nashville a little bit. The other thing I'll say is, learn the Nashville Number System. Remember my very first gig? The $1,000-a-week job? The first thing that happened when I sat down to play was that someone explained it to me. I was lucky. We also had a steel player who had just moved to town. He kept making mistakes. We would stop, try to help him work things out, and then he'd make more mistakes. Finally someone asked him if he had a chart. 'Someone gave me this weird math problem,' he said, 'but I haven't solved it yet!' It's expected that you know it, and it's so simple to know and use, you are crazy not to.

"I tell everyone I meet there is always room for other players here. More songwriters too. There's no reason not to give it a try. The key to success is hanging out, subbing, networking period. That's how the bulk of the work comes down. As a musician, you really can't make up a demo, then go knock on studio doors or label doors. You've just got to get out there! It's like pulling teeth to go out to the clubs sometimes. But I've never driven home thinking it was a waste of my time.

"Now I am able to stay home and write, then go out on the road for awhile. I treat writing seriously, like a business. Some writers just write when they are inspired; others write every day. I just started getting interested in writing—it's a new challenge and a new goal."

8

A Basic
Understanding of
Nashville's
Songwriters
Organizations

There are three songwriters associations in Nashville, and the best advice for someone who is just getting acquainted with Nashville is to join all three. You never know where the next step to a successful writing career might lead. They are all very different and vary greatly in the benefits you will receive from each one. Here is a very brief analysis of why you should join as soon as possible. A more comprehensive list of services follows.

NASHVILLE'S THREE SONGWRITER ASSOCIATIONS

Nashville Songwriters Association International (NSAI) is the largest and most respected organization, with national and international recognition. They have over a hundred chapters across the United States, so the chances are there is one close to you. If you belong to one of these regional chapters, then you can perform at a writers' night at the Bluebird Cafe (you don't have to be a member to perform at Open Mic). And, you can also get your songs critiqued by an NSAI panel of experts. The NSAI board of directors consists of Nashville's hottest hit songwriters. The Songwriters Guild of America (SGA) is a national organization that focuses very intently on protecting songwriters' rights and assists in negotiations with publishers. The Tennessee Songwriter's Association International (TSAI) is a grass-roots organization, with a small group of passionate members.

Each of these organizations has a myriad of services designed to assist you in your songwriting efforts at various stages of development. It would be ideal to plan around one of the programs they offer. I would highly recommend the NSAI Spring Symposium and Tin Pan South as don't-miss events. Attending one of these events and the other events offered every week will give you maximum exposure to the songwriting community. Although you are guaranteed to learn a lot about songwriting and the Nashville music industry, the most valuable benefit will be meeting publishers, A&R reps, Nashville's hit songwriters, and potential co-writing partners.

NASHVILLE SONGWRITERS ASSOCIATION INTERNATIONAL (NSAI)
1701 West End Avenue, Third Floor
Nashville, TN 37203
Tel: (615) 256-3354, (800) 321-6008
Fax: (615) 256-0034
Web site: *www.nashvillesongwriters.com*

Weekly Workshops:
The following formats alternate every Thursday night:

- Critique: Your songs are evaluated by the best in the business.
- Publisher Night: A chance to attract a publisher to your songs.
- Pro Teaching: The pros share how they did it.

Yearly Events:
- Spring Symposium: A two-day intensive program on songcrafting, including the opportunity to have songs critiqued and an excellent opportunity to meet key executives in Nashville.
- Tin Pan South: The nation's largest festival spotlighting the songwriters and the song, the festival is a weeklong event featuring all genres of music in all of Nashville's popular music venues. Also includes a golf tournament and Legendary Songwriters Concert.
- Song Camp: An intense, three-day retreat with six pro writers; large and small group sessions, with individual song evaluations by one pro writer.

Other Services:

- Office Facilities and Writers' Rooms: Telephones, typewriters, fax machine, computers, photocopier, single-tape dubbing decks, reference library, industry publications, bulletin board, copyright forms, phone message service—wow! Your Nashville office!
- 800 Number: Members are given a toll-free number to call with questions regarding Nashville and your upcoming trip.
- Newsletter: *NSAI Newswire* is a quarterly newsletter on NSAI happenings.
- Song Evaluation Service: Members can mail one song at a time to NSAI for evaluation.
- Online Workshops: Can't be there? Jump online!
- Counseling: The NSAI staff is available to answer questions.
- Books and Merchandise: Discount rates for members.
- Insurance Plans: Major medical, disability, accident and life.
- Pro-Writer Category: NSAI offers special services for member songwriters who have had their songs recorded by major recording artists, such as regular informal meetings with label heads.
- Regional Workshops: NSAI may have a workshop near you, or will help you set up a workshop in your own hometown.
- Active Legislation Involvement: Fights for songwriter rights on a national level through a Legislative Committee and various songwriting coalitions.

INDUSTRY INTERVIEW WITH BARTON HERBISON, EXECUTIVE DIRECTOR, NSAI

"If you are going to make it as a songwriter in Nashville, there are certain things you have to do. I do know the formula—it is:

"Number One: Talent. If your songs aren't great, forget it. Even the most gifted writers need to hone the craft, but you've got to have the gift to begin with. A lot of people just don't.

"Number Two: Hard work and persistence. Just as if you were starting as a professional athlete. You've got to give it all the physical energy you've got.

"Number Three: Luck. I believe you have to have luck to a large degree. The more opportunities you make for yourself, the more luck will come your way.

"Number Four: Desire. Songwriting is not an incident, it's a pursuit.

You may have the best song ever written, but you've got to work at the business of the industry to get that song into the right hands.

"Hit songwriters all have one thing in common; it's something they do every day of their life. A lot of people come up here and get someone to listen to their songs, then they think they are done. But it's just the beginning. The most common thing I hear from the great writers is, 'I had to do it. I didn't have any choice.' Great songwriters never question why they do it.

"NSAI is a reality check. We want to foster the dreams and shatter the myths. It breaks my heart when I hear that a writer/artist had given someone $30,000 to produce a record or spent $5,000 to get their songs demoed. Come see us before you spend that kind of money.

"What do you get from (membership in) NSAI? Nothing, except opportunity and resources. We don't make it happen for you. We give you the information you need. We try to shoot straight. If you are a songwriter, it's good to hang out at NSAI. We have three writers' rooms, and there is a great energy among the staff. There is magic in the building.

"And you've got to hang out at those writers' nights around town. Why?

"One, to build relationships. You'll meet someone influential who likes your songs and will make calls on your behalf. Two, to get feedback on your songs. And three, to perform, for those that can; your performing helps you with your songs.

"Songwriting is a calling, not an incident."

_____

For the past decade BARTON HERBISON served as chief administrative officer for U.S. Congressman Bob Clement of Nashville. In that capacity he joined NSAI in fighting battles to protect writers' intellectual property rights. Prior to that he worked as a reporter and spent fourteen years in country radio. Bart grew up in the rural west Tennessee town of Paris.

SONGWRITERS GUILD OF AMERICA ("THE GUILD" OR SGA)

1222 16th Avenue South, Suite 25
Nashville, TN 37212
Tel: (615) 329-1782
Fax: (615) 329-2623
E-mail: *sganash@aol.com*

Web site: *www.songwritersguild.com*
Los Angeles: (323) 462-1108; e-mail *LASGA@aol.com*
New York: (212) 768-7902; e-mail *SongNews@aol.com*
New Jersey: (201) 867-7603; e-mail *SongwritersNJ@aol.com*

Weekly Meetings:
- Ask-a-Pro: An informal monthly meeting with top industry professionals; i.e. producers, A&R execs, publishers, managers, lawyers, etc.—anyone and everyone you need to meet.
- Song Critique: An industry professional listens to your demo and gives you honest input.
- Hit Song Analysis: A hit songwriter reveals the behind-the-scene story on his latest chart single.
- Songmania: Writers' night at one of Nashville's popular venues.
- Weekly Nashville E-mail Newsletter containing events in Music City and member updates.

Other Services:
- Songwriting Workshops: Periodic workshops with top songwriters, publishers, and other industry professionals. Usually last two or three full days, and include panel discussions on important topics, writers-in-the-round, keynote speaker, and lots of networking time. Try to plan your trip to Nashville around one of these workshops, usually in July.
- The Guild Contract: The Guild has the best songwriters' contract in the business. It contains important items that a "standard" songwriters' agreement might not have, the most important being a reversion clause and the written right to audit a publisher's books. Guild members *are not required* to use a Guild contract, one of the biggest misconceptions about membership in the Guild.
- Contract Review: The Guild will review a publisher's contract and give you the information you need to bargain for a better deal.
- Royalty Collection: The Guild has a Royalty Collection Plan that insures that you collect royalties from all sources. They also keep a copy of your contract on file in case of an emergency. Guild members *are required* to use this plan, another misconception about Guild membership.
- Publisher Audits: The Guild has an ongoing program of audits of music publishers.
- Catalog Administration Plan (CAP): For writers who control 25 percent or more of the publishing rights to their recorded and published

works, the Guild offers the CAP at very low rates as compared to other catalog administrators.

• Copyright Renewal and Termination: All Guild members are given a one-year advance notice when their songs are due to be renewed or reclaimed from publishers.

• Catalog Evaluation: Financial evaluation of a catalog for tax or estate planning, catalog sale, or negotiation for renewal or termination rights.

• Group medical and life insurance.

• Newsletters: Local and national periodic publications.

• Legal/Legislative Work: Constantly seeks to strengthen your rights and increase your royalties through appropriate action directed at publishers, industry groups, the courts or Congress.

INDUSTRY INTERVIEW WITH EVAN SHOEMAKE, SOUTHERN REGIONAL DIRECTOR, SONGWRITERS

"My first impression of Nashville was that it was very similar to Georgia, where I grew up. Honestly, the only remarkable difference is that there are a large amount of Midwesterners in Nashville. I have never run across so many people from Michigan, Minnesota, and Wisconsin in my life! The thing I love most about Nashville is that you have the best of both worlds. It is not an overwhelming urban city, but there is lots going on to keep you entertained.

"For the first month, I just felt intimidated and overwhelmed. Rundi Ream and I would go to industry parties and I was shell-shocked! The biggest names in Nashville were right in the room with us. I had to stand back and just absorb the view. Eventually I got used to it as I met more people and became more comfortable.

"The question I get the most is how do we differ from NSAI. Basically the two organizations have different resources. NSAI works really well with new writers, and is very nurturing to those developing writers. SGA works more with mid-level to professional writers and performing writers. SGA has the ability to help writers from the very beginning of their career all the way through because we offer programs and benefits at each stage of their career, including managing estates and recovering copyrights.

"The most important thing we offer is our contract review service. In today's songwriting climate, there really aren't any standard contracts. The SGA contract is helpful as an educational tool. When a songwriter is offered a contract, we will go through it and make sure it is fair and beneficial to the writer. This service is for members only. Membership in the organization is $70 or $85 depending on a songwriter's income, plus a 5.75 percentage of mechanical royalty income (with a $1,750 cap). We also offer an online membership that allows writers to join without signing the Royalty Collection Plan. Sometimes the percentage charge puts off writers from joining SGA, but I look upon it as an insurance policy; songwriters never know if they need it but if so, it's there. The money is used to fund the organization, including representation before Congress. SGA is the only songwriters' association that is allowed to go before Congress, and sets royalty rates along with the Recording Industry Association of America (RIAA) and the National Music Publishers Association (NMPA). These three organizations went before Congress and changed the rates, which have gradually been increasing over a ten-year period.

"I really feel that if people are paying a membership fee, they should get free services from the organization. We don't necessarily try to make money on these workshops and seminars, but instead provide a service for the songwriter. One of the most exciting events we offer is SGA Week. The workshop is very unique, in that we 1) keep the costs very affordable, only $45 for three days, with a special rate at a local hotel; and 2) we limit registration to only sixty people, so everyone gets a lot of special attention. During SGA Week 2003, we had a panel titled New Artist Introduction, with Autumn House (A&R Capitol Records) Doug Howard (A&R Lyric Street Records) and Jeremy Witt (A&R Warner Bros. Records). The panel gave attendees an open invitation to pitch their songs to their new artists, even after the seminar was over! That blew me away because it is virtually unheard of these days to have that opportunity and they really went above and beyond what we had asked them to do.

"Jerry Vandiver (*For a Little While*, Tim McGraw) coordinates our Pro Pitch Meetings with producers, A&R and artists. We have very strict rules for these pitch sessions, and keep it very small. They are limited to ten writers, and the song quality must be very high. We have three categories: 1) self-published writers who have had three major cuts; 2) staff deal writers with one major cut; or 3) a non-pro writer who has gone through a screening process with a publisher who screens the songs for quality.

"SGA offers great and unique services to the professional songwriter and performing artist—but people don't know us well enough—they don't know what we do! I'm a change agent. I get in and change things, not just for the sake of change but to make things better and stronger. I plan to do that for SGA Nashville."

EVAN SHOEMAKE received a bachelor's degree in English from the State University of West Georgia and a masters degree in higher education from the University of Florida. He wound up in Nashville quite by accident when he completed a job placement application for NACA, the National Association of Campus Activities, and unknowingly checked "interested in the music industry" on the application form. The former southern regional director of SGA Nashville, Rundi Ream, came across his application and found that they had a mutual friend. She called and asked for a resume, and interviewed him twice over the phone. He was hired sight unseen and moved to Nashville to take the job in May of 2002.

Shoemake quickly moved from an administrative position to project and event coordinator, and after two short years, stepped into the southern regional director position. His number one goal is to make SGA a major player in the Nashville music industry.

TENNESSEE SONGWRITERS ASSOCIATION INTERNATIONAL (TSAI)

P. O. Box 2664
Hendersonville, TN 37077-2664
Tel: (615) 969-5967
E-mail: *ASKTSAI@aol.com*
Web site: *www.clubnashville.com/tsai.htm*

The Tennessee Songwriters Association International is a "hands-on" organization. Its members are encouraged to actively participate in the growth and development of the association. TSAI welcomes your ideas and energy and encourages your participation.

Weekly Meetings:
The following formats alternate every Wednesday night:

- TSAI Workshop: Deals with all phases of the music industry that will help you better understand the business and those who operate it.
- Critique Night: A chance to have your song critiqued by your peers and get the feedback to make it a better song.
- Celebrity Critique Night: The top industry executives give feedback on your songs.

- Pitch-a-Pro Night: An opportunity to pitch your songs directly to someone looking for hit songs, including producers, A&R reps, publishers, and artists.
- Pro-Rap Night: A chance to ask question of a topnotch guest speaker from the music industry.
- Legends Night: A chance to meet stars of the Grand Ole Opry and country music Legends and listen to them share their personal story.

Other services:

Monthly Newsletter: packed with information, tip sheet on who's looking for songs, interviews, ideas, songwriting updates, and other useful articles.

INDUSTRY INTERVIEW WITH JIM SYLVIS, EXECUTIVE DIRECTOR, TENNESSEE SONGWRITERS ASSOCIATION INTERNATIONAL

"The biggest problem I see all the time is that people come into town and have no concept of what is going on here. They are still writing songs in the genre of Faron Young or Ray Price or the like. They have the wrong concept of what country music is today. Aspiring songwriters need to come into town a couple of times and find out what's going on—just hang out and get a feel for the place.

"They need to listen to the radio stations that are playing current country music, not the golden oldies or classic country. And it would be a really good idea to join a songwriters' organization in your own home town, get your feet wet in networking with other songwriters, something that is essential in Nashville.

"Also it's important to get some feedback on your demos before you start pitching them around. Usually when new writers come into town, their demos are not anywhere near Nashville standards. So I would advise writers to spend enough time in Nashville to get to hear some Nashville demos and compare their own demos to those. Chances are, they will have to re-demo their songs in Nashville in order to get the right sound.

"I've been in the business a long time, running our songwriters' organization for seventeen years, and I've seen the same thing over and over. People come here completely unprepared. So my advice for everyone is to learn as much as you possibly can before you come here; and make at least a couple of trips to Nashville just to learn how things are done before you start pitching your songs. Certainly you would want to make a couple of separate trips here before you pack your bags and move. Nashville might not be at all what you are expecting."

9

A Basic Understanding of Nashville's Performing Rights Organizations (PROs)

Many songwriters do not realize that each of the performing rights organizations—ASCAP, BMI, and SESAC—can help them get started, even though it isn't necessary to affiliate with one of them until you actually have a song recorded. They are in the song business and are constantly on the lookout for great songwriters. If, in their opinion, your songs can become hits, they will be quick to help you find a publisher you can work with. If all three organizations tell you your songs need work, it might be wise to reconsider your songwriting goals. Although anyone's opinion is just that, an opinion, the performing rights organizations have a very good idea of what has commercial appeal, and their opinion carries a lot of weight. They tend to be very conservative and don't discourage writers unless they are sure there is little possibility of future success.

ABOUT NASHVILLE'S PROs

The main function of PROs is to collect performance money on your behalf, and they have several different departments to guide that process. Each PRO has a writers' representative department that spends its time looking for new songwriters, helping them find a publisher or record deal, helping place songs with artists, and generally servicing accounts. Your decision of which organization to choose usually depends on the personal relationships you have made in the company. Getting to know the people at each of the PROs is an important step in the song process.

Try to get your songs reviewed by each of the PROs before you come to Nashville. That may be very difficult to do, as these organizations receive as many CDs in the mail as publishers. At a minimum, try to get an appointment with a writers' representative as close to your arrival time as possible. These three organizations will be your most helpful contacts during your trip.

The three organizations have the same purpose, but are very different in the way they operate. Their purpose is to collect money from radio broadcasters, live concert auditoriums and clubs, restaurants, television, cable, and the Internet. They distribute the money they collect to their affiliates (writers and publishers). These collections are based on a percentage of advertising income and broadcast capacity of radio and TV stations, and the size of live concert venues. They differ greatly in the way they monitor the songs being played or performed, and also in the way they distribute the money.

ASCAP collects the most money, as they are the oldest organization and represent many standard songs. BMI is a close second in collections. SESAC collects considerably less money than the other two, but has proportionately fewer affiliates to whom they distribute the money. Check out all three, then concentrate on developing a close relationship with the one organization you feel most comfortable with. Don't rush to sign with a PRO. Since their main function is to collect for the performance of a song, there really is no need to sign up until your song has been recorded.

Although the letters in ASCAP, BMI, and SESAC stand for something (of course), they always go by letters only. So there is no need to remember what they stand for. It's included here just so you'll know.

ASCAP
(American Society of Composers, Authors and Publishers)
Headquarters: One Lincoln Plaza
                New York, NY 10023
                Tel: (212) 621-6000
                Web site: *www.ascap.com*

Nashville: 2 Music Square West
                Nashville, TN 37203
                Tel: (615) 742-5000
                Fax: (615) 742-5020

With offices in Los Angeles, Atlanta, Chicago, Miami, London, and Puerto Rico

How They Determine Who Gets Paid

ASCAP uses two methods: Census Survey (a complete count) and Sample Survey. In a one-year period, 200,000 hours of radio are sampled. This is done using the actual taping of radio shows, as well as the use of data from program logs and the number of spins reported by BDS. The use of music on the Internet is monitored by EZ-Eagle, an Internet anti-piracy and music licensing application.

How They Pay

Every performance generates a certain number of credits. Each credit is worth a certain dollar value (for example, it was $4.64 in 1998). Performance credits depend on several factors, including medium, type, station weight, time of day, and allocation applied to broadcast feature performances. In addition, ASCAP members can apply for Special Awards. Application forms are sent to every ASCAP member.

Special Writer Services

- ASCAP Foundation Country Songwriters Workshop (Spring)—for all writers
- ASCAP Foundation Pop Workshop (Fall)—for all writers regardless of affiliation
- ASCAP Music Business 101—Monthly educational sessions with industry speakers
- ASCAP Writers Series—Pro writer meets with developing writers for three months
- Straight Talk—Weekly informational meeting on ASCAP and Music Row
- Song Source—Feedback from ASCAP staff and industry professionals on one song
- Writers Rooms—ASCAP has three writers' rooms with Yamaha keyboards
- ASCAP Nashville Demo Studio—Digital 8-track studio for ASCAP members
- ASCAP Showcases—ASCAP members perform for Music Row executives
- Additional Member Benefits—Health, dental, term life, long-term care, etc.

INDUSTRY INTERVIEW WITH JOHN BRIGGS, ASSISTANT VICE PRESIDENT, ASCAP

"ASCAP is the world's largest Performing Rights Organization, with over 180,000 composer, lyricist and music publisher members representing all

genres of music. It is the only U.S. Performance Rights Organization (PRO) created and controlled by songwriters and publishers. Created in 1914, as the first U.S. PRO, the founding writers and publisher members of the period established an organization committed to protecting the rights of its members by licensing and collecting royalties for the public performance of their copyrighted works, and then distributing these fees to the Society's members based on performances. A few of those founders included Irving Berlin, John Philip Sousa, Jerome Kern, and Victor Herbert. From our past, present, and into the future, we have embraced pop, country, classical, urban, R&B, rock 'n' roll, Broadway and any form of music available. WC Handy, Jimmie Rodgers, Louis Armstrong, Johnny Cash, Gene Autry, Jimmy Jam, The Beatles, Aerosmith, Marvin Gaye, Billy Joel, and Garth Brooks are a few examples of ASCAP's immense diversity. In short, if you're a songwriter or a publisher, ASCAP should be your home.

"ASCAP's board of directors is made up solely of writers and publishers, elected by the membership every two years. Historically our president and chairman have always been songwriters. Songwriter legend Marilyn Bergman is the current president/chairman and our CEO is John LoFrumento. When you join ASCAP you become an owner with a voice in the only U.S. PRO owned and run by its members. Ownership for a creator in this industry is rare and our success is based on that premise.

"ASCAP is the only U.S. PRO to hold annual membership meetings where members have the opportunity to learn about ASCAP, ask questions, and to voice concerns. Members also participate in the affairs of the Society by serving on a variety of committees, such as the Symphonic and Concert Committee; Latin Music Council; Commercial, Promotional, Announcement (CPA) Advisory Committee, the Board of Review and others. ASCAP is the leader in efforts to protect our member's rights by vigorously opposing legislation that is harmful to creators and by initiating changes to the copyright law that will benefit creators.

"ASCAP collects, monitors, and pays on performances in mediums where the benefit/cost ratio is favorable to our members. In 2003 we collected over $668 million, continuing our tradition as the number one PRO in collections and distributions to our members throughout the world. In addition we maintain the lowest operational costs of any PRO in the U.S. by distributing around 86 cents for every dollar we collect. In contrast to our competitors, we provide full financial disclosures to our members and the public. Our distribution system is transparent and based on fairness. All similar performances are similarly credited regardless of the member and no changes in royalty rates are made without Board approval and member notification. Royalty checks go out eight times a year, four domestic and four foreign distributions. ASCAP has reciprocal agreements with foreign societies representing virtually every country that have laws protecting copyright. We were the first U.S. PRO to distribute royalties from the Internet and continue to pursue additional revenue sources for our membership.

"The ASCAP Plus Awards Program compensates those writers whose works are substantially performed in venues and media outside of our surveys. Each year, members have an opportunity to apply for ASCAP Plus Awards by informing us about their live performances, such as club and concert dates, tours, etc. An independent panel evaluates submissions and determines monetary awards to deserving members that have unique prestige value. ASCAP is the only performing rights society in the U.S. with a cash awards program, with a similar program open to foreign society writers.

"ASCAP presents educational workshops in film scoring, country, pop, R&B, gospel, musical theater, jazz, Latin, concert music and various other genres. We sponsor a number of industry showcases that provide visibility and create new opportunities for our members.

"With the rapid industry changes that impact our members, ASCAP continues to develop innovative programs that insure our member's interests are served for the long haul. A few examples include: U.S. Alliance—a member-owned credit union that services member's financial needs; Music Pro—insurance for medical, dental, studio, longterm care, etc.; Media Guide—Created and launched in 2003, Media Guide is a high-tech company utilizing a unique and sophisticated audio fingerprint technology to track and instantly identify music, ads, and public service announcements as they are broadcast. Media Guide is already providing real value from its national network of monitoring stations in more than 200 U.S. markets covering over 3,000 radio and television stations as well as cable channels. As of June 2004, Media Guide is tracking over 27 million radio broadcast hours a year for the benefit of its members. A full list of membership benefits is listed on our Web site at *www.ascap.com*. Joining ASCAP is simple. Click on 'how to join,' print a membership application, complete and send it to our New York office.

"Information is power. So my advice to aspiring songwriters is to research the genre of music you are pursuing. *Music, Money and Success*, written by Jeff and Todd Brabec, is a wonderful overview of the mechanics of the business. Ralph Murphy writes a column called 'Murphy's Law's of Songwriting' that deals with the craft side of writing. Ralph has written and published numerous hits and his suggestions are focused on describing what a publisher is seeking. You can find his column on our Web site. One of our member privileges is Song Source, a weekly song pitch session where ten ASCAP members will play one of their songs to a professional music publisher. Members can sign up on a first come first serve basis once every six months. We also offer Straight Talk, a weekly ASCAP music industry meeting. The educational presentation allows writers ample time for questions regarding ASCAP and the music industry and is open to all writers regardless of affiliation. To sign up for either of these sessions, contact our receptionist at (615) 742-5000.

"A common mistake that young writers encounter is not being informed. If you're writing songs for commercial radio, read trade publications like *Billboard* and listen to contemporary radio stations. Those stations play songs that are written by your songwriter peers and competitors. Hold your songs in competition, against those you hear. If you A/B your songs with theirs, you'll have insight to what the industry is seeking.

"Also, perspiration, not inspiration, is the key ingredients to sharpening your skills. Create a focused writing schedule and devote a minimum of twenty hours a week to sharpen your skills. Remember, the pros spend forty or more hours a week writing. One insightful response to a disgruntled writer who was complaining about not getting a break was given by songwriter legend Harlan Howard. The comment was, 'Kid, who invited you?' Anyone who knew Harlan will tell you about his love for his fellow songwriters but his advice to that writer was a great lesson. Harlan's tremendous success was based on his strong work habits and a warm positive attitude. Harlan's songs will always be remembered for their heartfelt honesty and we all lost a great mentor when he passed away.

"Today's songwriters face greater challenges than their predecessors with over 60 percent of the music industry shuttered in the past few years. Talent, dedication, and hard work are your key tools for succeeding in this challenging environment. ASCAP is focused on ensuring that the songwriter's voice is heard and will continue to provide tools and services that will support your creative endeavors."

JOHN BRIGGS can be described as multifaceted with a knack for signing to ASCAP, the largest performance right organization in the world, unknown performing artists who become top selling stars and household names. His ability to recognize talent has paid major dividends for ASCAP. A few of his credits include writer-artists Alan Jackson, Brian McKnight, Clint Black, Backstreet Boys, Brad Paisley, Jessica Simpson, Dixie Chicks, Deana Carter and the Cranberries.

Briggs convinced former ASCAP co-worker, Bob Doyle, to present one of his writer/artists to a music-industry panel for a showcase of Nashville songwriters. The show provided the outlet that led to the artist signing with Capitol Records. In a short time, the artist became the top selling solo artist of all time. His name: Garth Brooks. Following stints at Wishbone Publishing, Will N' David Music and Screen Gems/EMI Music, Briggs moved to ASCAP in 1985. His unlimited energy and hard work combined with his creative, business and leadership skills led to his position as Vice President Membership Group of ASCAP.

In April 2003, John launched *ASCAP LIVE! From the Wild Horse*, a two hour musical variety show that features ASCAP Signature, Rising Star and Uncut Diamond artists. A living room set provides the perfect intimate mood for host Shannon McCombs, who achieved fame on CMT and TNN, to explore the songwriter side of an artist. Taped in front of a live audience of over 1,000 per show, *ASCAP LIVE! From the Wild Horse* is rebroadcast nationally on XM and locally on WSM-FM. In a June 2003 article, *USA Today*, mentioned ASCAP's Uncut Diamond artist Ashley Gearing as a star of the future. John is actively involved with a number of music industry organizations. He serves on the Academy of Country Music board and is a governor with the Nashville chapter of NARAS, the organization that produces the Grammy Awards. John has been a keynote speaker, moderator and guest panelist for music industry organizations including Billboard, ASCAP, NARAS, CMA and NSAI. In 1997 he received the Alabama Governor's Award for his contribution to American music

BMI
(Broadcast Music, Inc.)
Headquarters: 320 West 57th Street
                                                    New York, NY 10019
                                                    Tel: (212) 586-2000
                                                    Web site: *www.bmi.com*

Nashville: Ten Music Square East
                                  Nashville, TN 37203
                                  Tel: (615) 401-2700
                                  Fax: (615) 401-2707

With offices in Los Angeles, Miami, Atlanta, London, and Puerto Rico

How They Determine Who Gets Paid

BMI tracks radio performances by using the daily logs of radio stations. They track every song a station has played over a three-day period, collecting logs for 600,000 hours in a one-year period. Music performed on network TV, cable TV, and local TV stations is reported to BMI on music cue sheets, which list all music performed on a program. The use of music on the Internet is monitored.

How They Pay

Each station is stratified by musical genre and market size, and each performance is multiplied by a factor that reflects the ratio of the number of stations logged to the number licensed. As performances increase, so do writers' royalties. BMI has midlevel, upper level, and super bonus–level rates for songs that reach the 50,000 to one million performance plateau. A number one song has the potential to earn $400,000 a year.

Special Writer Services

- BMI Roundtable (monthly): History of BMI and of Music Row. Gives good fundamental guidelines to a beginning songwriter.
- BMI Songwriters' Workshop (monthly). If you have been to a BMI roundtable, you can attend a songwriting workshop taught by award-winning songwriter Jason Blume.
- BMI Demo Derby with Jason Blume (monthly): For BMI members only. Professional feedback and constructive critiques of songs within a small, supportive group.
- BMI Music Connection Showcase (bimonthly in New York, Los Angeles, Nashville, Atlanta, and Miami): An artist showcase, including all genres of music.
- Screening room, writers' rooms.
- Affiliate loan program.
- Direct deposit.
- Insurance: equipment, health, dental, life.
- Legislative representation.

INDUSTRY INTERVIEW WITH DAVID PRESTON, DIRECTOR OF WRITER/PUBLISHER RELATIONS, BMI

"We have an open-door policy here at BMI. We will always make an appointment to see writers if they make the effort to call in advance. It's not necessary for a writer to have anything published in order to sign a two-year contract with us, and there are a lot of advantages to joining BMI. For example, we have a lot of great workshops for beginning songwriters, including BMI Roundtable, BMI Writers' Workshop with Jason Blume, and BMI Demo Derby with Jason Blume. Jason is a great songwriter and instructor, and has helped a lot of writers in various stages of development.

"BMI was formed because country and R&B writers of the early 1900s were not being recognized as viable creators of music. Only standards by writers like Irving Berlin and John Philip Sousa were licensed to be played on the radio. Stations weren't allowed to play other songs unless they had permission from the songwriters, which individually was impossible to do. So a group of 425 radio broadcasters got together in 1940 and started BMI. In 1958 Frances Preston opened a Nashville office in support of the growing country music industry. For this reason BMI has always been considered the home of rock 'n' roll, country, and R&B.

"BMI's real strength is that we log more music than anyone, with over 4 million song titles, including music from the Top 10 motion pictures of all time. We monitor over 500,000 hours of music annually, using both the radio station program logs and BDS reports on the country charts. We have also launched a new Web site, *www.songwriter101.com*, which has an in-depth Q&A section and has greatly enhanced BMI's service to its songwriters and publishers.

"BMI has also taken a leadership role in the development of a global copyright information system to create a 'virtual database' of musical works. We are working with CISAC Common Information System on a prototype so that performing rights organizations can exchange information directly among their mainframe computers.

"The atmosphere in Nashville right now is highly competitive; there are approximately 200 artists signed to major and independent labels in this town, and approximately 50,000 songwriters in Davidson county alone! A lot of artists write their own material, and they produce only one CD a year—twelve songs. That's not very many chances to get songs recorded.

"It's very important that songwriters realize, there are a lot of people out there trying to get their songs heard. The number one rule is: *Have a professional and courteous approach.* It's important to be persistent but polite. Doing your homework before you come is very beneficial. Know the names of the producers and publishers, writers and artists. That's a huge help. Having an artist in mind, an idea of who you think can cut your material, is very important. Read *Billboard* and study their charts; and read the label copy on CDs. Study all about the artists, the publishers, the producers. I meet with a lot of people who are really out of touch with the industry and aren't familiar with the current country artists. It's frustrating!

"If you move to Nashville today and you are a great songwriter, then you are looking at least at five years before you start having some success; the average is ten years. Even great songwriters have to work very hard to write a great song. Songwriters who work hard at the craft of songwriting will make major improvements over time. With developing writers, I always say, 'Come see me again in six months.' If they come back with the same songs, no changes, I'll realize that they aren't serious about it.

"This is especially true with artists. Once they start getting better, at some point they will get *a lot* better. That's when Nashville starts paying attention."

———————————————

DAVID PRESTON is a native Nashvillian and son of BMI president and CEO, Frances W. Preston. Mr. Preston graduated from Peabody Demonstration School and studied mass communication at Denver University. Prior to joining BMI, Preston was national sales manager with Premier Marketing Group. Mr. Preston is currently a director of writer/publisher relations in BMI's Nashville office. Mr. Preston is on the board of directors of the Tennessee State Museum and served as chairman for the NeA Extravaganza for 1996 and 1997. He is the entertainment chairman of the Nashville Zoo and was most recently awarded the Nashville Hit Award from the Nashville area Chamber of Commerce as the Art and Music Volunteer of the Year. Mr. Preston is married and has three children. Some of his favorite hobbies include travel, snow skiing, jet skiing, scuba diving, four wheeling, and coaching soccer.

SESAC, INC.

Headquarters: 55 Music Square East
Nashville, TN 37203
Tel: (615) 320-0055
Web site: *www.sesac.com*

With offices in California, New York, and London

How They Determine Who Gets Paid

SESAC began using BDS (Broadcast Data Systems) in 1994 with its SESAC Latina division. Because of its success with SESAC Latina, the company expanded its usage to all mainstream commercial radio formats in 1996. BDS is the same system used by *Billboard* magazine to compile its music charts, a standard for the music industry. With BDS, SESAC monitors more than 9 million hours of radio programming annually. In addition to BDS, SESAC now uses other technologies. SESAC became the first performing rights organization in the world to more comprehensively track performances generated by film, TV, cable, Internet, music libraries, and niche radio formats, such as Americana, Black Gospel, College, Contemporary Christian, Jazz, Smooth Jazz, and Southern Gospel.

Special Writer Services

SESAC occasionally engages its writers and artists to perform at high-profile music and broadcast events, such as the Vail Film Festival, SXSW (South by Southwest Music conference), and the National Association of Broadcasters annual conference.

INDUSTRY INTERVIEW WITH DENNIS LORD, SENIOR VICE PRESIDENT, BUSINESS AFFAIRS, SESAC

"One of the main differences between SESAC and the other performance rights organizations is that we use a much more comprehensive survey to determine our royalty distribution. It makes our payments more accurate. SESAC was the first PRO to use Broadcast Data Systems technology, and still does today. Almost all of the songs signed to SESAC are logged into the BDS system. Others are logged into a monitoring technology called "Audible Magic." SESAC surveys over 10 million hours of radio airplay annually, about ten times the amount monitored by ASCAP and BMI. That is a huge difference.

"BDS and Audible Magic technologies are fingerprinting technologies. Such technologies are becoming more available to the entire industry.

Currently BDS takes a fifty-nine second version of a song and logs it into their computer database. This could be much more efficient. There is new fingerprinting technology available today that takes only ten seconds or less of a song to be able to identify it. But BDS already has millions of songs logged in their database, making them the leader in tracking songs, even though their technology might not be the most current.

"Technology is progressing and evolving so rapidly that it is going to be completely changed by the time this interview is in print! Just about the time one of the PROs announces a huge new innovation, it is already outdated. I do believe that one day all PROs will use one common system worldwide. Then, choosing your PRO will really be about customer service!

"The most exciting new company using digital technology is SoundExchange, a PRO for artists, musicians and record companies. It was formed and funded originally by the RIAA, but now it has spun off. John Simson, who used to manage Mary Chapin Carpenter, leads this performing rights organization. Up until now, artists were not paid for the use of their music. Thanks to SoundExchange and a change in the copyright law in the late 1990s, artists and record companies are now being paid for the digital use of their music on XM & Cirrus satellite radio, iTunes, Amazon, etc. It is a very innovative company, which monitors every single digital impression of music. That is a great advance in audio tracking technology!

"I would advise independent artists to find a way to get their music fingerprinted by registering their songs with BDS and as many other finger printing companies as possible. There are many different fingerprinting companies, and I would contact them all. They can be found on the Internet. It might not be easy, or even possible in some cases, but it would be well worth the effort. An independent artist should also register their recordings with SoundExchange, especially if they have a Web site where their songs can be downloaded or played on the Web.

"SESAC is a bottom-line company—we are about making money for our affiliates and for SESAC. We are very, very good at licensing, and bringing in money for the use of our affiliates' copyrights. And that is why we are very careful about who we sign to SESAC. We are qualitative as opposed to quantitative; a writer has to be invited to join or be recommended by an industry professional. While we would love to be able to, we can't sign all writers who come to us wanting to join. We are targeted and selective; we want writers whose copyrights we think we can serve. Our writers include Bob Dylan, Joe Nichols, Teddy Riley, Paul Shaffer, and Neil Diamond, to name just a few.

"For that reason, SESAC does not have a lot of special workshops or Music Business 101 classes for aspiring songwriters and artists. We do writer/artist development very selectively. The key component is the writer—he or she has to be responsible for his or her own career. A very good example is SESAC 2003 Country Writer of the Year Jerry Salley. Jerry has been SESAC Writer of the Year for several years, having written hits for Toby Keith, John Anderson, Joe Nichols, Patty Loveless, Rhonda Vincent, and for the 2003 honor, *I'm Gonna Take That Mountain* for Reba McEntire. Jerry is a classic example of someone who is out there working hard every day and relying on himself to make things happen. Along the way we have helped when we could, with a news article, showcase, or other special event to spotlight Salley's music.

"We do a lot of research. It is used in tandem with the instincts of our creative staff to help determine what music is the most compelling. Do we have the most writers at SESAC? No. Do we have competitive music? Yes! The music we sign is ubiquitous. You will hear it everywhere—in bars, on radio, on TV, in stadiums, in restaurants . . . everywhere!

"One of my favorite genres of music is Americana. I have a personal belief it is the most vibrant, creative, artful genre of music out there—it is broadminded. It doesn't have borders or boundaries. I have spent some time working with members of the Nashville music community to help market and promote Americana music. I am a founding member of the Americana Music Association, and served on the board for several years. I am proud of the work we have accomplished. It has also been good for SESAC. We have been able to pick up a significant number of artists, like Kevin Welch, Kieran Kane, and Sonny Landreth. Several years ago SESAC recognized Americana as legitimate form in terms of the art of the music—it is pure. Therefore, we do monitor Americana music. But we believe that over the new decade it will be more economically vibrant. Right now the numbers for Americana are very small, although these artists do occasionally cross over to other genres of music.

"I guess I would paraphrase something Andrew Lack—the new chairman and CEO of Sony Music Entertainment, who recently went to Sony at age fifty-five with no music experience—said to distinguish SESAC in the marketplace. He said, 'At NBC, where I came from, it's all about profit! In the record business, I was surprised to find that it's all about market share!' At SESAC, that profit motivation works to the great benefit of our writers and publishers. That's why business at SESAC is good—better yet, great!"

DENNIS LORD is the senior vice president of business affairs at SESAC, the second oldest performing rights organization in the United States. In addition to overseeing all aspects of SESAC's corporate business affairs, Lord works with the writer/publisher relations staff, signing and developing songwriters and publishers in all musical genres, as well as film and television, throughout the United States.

Lord has experience in multiple aspects of the music business. Prior to joining SESAC, he was managing partner of Lord Entertainment, where he managed various artists, including guitarist Sonny Landreth. As an attorney, Lord focused his practice on entertainment law. He's been active in the Nashville Songwriters Association International, where he served on the board of directors and executive committee for several years and lobbied on behalf of songwriters at the federal level. Lord is currently a member of the board of directors of the Academy of Country Music, Gospel Music Association, Copyright Society of the South and an alternate member of the National Recording Preservation Board. In addition, he is also a founding council member and past president of the Americana Music Association, a trade organization dedicated to the promotion of roots music and the Americana genre.

Lord spent several semesters at Middle Tennessee State University at Murfreesboro as an adjunct full professor, teaching in the recording industry management program. He is also a songwriter with recordings by artists such as T.G. Shepperd and Travis Tritt, for whom Lord penned *Country Club*, Travis' first major hit.

10

A Basic
Understanding of
Nashville's
Networking System

Nashville runs on a 10-2-6 schedule, but people are pretty much in their offices by 8:30 A.M. or so. They don't leave until late, and when they do, it's usually to go to a writers' night, artist showcase, or . . . a party.

PARTY, PARTY, PARTY

There are a zillion parties in Nashville for everything under the sun. Every time a single goes number one on the Country Chart, the publisher throws a party for the writer. There are usually more than one publisher and writer involved, so there might be more than one party. Also, the PRO might throw a party for the writers and the publishers. The publisher will make up a banner for the occasion and hang it outside on his building. You will see these banners all over Music Row.

Record labels throw a party for an artist when his album sells gold, and another when it goes platinum. Sometimes these parties can be very elaborate, and everyone on Music Row is invited. Other times it's a small gathering at the record label offices. Sometimes the label will have a listening party when an album project is completed. These parties are usually held at the recording studio.

It's not too difficult to crash most of these parties, but it's best to tag along with someone who was invited or knows plenty of the people who are going to be there. Don't be surprised if you find yourself at one of these parties, but be sure to be on your best behavior! There is lots of great food and drink and many celebrities, so it's easy to get carried away with the ambiance.

These parties are given because of the importance of networking. It takes place on every level. Everyone wants to stay in touch with all the different people who worked on a project. Hopefully they will be back to contribute to another project in some way and make valuable contacts that will lead to future creative ventures. While you are in Nashville, be aware of these opportunities and take advantage of them if you can.

EAT, DRINK, AND BE MERRY

Music Row restaurants are not just for eating. Since hanging around publishers' offices is a very difficult task, hanging around Nashville's restaurants can be the reward for a job well done! And you'll probably have more success meeting people in the restaurants than at the writers' nights and publishers' offices combined. If you are uncomfortable going to a restaurant by yourself, all the better. You will be forced to ask that new writer you met at the Bluebird last night to join you. Lunch and happy hour are the best times to run into people—dinner would be more of a long shot. But don't skip these networking opportunities . . . you could hit the jackpot! Seriously, everyone you are trying to meet or get an appointment with is in one of the following restaurants:

Breakfast

The Pancake Pantry
1796 21st Avenue South
Tel: (615) 383-9333

This restaurant used to be in a tiny room next door to the current location, and there was a table right next to the kitchen that was reserved for Chet Atkins, Harold Shedd (producer, Alabama), Ray Stevens, and all of their friends. They ate there every morning. Alas, progress changes everything. Even the "Cake" is upscale now, bigger and better, with a long line out in front. I've never gone there and not run into someone I know.

Lunch

Sunset Grill
2001 Belcourt Avenue
Tel: (615) 386-3663

Without a doubt, *the* place where the industry hangs out, especially songwriters. Often seen: Pat Alger, Richard Leigh, Ralph Murphy. Start at the bar, then have lunch in one of the dining rooms, then drift to the outside patio for dessert and watch Music Row parade by. Or get there early and get a table on the patio, where you have a ringside seat to watch everyone who comes in and out.

Midtown Cafe
102 19th Avenue South
Tel: (615) 320-7176
Recently purchased by Sunset Grill, but retained its original menu.

Noshville Delicatessen
1918 Broadway
Tel: (615) 329-6674
Fashioned after a New York deli. Industry execs like it because it reminds them of home! Popular for breakfast too.

Granite Falls
2000 Broadway
Tel: (615) 327-9250
Industry execs, plus Marty Stuart and his clothier extraordinaire, Manuel, are seen here frequently. Friday night happy hour is a favorite among industry A&R execs and song pluggers.

The LongHorn
110 Lyle Avenue
Tel: (615) 329-9195
Popular writers' hangout.

The Palm Restaurant Nashville
140 5th Avenue South
Tel: (615) 742-7256
The place to be seen—and lunch prices aren't that bad!

The Tin Roof
1516 Demonbreun Street
Tel: (615) 313-7103
The most popular on Nashville's new "Restaurant (Music) Row"!

Happy Hour

Sunset Grill, Restaurant (Music) Row, and the LongHorn

The Trace
2000 Belcourt Avenue
Tel: (615) 385-2200

A big, upscale happy hour crowd. You'll find music industry mixed with Nashville's upper crust.

Dinner

Sunset Grill, the Trace, and, if you are someone else's expense account:

Morton's of Chicago
625 Church Street
Tel: (615) 259-4558

Music industry executives like to entertain their clients at the downtown Morton's or the Palm because it also reminds them of New York. A be-seen type of place; not the best for socializing, except with your dinner guests, of course.

THE ACKLEN STATION POST OFFICE

No kidding! Everyone has a post office box at the Acklen Station behind Sunset Grill on Acklen Avenue. You never know who you'll run into there, but you will be sure to run into someone important in the music industry. Faith Hill used to drop by every day to pick up mail for Reba McEntire! You might want to stop by there when you are in the vicinity. You could get lucky and stumble into just the person with whom you were trying to get an appointment.

GOLFING, FISHING, AND PLAYING TENNIS

Highly recommended for great networking opportunities. Music Row professionals are really into golf, and there is a tournament almost every week during the summer. Top record executives, producers, publishers, and songwriters all participate, mix and mingle, and compete on the course. The most popular music industry tournaments are the Vinnie (Vince Gill's tournament), HoriPro, and NSAI during Tin Pan South. For tennis players, the Music City Tennis Invitational is held the last weekend in April or the first weekend in May.

Songwriters love to go bass fishing. Many a great song has been written on the water, including the classic *Wind beneath My Wings*.

PROFESSIONAL ORGANIZATIONS

There are four very important professional organizations that you will want to research thoroughly. The CMA and NARAS (The Recording Academy a.k.a. The Grammys) produce popular network TV awards shows that are extremely important to the country music industry, and greatly affect an artist's career. An appearance on one of these shows is a guarantee of significant album sales in the immediate days following the broadcast. Membership in all four organizations is limited to persons who derive a significant amount of income from the music industry, and new members have to go through an interview process in order to be accepted. You may not be interested in joining these organizations, but you will definitely want to check with them before coming to Nashville. They host several different special events throughout the year that are open to nonmembers as well as members.

Country Music Association (CMA)
1 Music Circle South
Nashville, TN 37203
Tel: (615) 244-2840
Web site: *www.CMAworld.com*

- CMA Music Festival (formerly Fan Fair): Second week in June. A weeklong opportunity to meet all of the top-name country recording artists at their fair booth, and/or backstage at their record label showcase.
- CMA Awards Show: Second Tuesday in November. Subject to change at network discretion.
- CMA Close-Up: An outstanding magazine dedicated to country music, available to CMA Members only.

National Academy of Recording Arts and Sciences (NARAS or The Recording Academy)
1904 Wedgewood Avenue
Nashville, TN 37212
Tel: (615) 327-8030
Web site: *www.grammy.com*

- Grammy Awards Show: Held each February, this annual awards presentation on national television highlights the best of the best in many different genres of music. Winners are selected by a jury of their peers—members of NARAS.
- Educational Seminars: The Nashville chapter of NARAS hosts a variety of seminars, panel discussions and events that are sometimes open to the public. Check with NARAS for time and place.
- Annual Block Party: THE block party of the year held every May in the vacant lot on Wedgewood next to the NARAS office building.

Literally the "who's who" of Music Row attend to watch performances by Nashville's hottest acts, new and established. This is actually
a membership drive for NARAS.

Country Radio Broadcasters, Inc. (CRB or CRS)
819 18th Avenue South
Nashville, TN 37203
Tel: (615) 327-4487
Web site: *www.crb.org*

Country Radio Seminar: Formerly known as the DJ Convention,
CRS is an annual weeklong event the primary purpose of which is to
introduce artists, radio personalities, and programmers to one another.
There are lots of seminars, dinners, showcases, and record label parties
which maximize opportunities.

Americana Music Association (AMA)
1101 17th Avenue South
Nashville, TN 37212
Tel: (615) 438-7500
Web site: *www.americanamusic.org*

Americana Music Conference and Awards Show: Held annually the
third week in September, this three-day event provides great opportunities
for aspiring artists and musicians. Don't miss it! Americana Music Sampler:
A compilation CD of new and established Americana artists, distributed
globally. Artists may submit their product for consideration.

Two other genre-specific membership trade organizations are the
IBMA (*www.ibma.org*) and GMA (*www.gospelmusic.org*). The Gospel Music
Association was established in 1964 to expose, promote and integrate the
gospel in all forms of music. GMA hosts the Annual Dove Awards and
Conference the third week in April. The International Bluegrass Music
Association was established in 1985 to create a high standard of prof-
essionalism, a greater appreciation for bluegrass music, and success of
the worldwide bluegrass community. Judging by the phenomenal success of
bluegrass music today, it appears that IBMA has done an outstanding job!

BACK TO SCHOOL: RECORD INDUSTRY COURSES

Many of the people who work on Music Row are graduates of a
Recording Industry Program at either Belmont University or Middle
Tennessee State University (MTSU). Both colleges have a great curriculum
aimed directly at getting a job in the Nashville music industry. The biggest
advantage offered by both of these universities is their internship program,
which places students directly in the offices of Music Row businesses. They

also have state-of-the-art recording studios and film and video production facilities, and prominent Music Row professionals teach courses at both universities. If you are seriously considering a career in the country music business, then you would benefit greatly from attending either of these colleges. Both are very well integrated into the Music Row community, but they are quite different in structure.

Belmont University (Belmont)
1900 Belmont Boulevard
Nashville, TN 37212
Tel: (615) 460-5504
Web site: *www.belmont.edu*
Program: Mike Curb College of Entertainment/Music Business
     Belmont is a private university with a religious base. It requires some attendance at religious seminars and has some basic religious restrictions. Its close proximity to Music Row enables the students to closely interact with Music Row businesses. Belmont offers an extension program in Burbank, California, and Victoria University in Australia!

Middle Tennessee State University (MTSU)
P. O. Box 21
Murfreesboro, TN 37132
Tel: (615) 898-2578
Web site: *www.mtsu.edu/~record*
Program: MTSU Department of Recording Industry
     MTSU is a state university and, as such, offers affordable enrollment. It is the country's largest recording program with over 1,716 different majors. Music Row works equally with both MTSU and Belmont, but the greatest hardship is on the MTSU students who have to travel back and forth between Nashville and Murfreesboro, a forty-five-minute drive.

OTHER IMPORTANT RESOURCES

American Songwriter Magazine
50 Music Square West, Suite 604
Nashville, TN 37203
Tel: (615) 321-6096
Web site: *www.americansongwriter.com*
     Owner/publisher Jim Sharp is a Music Row veteran, having been in key positions at CBS and Monument Records and heading the Nashville office of *CashBox* magazine. Highly respected in the country music industry, he has been helping songwriters through *American Songwriter* for over thirteen years.

The magazine is very affordable at $22 per year, and contains lots of detailed information about Music Row and great interviews with Nashville songwriters, providing valuable insight into the challenges of the profession.

Nashville Star (USA Network)
c/o Tracy Gershon, Sr. Director A&R/Artist Development
Sony Music Nashville
Web site: *www.usanetwork.com/nashvillestar*

If you are a country music artist and feel your live performance is the best it is ever going to be, then you might want to consider auditioning for the hit TV Show, *Nashville Star*! The show has been an outstanding success for audiences, country music executives, and the contestants. Not only does the final winner get a record deal and national recognition, but all contestants attract fans, artist managers, and record label attention. But a strong word of caution! If you are just starting out and don't have a lot of experience under your big country belt buckle, the judges won't be kind! And they won't give you a second chance! So, be sure you are at the peak of your career before trying out for *Nashville Star*.

The place to start is in your hometown. Sometime in the fall, radio stations start announcing local auditions, which will most likely be in the most popular live country music venue nearest your city or town. You will also want to send in a live performance video. The *Nashville Star* Web site will announce that they are accepting video applications. Mail in your video by FedEx or UPS as close to the deadline as possible (to make sure your video winds up on the top of the heap!). Keep a close watch on the *Nashville Star* Web site and follow their instructions.

ABOUT MUSIC CONFERENCES

Approximately twenty-five years ago some very enterprising people realized there was a treasure trove of talent in Austin, Texas, just waiting to be discovered. The college town of Austin is rich with live music clubs, mainly situated in one area on Sixth Street. College students hop from club to club searching for new and different music, and the bands thrive on this appreciative audience. Organizers put together a music conference and invited top music executives from Los Angeles, Nashville, and New York to come and hear these bands. In another stroke of genius, they planned their conference during spring break, so that students from other campuses across the country could attend as well.

The conference is called South by Southwest (SXSW), and has grown to gigantic proportions. Originally, it was designed to showcase new emerging talent for the record industry, but the record companies were so receptive to the idea, they began to hold their own showcases of their hot new acts. Today, SXSW is a huge event attended by aspiring songwriters and artists, music industry executives, and journalists. SXSW now includes a film festival as well, and conference attendees are likely to meet some of Hollywood's top stars.

It didn't take long for other cities to recognize the impact a music conference would make on their own city, and music conferences began to spread like wildfire across the country and Europe. There is at least one a month in some city somewhere in the United States. Organizers are careful to pick dates that don't interfere with other conferences in the hopes of attracting large crowds of music industry executives. SXSW organizers produce many of these conferences themselves, with NXNE in Toronto, Canada, and NXNW in Seattle, Washington.

Besides showcases of both signed and unsigned talent, conferences include panel discussions on just about every topic under the sun, including songwriting, getting a job in the industry, and getting a record deal. They also have great networking opportunities including cocktail parties, golf tournaments, and riverboat rides.

Trying to find a music conference near you might take a little bit of detective work. Music magazines like *Spin* and *Rolling Stone* will have articles and, more likely, advertisements on various conferences. You can also call the Chambers of Commerce in the biggest cities near you. It will be worth the effort to track them down, as you will benefit greatly from these conferences no matter what level your stage of development.

11

Packaging Your Product

In Nashville, you will be expected to have your music on a CD. Lead sheets with the music written out are absolutely never used in Nashville. You cannot go into anyone's office with your guitar and sing a few songs—it is simply not done anymore. No one has that kind of time, and it's not the norm. Nashville has a strict way of doing things, and the song demo is at the top of the list.

THE SONGWRITER'S DEMO
Not too long ago a songwriter could take his guitar into a publisher's office and perform his songs live. Songwriters and publishers with a close working relationship may share new songs in this manner, particularly in the developmental stages of a song, but publishers require a "demo" to be made for each song so they can listen to it at their own convenience. There are two kinds of demos: 1) a simple guitar/vocal or piano/vocal; and 2) a full-blown demo. A simple guitar/vocal is the best way to pitch songs to publishers, but they are rarely pitched to producers and A&R executives. Their ears are used to hearing "full-blown" demos that have the entire production already in place. One of the most important functions of Nashville publishers is knowing how the producers and A&R reps like songs to be presented. Publishers produce their demos according to these preferences.

THE GUITAR/VOCAL (OR PIANO/VOCAL) DEMO
When a Nashville publisher is listening to your song, he is listening to the lyrics and story development. If a simple guitar/vocal is done correctly, that is all that is needed to shop songs to publishers in Nashville. It is perfectly

acceptable for you to record your songs yourself, but the sound quality should be very good—no hiss or background noises—and the vocalist must be excellent. The song needs to be delivered in a straightforward manner, with not too much inflection in the voice. The vocalist has to do a good job of following the melody accurately. The lyrics must be crystal clear.

It is important not to spend a lot of money on demos. Remember that it is a publisher's job to demo material, and they have their own ideas about how a song should be presented. Your goal is to make an excellent songwriter's demo to present to a publisher, who will then put his own money into a professional demo. If you spend a lot of money on a demo yourself, then you will have a major investment in the song that may in turn change your focus. You might spend too much time on one song when you need to move on to something else, or you might become inflexible regarding rewrites or the need to re-demo. Be very conservative with your demo budget.

Don't hire someone to write music to your lyrics. If you are a lyricist only and do not write music or play an instrument, then you need to find a co-writer—someone who is as involved in your lyrics as you are and whose music is a perfect interpretation of your words. This cannot be purchased at any price.

THE FULL-BLOWN DEMO

The majority of songwriters get carried away with how great their songs are; they want to go straight to the artist with their song. They can't imagine even needing a publisher, except for their contacts and connections. So they go ahead, skip the songwriter demo process, and go straight to demoing their songs. They are hoping that once the publisher hears it, he will take it directly to the artist.

A full-blown demo can represent a song more accurately, but a demo can make or break a song. A poor demo can ruin a great song, so great care should be taken in producing your demos. An overproduced demo is the biggest danger—you don't want your listeners to get distracted by the production. Also, Nashville demos have a certain sound that is similar to what is played on contemporary country radio, so your demos should be close to that quality. Also make sure that the vocals are turned up in the mix; in a Nashville demo, vocals take precedent over the music.

Nashville producers and A&R reps continually say that they like to hear guitar/vocals because they want to be free to think of their own production ideas. However, they are rarely pitched guitar/vocals by Nashville publishers. These publishers have their own demo studios, and spend a lot of money and time producing demos that sound like a master recording. This intense competition is what you are up against when pitching to A&R, producers, and artist managers. That's why you want to first play your demos for publishers, the songwriters' organizations, and all three PROs before pitching them to the rest of the music industry. You will learn a great deal about your songs, your demos, and the way the Nashville music industry thinks in the process.

As you can well imagine, there are lots of great demo studios in Nashville. It would be a good idea to have your songs demoed in Nashville, as opposed to a studio in your hometown, because it will be one more opportunity to get to know people in Nashville. Also, you will have a greater chance of getting a "Nashville sound" production; more like the demos producers are used to hearing. Following, is a list of some popular demo studios:

NASHVILLE'S TOP DEMO STUDIOS

Angello Sound Studio
526 East Iris Drive
Nashville, TN 37204
Tel: (615) 383-0888
Web site: *www.angellosound.com*
    Bobby Angello has been producing songwriter demos for many years.

Bayou Recording Inc.
1008 17th Avenue South
Nashville, TN 37212
Tel: (615) 340-9000
Web site: *allnashvilleradio.us*
    Voted one of the top five studios in town, but #1 in affordability.

Beaird Music Group, Inc.
2703 Greystone Road
Nashville, TN 37204
Tel: (615) 279-8030
Web site: *www.beairdmusicgroup.com*
    Larry Beaird has been producing songwriter demos for many years. He works well with songwriters who are new to the process and do not live in Nashville.

Brush Hill Studios
1421 Tempany Court
Nashville, TN 37207
Tel: (615) 870-1221
Web site: *www.bhstudios.com*

County Q

P. O. Box 40228
Nashville, TN 37204
Tel: (615) 298-1434
County Q is the most popular song demo studio in Nashville.

Earwave Productions

P. O. Box 40857
Nashville, TN 37204
Tel: (615) 298-3504
Web site: *www.davepomeroy.com*
Bassist Dave Pomeroy is a very popular session musician, session leader, producer, and live performer.

Island Bound Studio

1204 17th Avenue South
Nashville, TN 37212
Tel: (615) 320-5413
E-mail: *studio@islandboundmusic.com*
Also one of Nashville's top music publishers.

Juke Box Recording Studio

646 West Iris Drive
Nashville, TN 37204
Tel: (615) 297-9100
This popular Berry Hill studio is run by Dan Frizsell.

Money Pit

622 Hamilton Avenue
Nashville, TN 37203
Tel: (615) 256-0311
E-mail: *pitofmoney@comcast.net*
Owned by one of Nashville's top producers.

OMNIsound Studios

1806 Division Street
Nashville, TN 37203
Tel: (615) 321-5526
Web site: *www.omnisoundstudios.com*
Owned by one of Nashville's super-pickers! Originally named Omnisound Studio.

The Parlor
1317 16th Avenue South
Nashville, TN 37212
Tel: (615) 385-4466
Web site: *www.parlorproductions.com*
   Owned by one of Nashville's top publishers.

Studio 19
821 19th Avenue South
Nashville, TN 37203
Tel: (615) 327-4927
Web site: *www.studio19nashville.com*
   Larry Rogers owns several studios in Nashville and Memphis, and has produced songs for many hit artists over the years.

Song Cellar Production Service
P. O. Box 121234
Nashville, TN 37212
Tel: (615) 383-7222
Web site: *www.songcellar.com*
   Jackie Cook established his performing, writing, and recording career in Memphis before coming to Nashville to sing and play guitar for the legendary Roy Orbison. In 1984 Jackie started the Song Cellar in the basement of NSAI. Since then he has been involved in the production of over 4,000 songs. Some have won Grammys, others have made it to number one on the charts. The Song Cellar offers a variety of packages, from simple guitar/vocals to full-blown master quality demos.

Sound Control
2824 Dogwood Place
Nashville, TN 37204
Tel: (615) 292-2047
Web site: *www.soundcontrolstudio.com*
   Specializes in rockabilly and Americana music genres.

Swanee Recording Studio
3950 North Mt. Juliet Road
Mt. Juliet, TN 37122
Tel: (615) 754-0417
Web site: *www.doorknob-rec.com*
   Studio of producer Gene Kennedy. Door Knob Records is one of Nashville's oldest independent record labels.

Waltzing Bear Studio
1710 Grand Avenue
Nashville, TN 37203
Tel: (615) 329-2886
Web site: *www.waltzingbearrecords.com*

BEWARE OF SONG SHARKS

A "song shark" is anyone who will publish your songs for a fee. The most notorious song sharks offer a contract that says they will record your song, put it on an album with nine or so other songs, and present them to radio stations and/or record labels. There is nothing illegal about this practice—it just doesn't have anything to do with the music industry. Radio stations and record labels throw this product in the trash. You do not want your songs to be associated with these companies. Be very wary of anyone who wants to charge you a fee for publishing your songs.

You have to be equally careful when looking for a producer. There are a lot out there that have some pretty impressive credentials, but really aren't as connected as they used to be. Or even worse, they are still connected, but will produce some "vanity" projects for a little extra income. A vanity project is a CD produced for someone who really doesn't have a clue about the music industry. He is just content to see himself on an album cover, and doesn't really understand the big picture. If you ask the right questions, you should be able to weed out the song sharks.

The catch-22 is that it will probably take some output of money on your part to get things accomplished; professional song demos and/or an artist's package are expensive. Just make sure that if you need to hire a professional to assist you in this process, you hire someone who is well connected on Music Row.

PUBLISHER FEES

Publishers do not charge anything at all for their services. However, publishing is an expensive business, with the financial return greatly delayed. It can take up to two years to start collecting for a song that is currently on the singles charts. Some small publishers may need help with demo costs, and while this is not the most ideal situation for a songwriter, it is not unethical for publishers to ask for assistance in producing a demo of the material. If you have paid for your own song demos, and a publisher wants to start pitching your demo, then you have the right to ask for half of the publishing. If the publisher objects (which he will), offer to let him administer the rights for your publishing company and tell him that you would be willing to give up your share of the publishing in the event that some publishing has to be given away in order to get the song recorded (not as common a practice as is rumored). At a minimum, if you sign over all the publishing on a song that you paid to be demoed, get your demo money reimbursed.

THE SONGWRITER'S DEMO PACKAGE

The demo package consists of a CD and a lyric sheet attached. Every song that is pitched in Nashville has a certain look to it, and yours should look exactly the same. In some kind of reverse logic, CDs that stand out from the others are most likely to wind up in the round file (trash can).

The Cassette Tape

DO NOT USE CASSETTE TAPES UNDER ANY CIRCUMSTANCES!

As we have said many times, the music industry has changed drastically in the last few years, including the way music is delivered. The cassette tape is a dinosaur! Everyone still has a cassette tape deck and the capability of playing tapes, but the professionals on Music Row just don't use them anymore. You shouldn't either!

DAT, MP3, Ipod, Windows Media Player, Downloading, Etc.

Once upon a time the music industry thought that DAT would revolutionize the industry, making the cassette tape obsolete. Cassette tapes did in fact become obsolete, but not because of DAT technology. Digital audio was superior, but the tape proved to be very fragile, having a very short shelf life. No one uses DATs anymore, but they do have a DAT machine as well as a cassette tape player in their office, just in case one is needed. As for new music delivery systems such as MP3 or iPods, if you like them, use them and share your knowledge with others. Just be sure to have a CD as a backup.

The CD

The best way to pitch songs is by CD, because of the superior sound quality. One word of caution about CDs: Not all sound equipment is compatible. There has been a recurring problem with CDs on Music Row. Some CDs did not record, or will not play on different sound equipment. In a recent pitch session to top-notch producer Tony Brown, almost half of the CDs pitched to him would not play on his high-tech equipment! How embarrassing would that be to have your big chance to pitch a song to Tony, only to have no sound come off the CD! Be sure to double-check your CDs on the best equipment you can afford.

Put no more than three or four songs on your CD. Put your best song first, a novelty song (if you are pitching one) last. Your CD label should look something like the one shown on page 154. Put a copyright notice on your CD label, even if you have not registered your songs with the copyright office. If you have registered your songs and they were all registered in different years, use the most recent year for your CD.

Needless to say, putting the song titles and your name, address, and phone number on each CD is very, very important. Also on any insert, lyric sheet, letter, note, memo, fax, e-mail—each and every printed or electronically produced item pertaining to your songs. It is mind-boggling how many people forget to include some way to reach them on the CD itself, relying on a lyric sheet or business card to contain that information. CDs often get separated from the rest of a song's package, so all important information should be included on the CD itself.

There are several different types of CD cases, and so far there has been no preference for any one of them. Choose the one you like best.

The Lyric Sheet

Don't ever pitch a song without a lyric sheet. Important things to include are:

- Your name, address, and phone number.
- Copyright notice at the bottom of the first page (fit everything on one page).
- An indentation for the chorus, bridge, and tag. Many people do not look at the lyrics when they are listening to a song, but will glance at them occasionally. Your lyric sheet needs to be laid out so that whoever's glancing at it can find his place easily.

Lyric sheets are usually typed on 8 1/2″ × 11″ letter-size paper. You can then keep them in your briefcase to give to the listener when you are pitching your songs; or fold them into fours and attach to the back of the CD case with a rubber band when you are dropping off your CD. This is the most common way to pitch your CDs on Music Row.

Other ideas are:

- Lyric sheet with a hard CD case (similar to commercial CD packaging)—This case is best for an artist package, as you can put a photo, logo and other information on the front of the CD case, and the lyrics on the other side or inside a folded insert; or the back of the CD case. Usually, song titles are listed on the back, but if there are only one or two songs on the CD, the lyrics would fit on the back of the case.
- Lyric sheet with a thin CD case—Some publishers and producers prefer this case because they can fit more into a briefcase or travel

bag. The CD holder is one unit with the back of the case, so information can only go in the front. But there is room for a folded insert which could contain lyrics and bio info.

- Lyric sheet with a plastic envelope–style CD case—This is the best choice for songwriter demo, because the CD fits inside the flap, and a separate 8 1/2″ × 11″ lyric sheet can be folded and put in the back slot, along with a business card. For a songwriter pitching lots of songs in different combinations, this is the easiest format.
- Do not use a lead sheet (melody line and chords printed out). Lead sheets are hard to read and are no longer necessary due to the change in copyright law, which allows copyright registration with a CD instead of a lead sheet.

The Bio

Biographical information is completely unnecessary and should be avoided, unless you really have something important to say, i.e., songs you have had recorded or awards you have won. Publishers don't need to know where you went to high school or college and what bands you've played in, etc.

Miscellany

- Business cards: A card with your picture on it is very effective and helps a publisher remember you. Have lots of cards handy for all the people you are going to meet at writers' nights, restaurants, and publishers' offices.
- Manila envelopes: Some songwriters and publishers prefer to enclose their CD in a manila envelope. If you use this method, be sure you use a small size (6″ × 9″) and have professional, typed labels on the front. Do not seal the envelope; make it easy to get inside. An envelope is not necessary and strictly your personal preference.

A Nashville Song Demo Package

If you make your way into a publisher's or producer's office, you will see that the desk will be covered with CDs, stacked on top of each other in neat little piles. Each CD will be in a hard plastic case, and the lyrics to the songs will be neatly folded to the size of the CD, placed on the bottom and secured with a rubber band. You will see these neat little piles of CDs everywhere, including the receptionist's desk and little bins next to the receptionist's desk, put there to collect CDs for producers and A&R reps. Your songs should be packaged like all the others.

Example: Artist's CD Demo
The possibilities are endless for graphics and information contained on a CD
insert. Here is one idea for a basic design.

CD labels and inserts, lyric sheets, and business cards should be professionally done with a word processor, with the same type font and distinctive marketing imprint or logo. This is very inexpensive to do these days. If you don't have your own PC and printer, any of the quick copy stores can design something for you for practically nothing. Then you can either type in song titles on ready-made CD labels, or you can have them do it for you. You will probably be pitching the same songs to lots of different people, so you can get them made in bulk. Do not *ever* submit anything that is handwritten. It will not get listened to.

THE ARTIST'S DEMO

Your artist demo must be the best that you can possibly afford. You are going to need a professionally produced CD of master quality. If you are a really great writer and artist, you should try to get a producer or publisher to put up money to produce you in exchange for the publishing on your songs. That would be the most ideal situation. The next best thing would be to spend your money (or your investor's money) on the best producer you can afford. Following is a list of some of Nashville's best.

NASHVILLE'S TOP PRODUCERS

Chuck Ainlay
10 Music Circle South
Nashville, TN 37203
Tel: (615) 256-2676
E-mail: *ainlaycj@aol.com*
        Clients include George Strait, Travis Tritt, Peter Frampton, and Willie Nelson.

Mark Bright
10 Music Circle South
Nashville, TN 37203
Tel: (615) 255-1213
E-mail: *mark@teracel.com*
        Clients include Rascal Flatts, Heather Davis, and Amber White.

Gregg Brown
P. O. Box 128108
Nashville, TN 37212
Tel: (615) 242-6222
E-mail: *gregg@revelatorrecordings.com*
        Travis Tritt is a former client; now producing the Roostars.

Tony Brown
Universal South
40 Music Square West
Nashville, TN 37203
Tel: (615) 259-5300
Fax: (615) 259-5301
Entertainment Weekly named Tony Brown one of the one hundred most powerful people in entertainment.

Buddy Cannon
Bud Ro Productions
1706 Grand Avenue
Nashville, TN 37212
Tel: (615) 320-4880
E-mail: *bud_ro@hotmail.com*
Producer, songwriter, publisher, background vocalist, band member, and six-year label executive for Mercury Records.

Buzz Cason
Southern Writers Group Creative Workshop
2804 Azalea Place
Nashville, TN 37204
Tel: (615) 383-8682
E-mail: *bcason@musicnashville.com*
The co-writer of *Everlasting Love* tells his story in the autobiography, *Living the Rock 'n' Roll Dream* (See Reference Book section).

Don Cook
DKC Music/Sony/ATV Tree
8 Music Square West
Nashville, TN 37203
Tel: (615) 726-8300
E-mail: *don_cook@sonymusic.com*
Produces Alabama, Joe Diffie, and Michelle Poe, to name just a few.

Jerry Crutchfield
1106 17th Avenue South
Nashville, TN 37212
Tel: (615) 321-5558
E-mail: *crutchfieldmusic@aol.com*
Best known for former client Tanya Tucker. Still produces Lee Greenwood.

Garth Fundis
Sound Emporium
3100 Belmont Boulevard
Nashville, TN 37212
Tel: (615) 383-1982
Web site: *www.soundemporiumstudios.com*
    Fundis owns Sound Emporium recording studio and has produced
Trisha Yearwood and Don Williams, among many others.

Byron Gallimore
Song Garden Publishing
25 Music Square East
Nashville, TN 37203
Tel: (615) 244-8950
E-mail: *anncallis@mindspring.com*
    Publisher and producer of Tim McGraw, Faith Hill, and many other
top recording artists.

Byron Hill
Independent Producer
P. O. Box 120603
Nashville, TN 37212
Tel: (615) 973-9090
E-mail: *gbh333@aol.com*
    Clients include Gary Allan, Gil Grand, and Mic Dekle.

Dan Huff
Huff/Bright Productions
10 Music Circle South, Floor 2
Nashville, TN 37203
Tel: (615) 255-1213
E-mail: *Darrell@teracel.com*
    Clients include Faith Hill, Lonestar, Keith Urban, and Wynonna.

Michael Janas
1800 Holly Street
Nashville, TN 37206
Tel: (615) 228-0286
E-mail: *Michael.janas@att.net*
    Produces BR549 and Lynyrd Skynyrd.

Brent Maher
Moraine Music Group
2803 Bransford Avenue
Nashville, TN 37204
Tel: (615) 383-0400
Web site: *www.morainemusic.com*
    Maher is a songwriter, publisher, and producer of many artists, including the Judds.

Jozef Nuyens
The Castle Recording Studios
1393 Old Hillsboro Road
Franklin, TN 37069
Tel: (615) 478-3573
Web site: *www.castlemusicgroup.com*
    Nuyens is the owner of Castle Recording Studios and is a three-time Grammy nominated producer.

Warren Peterson
Javelina Recording Studio
P. O. Box 120662
Nashville, TN 37212
Tel: (615) 242-3493
Fax: (615) 777-3496
    Warren Peterson is publisher, producer, and owner of Javelina Recording Studios.

Allen Reynolds
Jack's Tracks Recording Studio
1308 16th Avenue South
Nashville, TN 37212
Tel: (615) 385-2555
Fax: (615) 385-2611
    Reynolds owns Jack's Tracks and produces Garth Brooks.

Frank Rogers
Sea Gayle Music
35 Music Square East
Nashville, TN 37203
Tel: (615) 742-1594
Fax: (615) 259-3470
    Clients are Brad Paisley, Darryl Worley, and Josh Turner.

Eric Silver
P. O. Box 128305
Nashville, TN 37212
Tel: (615) 297-0477
E-mail: *silver-703@comcast.net*
    Clients are Michelle Wright and Neal McCoy.

Dave Sinko
Sound Emporium
3100 Belmont Boulevard
Nashville, TN 37212
Tel: (615) 383-1982
E-mail: *sinko@comcast.net*
    Clients include Delbert McClinton.

Anthony Smith
Notes to Music/Words to Music
118 16th Avenue South, Suite #260A
Nashville, TN 37203
Tel: (615) 255-0360
E-mail: *ALSTunes2@MSN.Com*
    Smith coproduces Trini Triggs and SouthSixtyFive; he's also a hit songwriter and arranger.

Billy Joe Walker, Jr.
1708 Grand Avenue
Nashville, TN 37212
Tel: (615) 329-4244
E-mail: *marathonkeypub@aol.com*
    This highly acclaimed studio guitarist also produces Travis Tritt, Tracy Byrd, Brad Martin, and Mark Chesnutt.

Biff Watson
908 Neartop Drive
Nashville, TN 37205
Tel: (615) 356-3481
E-mail: *biff-bangs@mindspring.com*

Norro Wilson
Bud Ro Productions
1706 Grand Avenue
Nashville, TN 37212

Tel: (615) 320-4880
E-mail: *bud_ro@hotmail.com*

Wilson has won thirty-nine BMI awards as a writer, and twenty-seven number one awards as a producer for acts like John Anderson, Gary Morris, and Kenny Chesney.

Paul Worley
Warner Bros. Records
20 Music Square East
Nashville, TN 37203
Tel: (615) 748-8000
Web site: *www.wbrnashville.com*

Noted Nashville producer who produced the first Dixie Chicks hits; chief creative officer for Warner Bros.

Mark Wright
Sony Music
34 Music Square East
Nashville, TN 37203
Tel: (615) 742-4321
Web site: *www.sonynashville.com*

Wright is a hit songwriter and producer and executive vice president of A&R for Sony Music, Columbia, Epic, Monument and Lucky Dog Records.

THE ARTIST'S PACKAGE

An artist's package consists of a CD, 8″ × 10″ glossy photograph(s), a one page biography, and copies of any news articles or press releases (if any). One or two photographs are enough; one should be a headshot and the other a full-body pose. If you only have one photo, it should be a headshot. Black-and-white photos are fine if you are on a budget. The greatest financial outlay will be in the CD production; there is no need to put a lot of money into the artist package itself.

The CD should contain from four to ten songs, all original material. NO cover songs! Even though all aspiring artists frequently include some popular country standards in their live act, these standards or current country hits should not be included in the CD you will be pitching to industry executives and artist managers.

The main emphasis of the bio should be about the artist's music; what kind of message the songs portray, influences on the music, and reaction to the music from audiences, music critics, and industry executives. Some historical information can be included if it is relevant, such as when the artist first appeared on stage, whether the artist's family was musical as well, and any awards or special recognition. If there are any press clippings, they should be reduced to fit on one piece of paper, along with the logo (name) from the news source, and the date. Cut out the name from the front page of the news source, i.e. the *Tennessean*, and the date and page from the actual page the news article appeared. Shrink both of these items if necessary and paste at the top of the page, with the article underneath. If the article is too long to fit on one page, edit it down to one page only.

Put your CD, photos, bio and media page(s) inside a presentation folder. You can buy a presentation folder at your local stationery or copy store, or you can have one especially made. There are an infinite variety of folders to choose from, so you'll probably find what you are looking for on the shelf. Eventually all of these items will be separated from each other, so it is very important to put all of your contact information on the front page of every item, except the presentation folder itself. Contact info on the presentation folder should go on the inside left flap, or back. When opened, your bio will be on one side, with the media page behind it, and your photos on the other side. You can put the CD on either side, probably in front of the bio. There is usually a little slot to put a business card as well. This folder will then fit into a 10″ × 13″ envelope, to be used if you are dropping off your artist package to an industry executive, or if you have permission to send it by mail.

When putting together your artist package, remember that simplicity and consistency is the key. If you can spend a little money on graphic design, have something created that can be used on your CD, bio, business card, and mailing labels, so you have the same design or logo on all of your promotional materials.

THE ARTIST WEB SITE

Do you need a Web site? Yes, absolutely! Why? So people can find you instantly.

The World Wide Web is one of the most exciting technologies to come along in our lifetime. The Web is many different things to the people who use it to advertise, market their products, find bargains and cool stuff, or get information quickly. The priority for your personal Web site should be to help people find you. A very simple posting of your name and mailing address, along with a link to your e-mail address, is really all that is necessary. Of course, you will be tempted to provide much more, and the possibilities are endless. The best advice would be to put up something very simple at first, with plans to embellish your site later on. Keeping your budget in mind, your Web site shouldn't break the bank or take funds away from your CD project and live showcase opportunities. So design your Web site to provide information, not marketing your image.

Here are a few aspiring artist Web sites along with their Web designer's information:

- Artist/songwriter James Dean Hicks (*www.jamesdeanhicks.com*) is proof positive that fate and luck are two necessary ingredients needed to launch an artist's career. He has everything else, including great looks, talent, hit songs, and he's a really nice guy. But none of the labels have signed him to a record deal . . . can't understand why not?! His site was designed by Suzie Favor, a popular Music Row insider (*www.favorwebs.com*).
- Artist/songwriter Nancy Terzian (*www.nancyterzian.com*) moved to Nashville from San Francisco to further her songwriting career. She worked as a graphic design artist for Lynn Anderson's daughter Lisa Sutton, and then went out on her own. She has her web design company (*www.nterdesign.com*) and designed her own site.
- Amy Dalley, a new Curb recording artist (*www.amydalley.com*), has a very simple, easy to navigate Web site. Of course, that may be easier to create when you are drop-dead gorgeous like Amy! Site designed by Music Row studio backup singer and musician Thom Flora (*www.vaguenewworld.com*).

As we have mentioned several times, it is important to put your contact information on all of your promotional materials, and if possible, use the same graphic styling on each item. Graphic imaging can be a very powerful tool to make a statement about you and your music. An example of this can be found on the Web site of graphic artist Garrett Rittenberry, at *www.guerilladesign.com*. On his Web site, select "Case Study" and then artist Blake Shelton. Garrett provides a brief discussion of how graphics were used to create an image for Warner Bros. recording artist Shelton.

Another highly respected graphic artist, Luellyn Latocki, can help create your graphic image. Her stellar client list includes Garth Brooks, George Strait, and the Country Music Association. Her site can be found at *www.latockiteamdesign.com*.

12

Establishing Contact Before Your Trip

esides learning as much as you possibly can about the music industry
in general, there is a lot you can do to learn as much about the
Nashville music industry in particular. The more you learn before
your trip, the more successful your trip will be. It is very important to do your
homework *before* you go to Nashville. Although your first trip should be
regarded as a learning experience, Nashville is *not* the place to learn about the
music industry. You don't want to waste a publisher's time (and your own)
asking him what he does, how you are going to earn money for your songs,
etc. Likewise, a producer and record company executive do not want to waste
their time with someone they have to educate. That is the music industry's
biggest pet peeve. They especially get upset if you come in pitching a song
for someone who doesn't even have a record deal anymore, or even worse,
has passed away! Don't laugh; it happens all the time. Prepare yourself ahead
of time.

SUBSCRIBE TO MUSIC ROW PUBLICATIONS

If you haven't done so already as recommended in chapter 2, subscribe to
Music Row magazine. The Bible of the Nashville music industry, this publication contains information about everything that's going on in minute
detail. In addition to news about Nashville, this monthly magazine also
includes in its regular issues several comprehensive directories on various
topics. These are very important directories that will provide an update

to the listings in this book. As you can imagine, people move around frequently in this business, and *Music Row* magazine will be the best and most economical way to keep current. For example:

- **June** issue contains the "Annual Music Row Awards," which analyze the Top 50 country albums in a one-year period, and tell you the names of the session musicians who played on these albums.
- **July** issue is the "Studio Report," which lists the top studios and tells you a little about their equipment and the artists who record there.
- **September** issue publishes the "Artist Roster Report," which lists the A&R, management, booking, and publicity contacts for Nashville artists.
- **November** issue lists music publishers in its "Publisher Special."
- **April** issue—the most important issue—is "In Charge," which is a listing of Nashville's top decision makers. It includes a picture and brief bio of the person, along with a contact address and phone and e-mail or Web addresses. You can purchase any of these directory issues separately.

When you subscribe to *Music Row* magazine, you will also receive *@Musicrow*, sent every Friday to your e-mail address, which is a gossip column that tells you every little thing that happened on Music Row in a one-week period. If you did nothing else but start your own personal database with the people who are mentioned in *@Musicrow* each week, you would soon have a very comprehensive directory of Music Row decision makers. *@Musicrow* may be more than you need to know, and more than you need to spend right now; but you might want to go ahead and subscribe for three months or so just to get a feeling for what goes on in Nashville. Everyone on Music Row subscribes to *@Musicrow*, and everyone discusses its contents in their staff meeting on Monday morning. There are no secrets in Nashville, by the way. That's one reason your music is sure to be discovered if you are truly a great writer, artist, or musician.

ABOUT DEMO CRITIQUES

It is imperative that you have a Music Row professional critique your songs before you come to Nashville. There are only a couple of options available for this purpose; the performing rights organizations and the songwriters' organizations. This is a review of information covered in previous chapters, but just in case you missed it, here it is.

Performing Rights Organizations

BMI will probably be the most open to accepting your CD through the mail. It has what it calls "an open-door policy," which means that BMI will make an appointment with you if you call in advance, and someone will listen to your CD. The challenge for you will be in getting through to an individual, and not just BMI in general. You've got to glean some information out of the receptionist. Ask to talk to a "writers' representative," and be sure to get his or her name so if your call doesn't get through the first time, you can ask by name the next time you call.

ASCAP prefers to have writers go to its weekly "Straight Talk" session before they start making appointments and listening to demos. But you might get lucky and get to talk with a writers' representative. It's definitely worth spending some time to try to get someone to say "yes, send that CD!" SESAC needs a referral from a writer or publisher affiliate, or some other professional in the industry.

NSAI has a song critique service, but you have to be a member to be able to use it. You really should go ahead and join, and plan your trip to Nashville around one of NSAI's seminars or events. It has several during the year. The critique you receive from NSAI will be right on target. You can trust what the staff tells you. SGA staff doesn't critique songs. TSAI might, if you can talk them into it. They have a volunteer staff, so their time is limited.

Before you go to Nashville publishers, you will want to have had your demo critiqued by as many other professionals as possible. You really don't want a critique from a publisher—you want a song contract! Unfortunately, if a publisher agrees to listen to your song, he gets to give you his opinion of your song. Once you start playing your songs for publishers, you will get a myriad of differing opinions. That's why it's best to get as many professional opinions from non-publishers as you can before you start playing your songs for publishers.

STUDY THE TRADES

The "trades" are the two weekly magazines that chart the progress of country song singles. They are *Billboard's Country Airplay Monitor* and *Radio & Records (R&R)*. *R&R* was the preferred chart for the Nashville record labels for the past decade, but BDS technology finally won out, and the industry shifted over to *Billboard,* which uses the BDS fingerprinting system. When someone says to you, "study the trades," what he really means is that you need to know who the current artists are, what label they are on, and what their current single is. You certainly should be familiar with all the number one songs for the past year or so. The trades are the easiest place to find this information all in one place. The trades will tell you who the Top 100 recording artists are. *Billboard* goes even further and tells you who wrote their current single, who produced it, and who publishes it.

The reason it is imperative for you to have this information is that Music Row thinks in terms of "what's hot right now." Nashville songwriters write songs specifically for current country artists—songs that are similar to the artist's other hit singles. The country music industry is constantly criticized for producing product that all sounds the same. It is this method of doing things that causes this phenomenon. Although the labels and producers talk about the need to make some big changes, change will come slowly if at all. There are a lot of people involved in this process that will have to make the same changes.

There a lot of great country artists that aren't on a major label—Vern Gosdin, Gene Watson, John Anderson, Earl Thomas Conley, George Jones, Loretta Lynn. If you have written a song that fits one of these artists, then you need to know where to take it, and it won't be to a major record label or producer. There is no such thing as writing a great country song and playing it for everyone and letting them decide who should record it. Songs are written for specific artists and pitched to the specific people who work with that artist, only at the specific time they are looking for songs. It's a highly specialized process, which you will learn a little bit about from the trades and tip sheets.

STUDY CD LABEL COPY

What you *really* need to do is buy the CDs of the current country artists and study them inside and out. The "label copy," everything written about a CD, will give you lots of valuable information. There is a connection between everyone mentioned in the label copy, so you need to know who all these people are, especially the songwriters, publishers, and producer(s). It is a sad fact, but your songs need to sound like the songs on these CDs. The challenge is to write something just like these songs, only original! Somehow the top Nashville songwriters are able to do that.

The most important information on the CD label copy is the publishers listed. That's where you are going to get the information you need to call a Nashville publisher and get an appointment with him. Now you know some very specific information about each of the publishers listed; what writers they represent, what songs they publish, and which artists they have a close personal relationship with. You can use this information to your advantage when you call to get an appointment. You can also use this information to add to your own personal database directory. Now you not only know whom the top decision makers are in Nashville, you also know how you relate to the product they are marketing. You probably won't be crazy about all of the songs on the album—you may have written songs that are better. But you now have a reference point to work from.

ABOUT MAKING APPOINTMENTS

Your very first appointments should be with the PROs. It won't be necessary to make appointments with the songwriters' organizations. Their weekly workshops are open to everyone, so you just have to show up. You can drop in anytime at NSAI; someone is always available to help you. Plus, NSAI has lots of office facilities at your disposal, so you can make some phone calls while you are there.

You might have a hard time making an appointment with a writers' representative at ASCAP, because they provide a weekly "Straight Talk" session for new writers, which they will refer you to on your first trip to Nashville. BMI will make an appointment, you just have to ask. They also have a monthly BMI Roundtable. You may want to schedule your trip around this workshop, because it is the first in a series of workshops you can attend. SESAC requires a referral, but you still might stop by their offices when you are in town. It's worth a try.

Once you've had your songs evaluated by a writers' rep at one or more of the PROs, and/or some other Music Row professional, and they've given you some pretty positive feedback, then you are ready to contact the publishers. Here's your target list:

- **Publishers you've researched from the trades and CD label copy.** You now know a lot about these publishers now. Remember: There are a lot of staff members at these companies—professional manager, creative director, and song pluggers. You can get their names out of "In Charge" and the *Music Row* "Publisher Special."
- **Nashville's independent music publishers**. In chapter 5, there is some information about Nashville's independent music publishers. There is more information about them in "In Charge." Research as much as you can before you call. Tell them where you are from and that you will only be in town one week—this is your only chance to see them. It might work, as they are always looking for writers outside of Nashville. Also, be sure and drop the names of the people who critiqued your demo. That will help to get an appointment.

That should be enough to keep you busy for months trying to get an appointment with a publisher. This might be easier than you think, and is very, very important. The key to success in Nashville for songwriters and aspiring artists lies with the publishers. It is a little-known fact that publishers are the most important link in the chain. Publishers have direct contact with the artists, record companies, producers, and artist managers—as well as all other publishers and their staff songwriters. They know when an artist is recording and what kind of material he is looking for, and they relay this information to their staff writers. So, while evenings should be spent at writers' nights (meeting other writers, hopefully), days should be spent in publishers' offices—or trying to get in to see a publisher.

Since you have carefully prepared for your trip, you have with you a target list of publishers to call on. You know some of the songs they publish, a little of the history of the company, and you have a vague idea what they look like (you saw them in a magazine or at a writers' night). Now you are ready to hang out on Music Row.

The sign at the publisher's door says, "No Unsolicited Material." That's OK. Go on in. Chat with the receptionist, get her name, tell her who you are, stall, stall, stall. You are basically just hanging around as long as you can in the hopes you will run into someone you recognize. The chances of running into someone you saw or met at a writers' night is very good. Plan on it . . . be prepared. Have a CD ready to give to someone you might make a personal contact with. People are not taken aback when you hand them a CD. It's almost expected. Everyone does it. That's what Nashville is all about. There are CDs everywhere. You might even be able to leave one on the receptionist's desk, or maybe you can talk her into taking it.

Publishers do not accept unsolicited material for many good reasons. The one they emphasize the most is the fear of unwarranted lawsuits, songwriters who think their idea was stolen. Ideas and song titles are not protected by copyright. The truth is, publishers are bombarded with enough material from the people they know and do business with on a daily basis. They don't need outside material. And 99 percent of unsolicited material is really poor quality. So, even if there is a gem in there somewhere, it's not worth their taking the time to look for it.

Finding a Nashville publisher to represent your songs should be your first priority, way before pitching to record companies, producers, or artist managers. Nashville publishers are the pulse of the Nashville music industry. They are closely associated with the record companies, have their own artist production companies, and work closely with artist management. Publishers can also advance a musician's career, through songwriter demos and artist development projects. Careful study of Nashville publishers will be well worth the effort. The more you know about a publisher, the better your chances of getting an appointment.

13

When To Go: Important Industry Events Month by Month

H ere is a month-by-month guide to what's happening in Nashville. Once upon a time you could set your calendar by events on Music Row. That's no longer the case. If you want to attend any of the cool events described below, be sure to call first and check on the dates.

JANUARY

It would probably be a good idea to avoid this month altogether. The industry pretty much shuts down during the holidays, so people are just getting back from a long vacation. It's also a time when songwriters have made a new determination to get their songs heard, so publishers and producers get an exceptional number of calls this month.

FEBRUARY

By now most songwriters have forgotten about their New Year's resolutions and have quit blitzing publishers with calls—the publishers are concentrating on songs because the artists are in the studios. This is a high-activity time. Producers and artists are looking for material to take into the studio, and publishers are pitching songs and looking for new songs also. The only drawback for both January and February is the weather. It only snows occasionally in Nashville, but when it does, the town shuts down. The city has limited snow removal equipment, so businesses usually close when the weather report even hints at snow. Music Row, known to be efficient, punctual, and reliable, suddenly becomes undependable. However, if you are comfortable maneuvering in the snow and can be flexible about finding something else to do with your time if your schedule gets disrupted, February is an excellent month to get things accomplished.

The Grammy awards show takes place in February, usually in the second week. Since the Grammys are usually held in Los Angeles or New York, the entire Nashville music industry will be out-of-town for a week during the awards, which also hosts many nightly industry events. Check to see when it is before you plan your trip to Nashville.

MARCH

March is a great month to come to Nashville including ideal weather. There are two major events you should plan to attend, according to your own interests: the Country Radio Seminar (CRS) and NSAI's Tin Pan South. CRS was formerly called DJ Week and was held during the week of the CMA Awards Show. All the artists attend the event to meet with visiting radio air personalities and programmers, and to record radio spots ("Hi, this is Reba McEntire, and my favorite radio station is . . ."). During the day, there are in-depth panel discussions on every topic deemed important to country music, and at night, there are label shows in the clubs downtown. There is a New Faces show for the labels to introduce their hot new artists and a Super Faces show showcasing one of the industry's superstars.

Named after New York's songwriting district, Tin Pan Alley, Tin Pan South is a weeklong celebration of Nashville's most important citizen—the songwriter. There are seminars and panel discussions connected to the event, as well as a golf tournament and a Legendary Songwriter show. No songwriter should miss it.

APRIL

April is a great month to come to Nashville. February, March, September, and October are the busiest months, when artists and producers are in the studios recording their next album projects. Publishers are hustling to get songs to them at the last minute, and that is very often the time new songs are picked up. Although it's good to be involved in this activity, you are not likely to get much personal attention during those months. April and May are the ideal months for songwriters to approach publishers. There is still a lot of recording activity going on; publishers have exhausted their catalogs and are receptive to new material; everyone has more time available.

Tennis, anyone? Music Row hosts a tennis tournament the last week-end of April and first weekend of May. The purpose of the tournament is to provide networking opportunities for writers and industry executives and to raise a little money for Vanderbilt Children's Hospital. It's lots of fun and so popular many players come from out of state year after year. If interested, check out *www.musiccitytennis.com*.

MAY

Another great month to visit, but check first to see when the Academy of Country Music (ACM) Awards Show is held in Las Vegas. The show is on a Wednesday night, but you don't want to plan a trip to Nashville during that entire week, because everybody will be in Las Vegas! The HoriPro Golf Tournament takes place the Monday and Tuesday after Mother's Day—the golf course is literally strewn with every top music industry professional from Music Row, including Bob Beckham himself, president of HoriPro Entertainment Group.

JUNE

By June, recording activity has really wound down, as the artists go out on tours. June is a great time to come to town to meet with publishers, except during the CMA Music Festival (formerly Fan Fair). The festival is a huge country music festival produced by the CMA, which gives 25,000 fans the opportunity to meet and have their "picture made" (as they say in the South) with their favorite stars. Each label gives a great show featuring several artists from their roster. It's a good opportunity for you to meet the new artists and get a real feel for what they are like, but you won't be able to pitch them any songs. They have reserved this time for their fans, not songwriters. Pitching a song would be out of place. It's also not a good time to try to set up appointments, because everyone, including publishers and the staff of PROs and the songwriting organizations, is at the festival all day long. Record company executives work twenty-four-hour days during this week, planning their record label show, escorting and entertaining artists who are in town for the event, and trying to keep up with their regular duties. Don't even think about calling a record label this week!

The Nashville Songwriters Festival is a new event that you might want to check out for a June visit. Held at the Nashville KOA Kampground near the Opryland Hotel, the festival features four main stages to play on while you camp out, recharge your ideas and come up with some brand-new hooks. It's a great chance to meet some willing collaborators. For more information, go to *www.SongWritersFestival.com*.

JULY AND AUGUST

A good time to concentrate on developing a relationship with publishers. Artists are on the road, recording schedules are very light, and there is very little pressure on anybody. No one moves too fast during these months.

Temperatures are in the high nineties, with the humidity the same. Frequent summer showers are welcome to cool things off.

SEPTEMBER

Things start to get serious after Labor Day. Artists are back in the studio, producers are looking for material, and publishers are hustling to get songs recorded and to sign new songs. It's a great month to come to Nashville. You don't want to miss the annual Americana Music Conference, held the last week in September. Everyone in the industry attends this growing music conference, which concentrates its efforts on getting radio airplay for independent labels, and independent Americana artists.

OCTOBER

October and November are heavy studio months. It's a great time to come to Nashville—there is a lot of activity going on with writer showcases, parties, events. Everyone is focused on work and getting lots accomplished. The first week in October, the International Entertainment Buyers Association (IEBA) holds its annual conference in Nashville. It's a great opportunity to meet artist managers, booking agents and talent buyers—all the people who represent artists. Check out the organization at *www.ieba.org.*

NOVEMBER

At the beginning of the month, CMA Week completely dominates the industry. It is a weeklong celebration of country music centering around the nationally televised CMA Awards show. There are five black-tie events, where the men wear the same tuxedo every night, and the women wear five different spectacular evening gowns. Starting Sunday night, it's the NSAI Songwriters Awards Dinner, followed by nightly awards banquets hosted by ASCAP, BMI, and SESAC. The PROs honor their songwriter and publisher affiliates and members who had the most radio airplay during a one-year period. The CMA Awards Show is centered in the middle, on Wednesday night.

That's just the beginning. Every night after the awards banquets, several publishers have private parties to honor their writers. After the CMA Awards show, all of the record labels have private parties in honor of their artists who won awards or were performers on the show. And since all of these parties are by invitation only, the T.J. Martell Foundation sponsors events that you can attend simply by buying a ticket. Since so many people in the industry are not on the banquet guest lists (for award winners only), there are lots of folks who want to have fun, too. T.J. Martell offers a golf tournament, bowling tournament, silent auction, and celebrity concert.

Proceeds go to cancer and AIDS research. You might want to come to town during this time and join in the fun, but chances of getting much work done are slim.

DECEMBER

After Thanksgiving things really begin to slow down. There are holiday parties and many other distractions that start interfering with the song process. The business turns to year-end budgets and other housekeeping duties. Most record companies are closed for at least two weeks or more, and many publishers follow suit. Although some publishers may stay in town to get things done, finding someone to take an appointment may be difficult. Best to wait until next year.

14

The Logistics of Your Visit

After you have recorded your CD, picked your travel dates, and decided what your goals are, you still have to work out the practical details of your trip. Once you make up your mind to go to Nashville, you won't want to be thwarted because you inadvertently brought the wrong clothes, or booked a hotel room in the middle of nowhere.

WHAT TO BRING

- **Guitar**. If you compose songs using a guitar, then you will certainly want to have yours with you. As you will see when you attend your first open mic night, songwriters perform at all stages of ability. If you can perform your own songs with a certain agility, then you don't have to have a great voice or be able to hit all the high notes.
- **Boom Box**
- *Music Row's* **"In Charge" and this book (of course!)**. You'll want to have "In Charge" with you to refer to constantly. You will run into people who will mention someone you are not familiar with. You can look them up.
- **Personalized stationery and envelopes; lots of business cards; postcards with your picture or logo on one side, blank on the other; and stamps.** You never know when you might need to confirm some business agreement in writing, so bring stationery and envelopes just in case. Hopefully, you will be able to book yourself at a songwriters' night or open mic night

with enough notice to send out invitations. Use your postcards for that. You can handwrite a few to key Music Row executives (get addresses from "In Charge").

- **Or you could get a set of mailing labels**. You might get booked on a really great show, and you will then want to do a big mass mailing to the industry. You can get your blank postcards printed while you wait, stick on the labels and drop them in the mail. The industry people will get them the next day, and yes, they do pay attention to this type of invitation. It can be a simple invitation on an 8 1/2" × 11" piece of paper, folded once or twice, if you didn't make up postcards. But don't stick an invitation to a showcase inside an envelope. Chances are slim it would be opened.
- **Portable PC**. Are you proficient with e-mail? Have your e-mail database ready to send out a broadcast e-mail invitation to the industry, announcing the time, date, and place of your showcase or open mic night. And, you can send follow-up e-mails to people you have met, or to send a thank-you for any meetings you may have had.
- **Umbrella**. It rains a lot in Nashville, and you'll be glad of it in the summertime, when the humidity is 100 percent!
- **Antihistamine and allergy medicine**. Nashville is hard on those who suffer from allergies, and even might bother some who don't usually react to pollen. There are lots of beautiful things growing here that generate fuzzy and airborne byproducts.

WHAT TO WEAR

Everyday is casual day on Music Row. Even the top executives wear jeans with a nice dress shirt and sport coat. It's OK to go without a tie. The best advice is to dress in your favorite clothes; the ones that make you feel and look great. Stay away from Western gear unless that's your regular clothes and the ones you are most comfortable in. You won't see many cowboy hats on Music Row, except for the aspiring artists hoping to attract attention; but you will see people wearing cowboy boots or tennis shoes.

You'll need an overcoat mid-October through mid-March; temperatures hover near 30 degrees during the winter. In the summer, temperatures stay around 80 degrees to 90 degrees, but the humidity makes it feel like 180! You'll be grateful every time you step into an air-conditioned room. Spring and fall only last for a minute or two.

You'll be doing a lot of walking, so bring some really comfortable shoes. Save pretty heels or dress shoes for writers' nights and you might get lucky and get invited to one of the many Music Row parties. You can spiff up then with some special accessory. But don't plan on anything too dressy.

TRANSPORTATION

Almost everything on Music Row is located in a small area, and there are medium-priced hotels and motels nearby. Unfortunately, nothing is really within walking distance; the Row itself is fairly stretched out, with long blocks and long distances between companies. Plan to rent a car; then plan to park that car a good distance away from where you want to go. You'll probably stay within a few miles of the Row, drive to the Row and park your car, then walk to many of the places you want to go to. There is no public transportation to speak of, and taxis are more or less used to get to the airport and back, and that's about it.

If you absolutely can't drive or rent a car, you will still be able to stay fairly close to the Row and walk to most of the places you need to go to. Just be prepared to have to deal with the weather. If this is your only option, then plan your visit for April or October, towards the first of the month. That's the prettiest time in Nashville anyway, and the most pleasant weather. You just can't count on the nice weather lasting very long.

Even if you do rent a car, you won't have to do much driving. You will probably get by with less than a tank of gas, so rent accordingly.

WHERE TO STAY

It's not going to cost an arm and a leg to stay a week in Nashville if you are not picky about your accommodations. There are even places listed in the classified section of the *Tennessean* for $55 per week! Sounds too good to be true and probably is, but even the range of $100 to $150 is pretty reasonable. Occasionally something in that range becomes available right on Music Row. As soon as you know when you'll be coming, get a copy of the *Tennessean* from a bookstore that carries out-of-state newspapers, or contact the *Tennessean* at *www.tennessean.com*. Most accommodations in this price range will be in the airport, Dickerson Road, Madison, or Gallatin areas. These areas are not near Music Row. With traffic, they are probably thirty to forty-five minutes away, with the airport area being the closest.

There are very nice medium-priced hotels and motels almost within walking distance from Music Row, but not quite—depending on your stamina and the weather.

Comfort Inn
I-40 and Demonbreun
Tel: (615) 255-9977
$69 per night—no weekly rates
This used to be Shoney's Inn and is very popular with visiting artists such as Merle Haggard. Within walking distance of Music Row.

Courtyard by Marriott
West End Boulevard
(800) 321-2211
$92 per night—no weekly rates
   Also within walking distance to Music Row.

Guesthouse Inn & Suites/Medcenter
1909 Hayes Street
Tel: (615) 329-1000
$72 per night—no weekly rates
   Guesthouse has special rates for people in town for outpatient medical treatment. It is a little off the beaten path but not too far away—and has a free shuttle to Music Row.

Days Inn-Vanderbilt-Music Row
1800 West End Avenue
Tel: (615) 327-0922
$59.95 per night—no weekly rates
   Close to Music Row; Bazante's, a popular Nashville restaurant is in the motel.

Best Western on Music Row (formerly the Hall of Fame)
1407 Division Street
Tel: (615) 242-1631
$59.95 to $89.95 per night
   The closest motel to Music Row; contains the Hall of Fame Writer's Lounge.

The Spence Manor
11 Music Square East
Nashville, TN
Tel: (615) 259-4400
$450 for seven days; $1,650 per month; negotiable
   Built on Music Row expressly for the privacy of the music industry—has a guitar-shaped swimming pool and large apartment suites.

Loews Vanderbilt Plaza Hotel
2100 West End Avenue
Nashville, TN
Tel: (615) 320-1700
$199 per night; has special rates around holidays and other occasions for around $100 per night.

The Vanderbilt Plaza, as it is known, is where all the music industry executives stay when they come to town. It's down the street at 21st Avenue South and West End Avenue. It's not necessary to stay here to impress anyone or, hopefully, run into anyone.

Embassy Suites
1811 Broadway
Tel: (615) 320-8899
Ranges from $130 to $160 per night
New to the Music Row area, the Embassy Suites does have an extra sitting room for those who are planning to invite other songwriters over to collaborate on some songs, and the hotel provides a great breakfast and happy hour for guests.

Other Less Expensive Areas

You might save a little money if you stay further out from Music Row and Downtown Nashville; stick to the airport, Murfreesboro Road, or Nolensville Road–Harding Mall areas. They are each about twenty minutes away from Music Row and aren't bad neighborhoods. The Economy Inn (Roadway) on Murfreesboro Road has weekly rates of $182.50, which includes tax for a seven-night minimum, or $45 plus tax per day—call (615) 361-6830. You can search the Nashville yellow pages for other motels in these areas online at *www.yp.bellsouth.com*.

15

Your One-Week Itinerary

The following is an *imaginary* one-week schedule. Actually, one week would be a pretty long time. If you need to narrow it down, the best time would be to arrive Monday afternoon, work hard Tuesday, Wednesday, and Thursday, and then leave Friday afternoon. The most important songwriters' showcases, the ones featuring hit Nashville songwriters, are on Wednesday or Thursday nights. There's not much happening on weekends, except for the Bluebird Cafe's Sunday night shows.

General Guidelines

These are general guidelines, and it's NOT recommended that you strictly adhere to this schedule. You might meet a great writer and wind up doing nothing else but writing a hit song on your trip. This itinerary will simply give you an idea of some of the things you might consider doing while you are in Nashville—the primary purpose of this schedule is to get you out of your hotel room and on Music Row where you will get more accomplished!

It really doesn't matter whether you arrive on Sunday or Wednesday or whenever. But some of the things included on this one-week itinerary are very important. They are:

- **Obtain a copy of the *Nashville Scene* and the *Tennessean*.** The *Nashville Scene* (*www.nashvillescene.com*) is a weekly alternative newspaper that is available free at area restaurants and stores. It comes out on Thursdays, so if you arrive on Sunday or Monday, you may have trouble finding a copy. You can always get one at their office, 2120 8th Avenue South, Nashville, TN 37204-2204. If you are seriously considering a move to Nashville, you may want to subscribe to the *Scene*. It will give you an in-depth view of current issues affecting the city. The *Nashville Scene* has a comprehensive music section and lists the addresses and phone numbers for all the music clubs, providing detailed information about open mic nights, writers' nights, and showcases. There is very little coverage on country music since it is not a part of the live music scene in Nashville, but you should check out all the clubs for songwriters' nights and you will need the addresses as well. The *Nashville Scene* will be very helpful to you.

While you are in Nashville, you will also want to get a copy of the daily newspaper, the *Tennessean* (*www.tennessean.com*). They have regular feature articles on country artists, the Music Row business community, anything and everything affecting the country music industry in Nashville. They also have a daily preview of what's happening on the live music scene that evening, with recommendations of what to see.

In addition, on Wednesdays, the *Tennessean* publishes a free guide to what's going on through the next seven days, available wherever you can find the *Scene*. Called *The Rage*, it contains detailed information about the bands and writers that are playing about town. Another great publication available free on the newsstands is the *Nashville Music Guide*. It is a monthly publication so the performer information might not be as current as the other publications, but it contains much more detailed information about the open mic and writers' nights.

- **Attend a writers' night every night**. And try to get to more than one if possible. Some start at 6:00 P.M., and others start at 9:30 P.M.— so you can go to two per night.
- **Perform at as many open mic nights as possible**. It's the best exposure you can give your songs. Most writers' clubs have open mic nights at 6:00 P.M., and then again at 10:30 or 11:00 P.M. All you have to do is show up and signup, and you'll probably get on.
- **Attend the workshops at NSAI, SGA, TSAI, ASCAP, and BMI**. If you do nothing else but attend these workshops, you will make very valuable contacts.
- **Spend at least one day just stopping by the publishing companies, dropping off CDs**. Don't expect to get to see anyone in particular, but get a feel for the offices, get to know the receptionist, try to find out names of the people who work there. Then, when you are back home calling on the phone trying to get permission to

send another CD, you'll have a good idea how that office works. Each one is different. Not every company is right for you. Be selective about the companies you approach. Have your CD handy to give to someone if the occasion arises (plus invitations to any open mic nights or writers' nights you book). Don't hesitate to offer your CD to someone.

- **Hang out at area restaurants**. As I mentioned in chapter 10, the people at the bars in the LongHorn, Sunset Grill, and Friday nights at Granite Falls are all industry people. If you prefer not to drink, then have some juice or bottled water, and strike up a conversation with the folks around you. You may be dying to get a certain song to a specific producer or A&R rep; your chances of running into him at a nearby restaurant are very good. Don't go up to him when he is eating, but look for another opportunity.
- **Set appointment goals**. Try to get an appointment with all three of the PROs, and at least one publisher.
- **Set songwriting goals**. Try to get at least one song started with a co-writer while you are in Nashville. Then you'll have at least one good solid contact in town.

DAY-BY-DAY, HOUR-BY-HOUR SCHEDULE

This is an imaginary schedule, one to use only as a guideline, especially when you are not sure what to do next. The most important item on this itinerary is the open mic nights—that's where your direct competitors are hanging out, and you can get a firsthand look at what you are up against. Your first task will be to get comfortable in this environment. If you can impress this audience, chances are you will impress the rest of Music Row.

Sunday

Arrive in the afternoon; pick up a copy of the *Nashville Scene, Nashville Music Guide* and the *Tennessean*. Your hotel might have a copy, or they are found outside most restaurants and markets. Carefully look over all the open mic, writers' nights, and showcases and select the ones you plan to attend. Fill in your itinerary with the clubs you plan to go to. We've made some suggestions incase you can't decide! Take a walking tour around Music Row.

Sunday Night

Observe these two important showcases at the Bluebird Cafe:

- **6:30 P.M.—Bluebird Cafe Sunday Spotlight**. This show is very special and very different from what you normally see at the Bluebird. This is a mini-artist showcase for qualifying writers and artists and the best opportunity to showcase for writers who are not backed by a Nashville publishing company. Worth checking out.

- **8:00 P.M.—Bluebird Cafe Writers' Night**. The ultimate writers' night. Writers who play this show have gone through a long audition process.

Monday

- **9 A.M.—Breakfast at the Pancake Pantry**. Many Music Row executives have their first meeting of the day at this popular breakfast spot. Afterwards, go around the corner and stop by the Acklen post office.
- **10:00 A.M.—ASCAP**. Sign up for ASCAP's "Straight Talk." See if you can meet with a writers' representative.
- **10:15 A.M.—BMI**. Find out when BMI Roundtable is being held, and sign up if you will still be in town. See if you can meet with a writers' representative. They also have a telephone in the lobby you can use for a limited number of calls.
- **11:00 A.M.—SESAC**. Check in and chat with the receptionist. Ask to speak to a writers' representative.
- **11:30 A.M.—SGA**. Introduce yourself and get SGA's schedule for the week. They may have a workshop this afternoon, or you might be just in time for the noon workshop! SGA has weekly workshops on Mondays, but the time varies between noon, 5 P.M. or 5:30 P.M. Whatever it is this week, sign up!
- **12:00 noon—Lunch**. Sunset Grill (or SGA Workshop).
- **2:00 to 3:00 P.M.—Appointments with publishers**. If you don't have any appointments, then just start walking down 17th Avenue, dropping in on the publishers that are on your list. Try to make an appointment but be prepared to leave your CD.
- **3:00 P.M.—Head out to the Bluebird Cafe (thirty minutes driving time)**. Get in line to sign up to play the Bluebird Cafe with Barbara Cloyd. Sign-ups are from 5:30 to 5:45 P.M.—only fifteen minutes to sign up everybody. They can only take so many, so get there early. The earlier, the better. Take the *Scene* and the *Tennessean* with you; you can study the writers' nights while you are waiting, and discuss other writers' nights and Open Mic nights with the people in line.
- **6:00 to 9:00 P.M.—Open Mic Night at the Bluebird Cafe**. (If you have to choose between the Bluebird Cafe Open Mic Night and the SGA Workshop, go with SGA. You will have lots of Open Mic opportunities while you are in town.)

Tuesday
- **9:00 A.M.—Breakfast at Noshville.** Another big favorite of Music Row executives.
- **10:00 A.M. to 12:00 noon—Visit NSAI and SGA.** Staffers will take the time to answer your questions about Nashville and the music industry and give you any assistance you may need. Take the time to nurture a working relationship with people in the organization; they may become your very important link to Nashville.
- **12:00 noon—Lunch at the LongHorn.**
- **2:00 to 4:00 P.M.—Stop by the publishing offices on 16th Avenue South.**
- **4:30 to 6 P.M.—Happy hour at The Trace.**
- **8:00 P.M.—Douglas Corner Open Mic Night with Rick Campbell.**
- **9:30 P.M.—Attend a writers' night at Hair of the Dog.**

Wednesday
- **9:00 A.M.—Breakfast at the Pancake Pantry.** Afterwards, stop by the Acklen post office again.
- **10:00 A.M. to 12:00 noon—More appointments with PROs, Songwriters Organizations, and publishers.** Couldn't get any appointments? Then stop by ASCAP, BMI, or SESAC again and see if you can get an appointment with a writer's representative. Be persistent. Don't give up. Make it a goal to meet with someone at each of these companies this week and be sure to attend ASCAP Straight Talk and BMI Roundtable. Make a few calls to publishers from each of these locations.
- **12:00 noon—Lunch at the Tin Roof.**
- **2:00 to 4:00 P.M.—Stop by publishing offices and *American Songwriter* offices.**
- **5:00 to 6:00 P.M.—Happy hour at Sunset Grill.**
- **6:30 P.M.—TSAI Workshop at Belmont University.**
- **9:00 P.M.—Attend a writers' night at Commodore Lounge with Debi Champion with late open mic.**

Thursday
- **9:00 A.M.—Breakfast at Noshville.**
- **10:00 A.M.—Call publishers for appointments.** By now you should have a pretty clear idea of whom you would like to meet with while you are in Nashville. Try to get an appointment, but don't linger by the phone.

- **10:30 A.M. to 12:00 noon—Still no appointments**? Drop by the offices on 16th Avenue South (Music Square East).
- **12:00 noon—Lunch at the LongHorn**.
- **2:00 to 4:00 P.M.—Still no appointments**? Drop by the offices on 17th Avenue South (Music Square West).
- **5:00 to 6:00 P.M.—Happy hour at the Tin Roof**.
- **6:30 P.M.—NSAI Workshop, Musicians Union (enter back door)**—This is probably the most important appointment on your schedule—don't miss!
- **Also 6:00 P.M.**—Take the Stan Mott club tour, starting with It's All Good Cafe, Open Mic with David Lee Slater at 6:00 P.M.; Writers' Night with Jack Scott at the French Quarter Cafe, and Hobo Joe's late Open Mic with Shawn Harnett (*www.shawnharnett.com*). You can visit East Nashville on other nights, but Thursday is the night they all have open mic opportunities (check listings as this may have changed!).

Friday

- **10:00 A.M.—Time to get on the phone**! Spend Friday morning on the phone calling all the contacts you made, thanking them for their help, etc. Nashville is a genuinely friendly city that does business on a personal level. Let them know you appreciate their friendship and will be in touch.
- **12:00 noon—Leisurely lunch at Sunset Grill**. Music Row relaxes on Friday afternoons, most people taking off early. This would be a great time to co-write with that new writer you met at an open mic night!
- **5:00 to 6:00 P.M.—Happy hour at Granite Falls**. Industry hangs out here on Friday nights.

Saturday

Finish that song. Plan your next trip. Relax and go visit Cheekwood or the Frist Museum, walk Radnor Lake and enjoy the rest of Nashville.

16

Common Mistakes

Most people come to Nashville thinking they are going to set the town on fire and things will start happening for them right away. They fall into several different categories:

BIG FISH IN A SMALL POND

Good country singers, songwriters, and musicians who have a big following in their hometowns are surprised at the reaction they get when they come to Nashville. Their music is popular and widely received at home, and everyone is crazy about them! Everyone around them encourages them to take their music to Nashville. Once here, they are thrown into an environment rich with talent. No matter how great they are, they lack the advantage of having personal relationships in the recording studios and publishers' offices. Even though they may be outstanding, it will take awhile for the people of Nashville to get to know them, trust them, and take a chance on substituting them for someone they already know can get the job done.

"HOLIER THAN THOU" ATTITUDE

People from a major music city such as Los Angeles or New York who have a great track record in other areas of music, tend to think that gives them an edge in Nashville. It doesn't. Nashville is a separate entity in itself, and no matter what your success in other areas, everyone is on equal footing in Nashville. Many songwriters make their move to Nashville when they have a single on the charts. Although that success may open a few doors, it still doesn't change things. It is going to take time for anyone new to Nashville to develop relationships.

DISPLAYING AN ATTITUDE

One of the toughest things about putting yourself on the line and exposing yourself to criticism is that you are going to get an awfully lot of differing opinions from strangers. It's a painful experience and one that doesn't make much sense. Everyone you meet is going to give you different advice. Keeping a cool head and remaining objective about this whole process is very challenging. Try to look upon your first trip as a learning experience. Don't go expecting to impress anyone. And try not to overreact or become defensive. Many a frustrated songwriter has left town in a huff under such duress.

TRYING TO BUY YOUR WAY IN

You would think that your life would be a whole lot easier if you had enough money to help make your dreams come true. But the truth is, lots of money doesn't really help that much, and more often than not it gets in the way. Nashville isn't really impressed with how much money you have, so if you are lucky enough to have a rich uncle or an investor, keep it a secret. There have been many wealthy businessmen who have come into town, set up lavish offices, even built new buildings on Music Row, only to quietly leave town a few years later. An investor's money should be used to hire the very best entertainment attorney as a spokesperson and contract negotiator, to produce a master quality demo (four songs only—a ten-song CD is not necessary) using a top Nashville producer and studio musicians, and to hire a top-notch publicist. An investor should not play a high-profile role in marketing an aspiring artist or musician, but rather remain behind the scenes. Talking about money detracts from the most important topic—your talent!

"SELL" SOME SONGS

"Selling songs" is a common term that is used by people that are not in the music industry and don't understand what a publisher really does. It is not possible to sell a song. When a publisher signs a song to a contract, no money transaction takes place. A publisher never "buys" a song. When you "sell" a song, it's like "selling" your smile or your personality. People can "buy into" your winning smile, but they don't pay for it, they just believe in it. Don't use this term under any circumstances.

SENDING CDs THROUGH THE MAIL

Please don't take the address listings contained in this book and mail everyone your CD project. It is a big waste of your time and money. Publishers, producers, and record companies receive hundreds of CDs in the mail each week. They have different ways of handling these CDs, but for the most part, they don't open the packages and they don't listen to the CDs for the following reasons:

- It is not cost-effective. It takes way too much time to sort through the bad songs in the hope of finding one good one.
- They have their own source of songs.
- They are afraid of nuisance lawsuits by songwriters who feel their ideas have been stolen.

WRITING FOR PERMISSION TO SUBMIT A CD

This is almost as bad as sending in your CD without permission—a waste of time and money. Don't do this. One songwriter sent a clever questionnaire to all of the top music publishers in Nashville. It was very well written, easy to fill out, and came with an SASE (self-addressed, stamped envelope). She simply wanted to know how they went about selecting songs for their catalog, and would they listen to one of her songs if submitted to their attention. Surprisingly enough, almost all the publishers took the time to fill out the questionnaire but all of them said "no," she couldn't submit material. Only one never answered. But what amazed her the most was that one publisher returned her envelope unopened with a rubber-stamped response on the front saying "No Unsolicited Material." How did they know what her envelope contained?, she wondered. Easy. Publishers receive hundreds of letters asking permission to send material. Request letters are very easily spotted and receive negative or no response.

APPROACHING A PUBLISHER INCORRECTLY

Publishers receive a dozen calls a day that go something like this:

"Hello, I'm calling to see if you are accepting unsolicited material at this time."

"Hello, I'm a songwriter and . . ."

"Hello, I have a song demo I'd like to send you."

"Hello, I'd like permission to send you a song demo."

It's too easy to say "no" to those inquiries. Be much more specific. Find out as much as you possibly can about the company you are calling before you call. You can easily find that information in *Music Row* publications and *American Songwriter* magazine. Between these two publications, you should have enough leads to make several calls a week. It will be the quality of contacts made, and not the quantity, that will determine your success. Use the same sales techniques you would for any other sales job. Perhaps a book or course on sales would be helpful when making cold calls to publishers.

PACKAGING PRODUCT INCORRECTLY

Incorrect packaging is the trademark of an amateur. You want to be very mindful of what your package should look like. Don't make following very common errors:

Never, ever write by hand on a CD label. The labels must be graphically produced on your computer. There are so many computer software programs to choose from, it is very inexpensive to produce a great-looking CD label. If you'd rather not print your own labels, one of the many copy stores can do it for you at very little cost. Same for an insert card and lyric sheet. You need all three to have a uniform, professional look to them—nothing handwritten! CDs are little different, in that you can burn your own individual CDs, one at a time. If you are using the type of CD that you can write on with a marker, then your own handwriting is acceptable. But the CD insert and lyric sheets will still need to be professionally done.

Don't send long personal letters and snapshots under any circumstances. If your career goals go beyond songwriting, then you will need a professional bio and photo. See chapter 11 on how to prepare these materials.

Once you have identified the publisher you wish to contact, established a personal relationship with an individual in that company, and obtained her permission to send your CD, follow these helpful hints:

Write "Requested by _____" on the front of the envelope. Even with this notation on the front, sometimes a CD package won't get by the receptionist, because they are so used to rejecting this type of package. Lots of people use the notation "Requested Material" even when they haven't received permission to mail the CD, so you have to be more specific—who requested the CD and what's on it? Give as much information as possible on the front of your package.

If you don't have nice-looking professional labels with a nice business logo (which is not really necessary), then mail your package in a colored envelope. Use something other than manila or white. That way, when you make a follow-up call, you can tell the receptionist or publisher what your package looks like. It's probably sitting on their desk or in a box right next to it, under a pile of other CDs.

Make a follow-up call around the time you think the package will arrive. If you wait a month, it will be too late. Find out what happened to each and every package you send out. And don't be surprised if you have to mail out another copy.

Don't ask for your CD to be returned. Once you mail it, it's gone. Don't ever send your last copy, or only original copy.

NOT UNDERSTANDING THE INDUSTRY

Nothing frustrates an industry professional more than having to explain the basics of the industry—what a PRO does, why you need a publisher before approaching a producer or an A&R rep, etc. Do your homework thoroughly before you plan a trip to Nashville. If you wanted to design automobiles for a living, you wouldn't walk into General Motors without first having a degree in automotive engineering. The Nashville music industry is just as specialized, albeit a lot less technical! You have to know exactly who you are meeting with, what he does, what he can do for you, and specifically what you can do for him. What if he says yes? You have to know what the next step is without him telling you, so you'll know if you are being treated fairly and getting what you deserve. Don't even think about coming to Nashville to pitch your songs or artist package before you have a thorough understanding of how everything works and the unique things you have to offer.

STAYING IN YOUR HOTEL ROOM WAITING FOR RETURN PHONE CALLS

This used to be more of a problem than it is now, since the widespread use of cell phones has changed the way we communicate. Now when you call, you can leave your cell phone number instead of your hotel number, and you won't have to worry about someone not being able to reach you. If you don't have a cell phone, it might be a good idea to rent one when you rent a car. That way, you'll be a lot more accessible and you won't have trouble making calls either. The main point is not to waste time waiting for someone to return your call. If you have a potential list of people you want to try to connect with (and you should have such a list), you can make calls first thing in the morning, then get out on Music Row. Get friendly with that person's assistant or receptionist, and stop by his office and introduce yourself to him when you are in his vicinity. Keep trying each day you are in Nashville, but don't make it a priority. You will get a lot more accomplished out on the Row than in your hotel room waiting for someone to call you back.

17

Planning Your Artist Showcase

The importance of careful planning cannot be emphasized enough in regard to showcasing in Nashville. Even though showcases are a common occurrence on the Row, they provide the highest visibility an artist can obtain. If you bomb, *everybody* knows about it. The news travels fast! Don't take a casual attitude regarding your own showcase—be prepared!

You should have a very specific purpose for presenting a showcase, the best reason being a request from a record company executive. Be aware of the artist roster of each record label, and how you may or may not fit in. Showcasing for publishers is a very good idea as well. Nashville publishers are very closely involved with artist development—many publishers have their own production companies and actively work with aspiring artists.

SHOWCASE GUIDELINES
Perform Original Material Only
Producers do not want to hear cover songs no matter how great your version of *Rocky Top*. Don't be tempted to break this rule, because even if you have a very unusual arrangement of a well-known song and it's the best part of your act, there is a strong prejudice against performing cover songs in Nashville. People will think you aren't aware that this is a no-no, and that you don't know much about the Nashville music industry.

Make Sure Your Songs Are Awesome
Before you give an artist's showcase, get feedback on all of the songs you are planning to perform. Although you are looking for an artist's deal and

not a songwriting deal, the songs you perform are still going to be the most important part of your showcase. That's just the way it is in Nashville, the ultimate song town. There are many aspiring artists in town who are great entertainers and have great voices. Unfortunately, they also think their songs are great when they aren't, and keep on performing them. It hurts their chances of ever getting a record deal.

Limit Your Show to Forty-Five Minutes

Actually, thirty minutes would be OK, too, if they include six great songs: two ballads, maybe one heartfelt acoustic number, two mid-tempo, and two rocking up-tempo. Music Row *loves* rocking up-tempo songs, and has a hard time finding great ones.

Start on Time

The best time for a showcase is 6:00 P.M., at a club conveniently located near Music Row, somewhere producers can stop by after work. Don't wait for the room to fill up; go ahead and start at the time advertised. It will be expected and appreciated by the people who are already there. Producers only need to hear a few songs to know if you are what they are looking for.

Schedule for Weekdays

Plan your showcase for Tuesday, Wednesday, or Thursday evening. Avoid weekends, as the industry folks are not out and about. Showcases are work for the music industry, not entertainment, and no one wants to work on a Friday or Saturday night, certainly not Sunday, with the exception of the Bluebird Cafe. The regular Bluebird Sunday night show does draw some industry people, especially if one of their friends, a well-known hit song-writer, is headlining the show.

Offer Free Food and Drinks Sparingly

The music industry does not expect free food and drinks, except at places where it is not otherwise available, like sound stages. It's best to not offer food and drinks, even if you have an unlimited expense account. If you have personally invited certain executives, and you want to thank them for coming, you can make arrangements with the club to honor drink tickets. You can then give drink tickets to your special guests and settle with the bartender at the end of the evening.

Plan Seating

Plan reserved seating for record executives. These clubs are small and have limited seating. Usually a table in the back of the room is the best. Make up a table tent that says "Reserved," not "RCA Records" or the person's

Johnny Bond
Publications
presents...

Betsy Meryl Hammer

at the
Bluebird Cafe
Tuesday, July 23rd
6P.M. Sharp!

For further information:
615.297.7320

Example: Artist Showcase Invitation
Picture postcard invitation. You can send a mass mailing of postcards to your entire database, then hand-deliver personal invitations with your CD along to key industry executives.

name, or they will be hounded to death. Hire a hostess who can recognize the people you have invited. Ideally, you will have hired a Nashville publicist. They know how to get people to your showcase, and they know all the people. The publicist or hostess will escort important guests to their reserved seats. If they don't show in the first fifteen minutes of your show, have the hostess pick up the reserved sign and let anyone sit down, particularly if it is crowded and the seats are needed. Industry execs don't mind fending for themselves.

Send Out Invitations Via E-mail and Snail Mail

Music Row executives are starting to receive some very cool e-mail invitations. You can use your imagination and expertise in this area, but remember that simplicity is the key. Put "You Are Invited" or place/date/time in the subject line of your e-mail. Then, in the body of the e-mail at the top, put the place/date/time with your photo underneath, and a link to your Web site. You may also want to mail out invitations as not everyone will open e-mails—a picture postcard is perfect. Send them out a week or so ahead of time—two weeks maximum. If you send them too soon, you will be forgotten. If you are not going to do a picture postcard, then do a flyer or 5 1/2" × 8 1/2" heavy stock card that will go through the mail. Don't put an invitation in an envelope, because it might not be opened.

Make Follow-Up Phone Calls

You and your publicist, if you hired one, should start calling on Monday for your Tuesday, Wednesday, or Thursday show.

Make a Quiet Trial Run

Do at least one showcase in Nashville, better two or three, before you invite the music industry. Don't send out invitations; don't invite people personally; don't spread the word. Simply book a date in one of the clubs. It will automatically show up in the *Tennessean* and the *Nashville Scene* club listings. Put on a great show, just as if you had invited the entire music industry (there will probably be some industry people there anyway). Have a professional there to evaluate your performance; maybe the publicist you are thinking about hiring, the people you have met at the Performing Rights Organizations, or a publisher who has shown interest in your songs. This trial run will help you determine if you are ready for the real thing. It won't hurt to keep staging low-key trial runs until you are confident in your show. Just keep in mind that news travels fast on Music Row, and if you are really talented, the word will get out.

VARIOUS TYPES OF SHOWCASES: A GUIDE TO SHOWCASE CLUBS

The most common showcase is a 6:00 P.M. show at a club close to Music Row. These clubs have close, intimate, informal settings where producers can get in and out in a hurry. Producers and other industry professionals will probably not arrive on time or stay for the entire show. Two or three songs will tell them what they want to know. Again, you do not (and should not) provide complimentary food and drinks. Industry professionals do not expect it at these clubs. Your show will appear automatically in the *Tennessean* and the *Nashville Scene* club listings, and will be open to the public. This is the most inexpensive and the easiest way to put on your artist's showcase, as well as the most popular for the industry.

All live music venues are listed each week in the *Tennessean's* entertainment publication, *The Rage*, and the *Nashville Scene*. Listed below are the most popular clubs for showcase purposes.

3rd & Lindsley Bar & Grill
818 3rd Avenue South
Nashville, TN 37210
Tel: (615) 259-9891

Known mostly for blues and jazz, they don't host a writers' night and don't have many country acts perform here. But it's a great room. You might want to check it out!

12th & Porter Playroom
114 12th Avenue North
Nashville, TN 37203
Tel: (615) 254-7236
Web site: *www.faisons.com*

Popular showcase club with the largest stage of the clubs listed here. If you have a large band, you may want to perform here. Also, the Playroom is connected to a popular restaurant, 12th & Porter. If you provide complimentary hors d'oeuvres and put this information on your invitation, the industry will know that great food will be available!

The Basement
1604 8th Avenue South
Tel: (615) 254-1604

Steve West's new club. West used to own 328 Performance Hall, a very popular music venue, which was torn down to make room for a bridge connecting East Nashville and Downtown. This small intimate club is great for industry showcases.

Boardwalk Cafe
4114 Nolensville Pike
Tel: (615) 832-5104

Great showcase room has writers' night at 6:00 P.M. and open mic at 9:00 P.M. on Mondays.

Commodore Lounge
2613 West End Avenue
Tel: (615) 327-4707

Located in the Holiday Inn Hotel, "Commodore" refers to the Vanderbilt University mascot—but you won't run into Vandy students here. Writers' night on Tuesdays and Thursdays at 6:00 P.M.

Douglas Corner Cafe
2106-A Eighth Avenue South
Nashville, TN 37204
Tel: (615) 298-1688

Writers' hangout. Nashville's greatest writers perform here every night. You should spend a lot of time here on your trip to Nashville. It's a great place to showcase, too.

French Quarter Cafe
821 Woodland Street
Tel: (615) 227-3100

Writers' Night on Wednesdays hosted by the Bluebird Cafe's top writers' night hostess, Barbara Cloyd. Barbara can help you get discovered in Music City, U.S.A.!

The Mercy Lounge
1 Cannery Row
Tel: (615) 251-3020

Popular new club in one of Nashville's oldest performance venues.

Radio Cafe
1313 Woodland Street
Tel: (615) 228-6045

So named because of the collection of vintage radios displayed in cases along the walls. Popular, small club for aspiring artists and writers.

The Sutler
2608 Franklin Road
Nashville, TN 37204
Tel: (615) 297-9195

Lots of charm with great vibes. They don't have a writers' night, but they do feature all kinds of music. Check it out.

The Trap
201 Woodland Street
Tel: (615) 248-3100

Owned by Music Row executives, this is a very popular showcase venue.

The Sound Stage Showcase
The sound stage showcase is a 6:00 P.M. show at a sound stage like the Castle Door, S.I.R., or SoundCheck. It is in a formal setting and is by invitation only, no public will be in attendance. This showcase will not be listed in the *Tennessean* or *Nashville Scene*. Food and drinks must be catered, and will be expected. The sound quality and focus on the showcase will be superior

to a local club. Careful consideration should be taken before choosing this format. If a specific producer or record company has requested a showcase, they might prefer this format. Do not use a sound stage unless you are assured attendance.

Your invitation should include a separate reception time, giving people a chance to mix and mingle and have refreshments. No matter how well the reception is going, start the showcase on time.

The Castle Door
115 16th Avenue South

Great room, convenient location, lots of services including catering and video/audio taping capability. Under new ownership and closed for remodeling at the time of this printing.

Soundcheck
750 Cowan Street
Tel: (615) 726-1165

Soundcheck has one big room and a smaller room. It is off the beaten path in North Nashville, but everyone knows where it is and will go there to see a showcase.

Studio Instrument Rentals (S.I.R.)
1101 Cherry Avenue
Tel: (615) 255-4500

The sound gurus of Music Row. They have a small room for showcases with a "cool" factor attached to it. Or you can rehearse your showcase here before you perform for the industry. But even if you decide to showcase in one of the regular clubs listed above, you may still have to rent some sound equipment. S.I.R. and Soundcheck can take good care of you.

Late-Night Showcase

A late-night showcase starts at 9:30 P.M.—some artists prefer a later time, and the industry is pretty good at getting out for a late-night show. It is the music business, after all! This show is similar to the most common showcase (6:00 P.M.), except that the public attendance will be larger and industry attendance smaller, unless you've done a great job at attracting some professional interest in your showcase. The same venues apply, plus one other very important club:

The Bluebird Cafe
4104 Hillsboro Road
Nashville, TN 37215
Tel: (615) 383-1461
    Best room, best vibes, and best ambiance. There is no talking allowed during performances at the Bluebird, so you have a guaranteed attentive audience. You could consider a 6:00 P.M. show at the Bluebird, but traffic is a problem. Best to stick with a late-night show.

Other Showcase Venues
There are a few other live music venues that have a reputation for presenting exceptional music, and a showcase at one of these clubs might lend an aura of intrigue. You might attract some industry professionals just because it's something out of the ordinary. In Nashville, it's best to stick with the norm. The closer your showcase follows traditional patterns, the more professional you appear. That said, here are some nontraditional but attention-getting venues:

Exit/In
2208 Elliston Place
Nashville, TN 37203
Tel: (615) 321-4400
    Once a famous club for showcasing cutting-edge alternative music, the Exit/In is rich in history. It has a huge stage and great layout for a showcase.

The Station Inn
402 12th Avenue South
Nashville, TN 37203
Tel: (615) 255-3307
    If your music is grassroots country, bluegrass, Americana, alternative country, or traditional country—this is the place for you!

The Clubs on "Lower Broad"
There is a cluster of honky-tonks on Broadway, between Fourth and Second Avenues, which play some pretty twangy country cover tunes. Clueless aspiring country artists, who don't know a thing about the music business, hang out here dreaming about getting discovered. You will spot them in an instant, both on- and offstage. This two-block area personifies the image of the Nashville music industry, not the reality. However, if you really want to have fun, forget the business for a minute and club hop on "Lower Broad." Locals and tourists alike dance, drink, and sing along to their favorite songs. Gibson's is a very classy coffeehouse with yummy desserts and a wide range of music; the rest offer diehard country classics.

The Arista Records recording artists, BR549, were discovered at Robert's Western World, and it could happen again. Wolfy's presents all kinds of music, including swing. If you are a very traditional country artist, you might want to showcase in one of these clubs. But don't make the mistake of thinking that "Lower Broad" is what Nashville is all about. This is a tourist area and doesn't represent the Nashville music industry at all.

Legends Corner
428 Broadway
Nashville, TN 37203
Tel: (615) 248-6334

Robert's Western World
416 Broadway
Nashville, TN 37203
Tel: (615) 244-9552

Tootsie's Orchid Lounge
422 Broadway
Nashville, TN 37203
Tel: (615) 726-0463

Wolfy's
425 Broadway
Nashville, TN 37203
Tel: (615) 251-1621

GETTING THE RIGHT PEOPLE TO YOUR SHOWCASE

Don't expect industry professionals to automatically show up just because you sent out invitations. They get a lot of invitations each week and don't attend unless they have a truly good reason to go. If they were a little curious about your showcase and didn't attend, they can easily find out how it went just from the street talk. If it was positive feedback, they'll make a mental note to go the next time. Yes, there probably will have to be a next time—even Garth Brooks wasn't signed on the basis of his first showcase! You will have to work *very hard* to get key industry executives to your showcase. Here are some ideas on how to get help.

NASHVILLE'S TOP PUBLICISTS

The publicists listed below are experts at getting the right people to attend an artist showcase. They know exactly whom to invite, what the invitation should look like, when it should be mailed, and what to say when they make follow-up calls. They know everyone in town and their schedules. They will know if there are any conflicts with your show and if it should be rescheduled. They know how to time press releases and how to get the best press coverage. Their calls will be taken or returned by the key decision makers. Just like Nashville's entertainment attorneys, a good publicist will be hard to find. Their reputation is on the line every time they invite industry leaders to a showcase. They cannot afford to waste anybody's time. So they will have very strict requirements that must be met before they agree to represent an aspiring artist. If all of the publicists listed below decline to represent you that will be a sign that you aren't ready yet.

Alison Auerbach PR
3314 West End Avenue, #503
Nashville, TN 37203
Tel: (615) 297-1033
E-mail: *alisonapr@aol.com*
  Represents Vince Gill, Buddy Jewell, and John Michael Montgomery.

Aristomedia
1620 16th Avenue South
Nashville, TN 37212
Tel: (615) 269-7071
Web site: *www.aristomedia.com*
  Represents Jo Dee Messina and many aspiring artists.

Brokaw Company
P. O. Box 125
Nashville, TN 37202
Tel: (615) 384-6964
E-mail: *sljallen@aol.com*
  Represents Mark Chesnutt and others.

FORCE
1505 16th Avenue Southx
Nashville, TN 37212
Tel: (615) 385-4646
Fax: (615) 385-5840
  Nancy Russell represents Loretta Lynn, the Wrights, and Alan Jackson.

Front Page Publicity
P. O. Box 60628
Nashville, TN 37206

Tel: (615) 383-0412
Web site: *www.frontpagepublicity.com*
　　Kathy Allmand represents the Dixie Chicks, Martina McBride, and Naomi Judd.

Gurley & Company
P. O. Box 150657
Nashville, TN 37215
Tel: (615) 269-0474
Web site: *www.gurleybiz.com*
　　Cathy Gurley is a former publicist for CMA.

Hofer Company
2121 Fairfax Avenue, #3
Nashville, TN 37212
Tel: (615) 269-9803
　　Betty Hofer was with Sony/ATV/Tree for years. Represents Bill Anderson.

Holley-Guidry Co.
3415 West End Avenue, #101-D
Nashville, TN 37203
Tel: (615) 460-9550
E-mail: *thehgcompany@aol.com*
　　Husband and wife team Randy Guidry and Debbie Holley represent Tracy Lawrence and Bryan White. Also are managers for Bill Gentry and Ruby Lovett.

Hot Schatz Productions
1024 16th Avenue South, 2nd Floor
Nashville, TN 37212
Tel: (615) 782-0078
E-mail: *hotschatzpr@csi.com*
　　Shatzi Hageman is a former publicist for Sony Music. Represents Trace Adkins.

Joe's Garage
4405 Belmont Park Terrace
Nashville, TN 37215
Tel: (615) 269-3238
Web site: *www.joesgarage615.com*

Former *Hits* magazine writer Holly Gleason represents Brooks & Dunn, Chris Cagle, Kenny Chesney, John Michael Montgomery, and Terri Clark.

PLA Media
1313 16th Avenue South
Nashville, TN 37212
Tel: (615) 327-0100
Web site: *www.plamedia.com*
Pam Lewis was Garth Brooks' first and only publicist—instrumental in the development of his stellar career.

The Press Office
2607 Westwood Drive
Nashville, TN 37204
Tel: (615) 269-3670
E-mail: *publicity@thepressoffice.net*
Represents John Anderson, Vince Gill, Ralph Stanley, and many others.

Rubin Media
P. O. Box 158161
Nashville, TN 37215
Tel: (615) 298-4400
E-mail: *rubinmedia1@aol.com*
Ronna Rubin is a former publicist for Warner/Reprise and represents Jo Dee Messina, Maura O'Connell, and Clay Walker.

Schmidt Relations
209 19th Avenue South, #229
Nashville, TN 37203
Tel: (615) 846-3878
E-mail: *jessie@schmidtpr.com*
Jessie Schmidt represents Tim McGraw, Rascal Flatts, and The Grand Ole Opry.

So Much Moore Media
P. O. Box 120426
Nashville, TN 37212
Tel: (615) 298-1689
Web site: *www.somuchmoore.com*
Martha Moore is a former publicist for Mercury and CBS Records. Represents many Americana artists.

Star Keeper PR
P. O. Box 128195
Nashville, TN 37212
Tel: (615) 329-0460
E-mail: *starkeeper@carterandcompany.com*
    Represents Tracy Byrd.

Turner & Co.
4487 Post Place, Suite 177
Nashville, TN 37205
Tel: (615) 356-9115
E-mail: *turnerco@bellsouth.net*
    Judy Turner is a former CMA publicist.

Whiting Publicity & Promotions
P. O. Box 331941
Nashville, TN 37203
Tel: (615) 327-9857
Web site: *www.shinetime.com*
    Chuck Whiting represents the book *Love Always, Patsy (Cline)*, Arts on the Row, and the SGA.

Enlist the support of your attorney. Nashville entertainment attorneys will also be able to get the right people to your showcase, but they won't do the legwork for you—that is, you will have to mail out invitations and make most of the follow-up calls yourself. Your attorney will make a few phone calls to key targeted individuals at the record labels, as well as major producers and publishers. You really don't need an attorney until you already have some label interest and are close to getting a deal. An attorney can help speed up the process and create a "buzz" about you. If one label seems interested, they all will want to check you out. Attorneys are great at making that happen.

Send out invitations. You can produce your showcase on your own without a publicist or attorney—just be sure to follow the showcase guidelines very closely. Mail a postcard with your picture on it, plus time, place, etc., to everyone on the database listing at the end of this book. Get some friends to help make follow-up phone calls and call everyone on the list. Send a reminder fax and/or e-mail the morning of the showcase. There is a lot going on every night in Nashville, and people's decisions can be influenced at the last minute. If they have to be somewhere at 8:00 P.M., they might just stop by your showcase at 6:00 P.M. even if they don't have it on their schedule.

Once your showcase is in motion, relax and enjoy your time in the spotlight. It's your night, and you are giving it your all. Don't place all your hopes and expectations on this one night, thinking that it's your one big opportunity. Lots of things can interfere with success, the most common problem being scheduling conflicts. There might be some industry function you didn't know about, or someone else might be having a showcase at the same time. Even if the attendance isn't what you had hoped for, give a performance just as though the head of RCA Records was sitting in the front row. You never know, someone who works for him might be somewhere in the room.

18

Making the Decision to Move to Nashville

Y ou can't go wrong if you pack up the moving van and head towards Nashville. It is a wonderful family community, with many of the attractions of a big city and all of the charm of a small town. Even if you move here for a few years only to return home later, you won't regret the time you spent here. Of course, we are talking about the quality of life, the wonderful southern hospitality, the beautiful historic architecture scattered throughout the city, and the relative ease of getting around town. We aren't really talking about your experience on Music Row and your chances of success.

SHOULD YOU OR SHOULDN'T YOU?

Most of the songwriters who move here get caught up in the comforts of the city. Nashville has an almost zero unemployment base and there is a wide diversity of jobs in print publishing, computer technology, hospitals, insurance, real estate, automotive, banking, and lots of jobs in the service industry. Writers will move here, get a great secure job, meet a beautiful southern belle or a Rhett Butler, get married, have children, and wonder where the time went. They came here to write songs and made some great contacts when they first started out, but somehow time slipped away and they lost sight of their initial goals. Come to think of it, what's so wrong with that?

The greatest danger in moving to Nashville is facing all the opportunities there are to distract you from your original purpose for moving here in the first place. With that in mind, your decision to move here and become a successful songwriter or artist should be based on your willingness to live a Spartan songwriter's existence, putting financial prosperity on the back burner for a few years. If it's money you are seeking, you shouldn't even be considering a career in the music business in the first place. Money is only a side benefit that may or may not ever materialize. The true reward is to be able to share your creative talent with an appreciative audience. Here are some great jobs for aspiring songwriters, artists, and musicians that will guarantee that you meet and chat with Nashville's top decision makers.

IDEAL JOBS
The Bluebird Cafe or Douglas Corner
The very best job you can possibly get is the one that is right in the apex of the songwriting community. The Bluebird Cafe should be the first stop on your job search. Amy needs waiters and waitresses, a bartender, a cook, a sound engineer, a maintenance person, and office workers. These jobs don't come open very often, but every once in awhile they do, so stay tuned and ready to step in when the occasion arises.

Next stop, Douglas Corner. The same jobs are needed there, too, except they really don't need a cook. In Tennessee, establishments serving alcohol must also serve food, but that doesn't always mean cooked meals. You might consider applying at some of the other songwriter hangouts, but their customer base will not be as saturated with hit songwriters and industry executives as the Bluebird and Douglas Corner.

Some entrepreneurial writers come to town and start their own writers' night in a club or restaurant. That's a great idea because you can select the hit songwriters you want to meet and invite them to your writers' night, you get your name in the paper every week, and you meet just about every writer in town. But it's a lot of hard work, doesn't pay anything, and might distract you from the main reason you moved here—to write songs.

Music Row Restaurants
The next best jobs are waiting on tables at Music Row area restaurants— Sunset Grill, The Trace, the LongHorn, Midtown Cafe, and Noshville would be the best places to meet people; but there are lots of restaurants in the vicinity, and music industry execs eat in all of them. Nashville restaurants have a very relaxed atmosphere, even the stuffy ones (actually, there aren't any stuffy ones!), and waiters can chat with customers. You'll get to know the people who dine in your restaurant. And everyone else working there is a writer or aspiring artist!

Randstad Staffing Services
Another ideal job is with a temp agency. *The* Music Row temp agency is Randstad Staffing Services. Their office is located in the cool Elliston Street area, at 2317 Elliston Place, Nashville, TN 37203. Their phone number is (615) 342-9004; Web site: *www.randstadstaffing.com*. Carolyn

Hill is the senior agent and Music Row guru, and you can reach her directly at *Carolyn.hill@us.randstad.com*. Tell Carolyn you want only music industry jobs and that's where she'll send you. She can also get you a permanent job in the industry somewhere, but it's a good idea to temp for a little while to find out which companies you like the best. Also, you will have a chance to meet more people, which may lead to a permanent job.

It's tough to get a full-time job in the Nashville music industry because of the local colleges' intern programs. Students at Belmont and MTSU recording industry programs get class credit for working for free at various entry-level positions in the music industry. So the businesses on Music Row don't have to hire anyone for these positions. They often have many interns from both colleges working for them. And then, as you would suspect, when a job does open on a higher level, interns are first on the list for that job. So the jobs rarely become available to someone outside the company.

It is not uncommon for non-students to offer to work for free also, in the hopes of ingratiating their way into the company. It's worked from time to time. Some companies have a very strict policy about working with interns and only accept qualified students; others are more lax. If you decide to go that route, it won't be hard to find out what the policies are.

Service Organizations

Jobs with the various nonprofit trade and service organizations are interesting, fun, and multifaceted. There are lots of different organizations and associations besides the ones mentioned in this book. Usually they operate on a streamlined budget and produce imaginative, challenging, and creative fundraising events. The entire Nashville music industry supports these various groups with corporate sponsorships and helps produce and manage some of their events. Industry execs also serve on lots of different committees in support of these organizations. So there is a great opportunity to work alongside a top industry executive who is volunteering his services for the organization and, ultimately, the Music Row community. The top choices would be NSAI, NARAS, CMA, CRB, and the Country Music Hall of Fame Museum.

Even if you don't get a job with one of these associations, it would be a good idea to volunteer your time to help out on one or two projects. It's a great way to meet people in the industry and, who knows, you may work your way into a job after all.

Catering and Special Events Companies

The Nashville music industry is big on parties, and there are lots of parties and special events every month. If you work for a catering company or special event company, chances are very good that you will be doing dinners and special events for the music industry. That includes the catering departments of area hotels. Included here is contact information for the most popular caterers and special event companies.

Event Managers

Helen L. Moskovitz & Associates
95 White Bridge Road
Nashville, TN 37205
Tel: (615) 352-6900

What A Trip! Inc.
1605 17th Avenue South, Suite 200
Nashville, TN 37212
Tel: (615) 269-0039
Web site: *www.whatatrip1.com*
    Music Row veterans Grace Reinbold and Darlene Williams put this specialty event company together seven years ago and have been having fun ever since!

Caterers

Kates Fine Catering Inc.
619 West Iris Drive
Nashville, TN 37204
Tel: (615) 298-5644

The Clean Plate Club
718 Thompson Lane
Nashville, TN 37204
Tel: (615) 661-5866

TomKats, Inc.
9003 Overlook Boulevard
Nashville, TN 37027
Tel: (615) 256-9596
Web site: *www.tomkats.com*

Hotels

Loews Vanderbilt Plaza Hotel
2100 West End Avenue
Nashville, TN 37203
Tel: (615) 320-1700

Utilizing Your College Degree

If you really can't imagine yourself in one of these "ideal" jobs, there are lots of great opportunities waiting for you in your field of expertise. Many major corporations have offices in Nashville: Dell Computers, Hewlett-Packard, Toshiba, Bank of America, BellSouth, Columbia/HCA (healthcare), Saturn, Nissan, Vanderbilt University and Medical Center, Gibson Guitars, to name but a few. The Nashville Area Chamber of Commerce has a JobsLink Program on the Internet to help businesses find skilled employees with credentials outside of the city. You can contact them at *www.nashvillechamber.com*. They also sell an employment packet to assist with a job search. It contains the Chamber's business directory plus a list of top employers, wage and salary information, and a list of executive search firms and personnel agencies. It's a little pricey at $40, but if you are serious about finding a job in Nashville, the packet and JobsLink Web page will be very helpful.

WHERE TO LIVE

Nashville has so many beautiful neighborhoods, it's hard to know where to start! Unfortunately it also ranks as the eleventh most congested city in the nation, with longer traffic delays than Boston, New York, and Chicago. One problem is that the neighborhoods are not really near the jobs, so Nashvillians spend a lot of time in their cars. There is no transportation system to speak of.

It might be a good idea to get a job first, then pick a neighborhood with the easiest route to commute. There are lots of beautiful neighborhoods with unique qualities to choose from, so don't get your heart set on one before you find out where you are going to be working. BMI's former president and CEO Frances W. Preston always tells every songwriter, "Get a job first, then move here."

Music Row

Music Row is right next to Vanderbilt University, so there is a lot of transient housing in this area. Vandy students tend to have a little bit of money to spend, so the area has some very nice condos and community living spaces that are frequently vacated corresponding to semesters. There are even some very nice condos and apartments right on Music Row. There are also some that are not as attractive but relatively inexpensive.

Music Row is a mix of businesses and residences. Horton Street is the dividing line. North of Horton is primarily businesses, many of them with offices in beautiful old houses. South of Horton is mostly residential, but many houses are being purchased by music industry companies and turned

into offices. If you are into renovation projects, there are still a few run-
down houses that could be saved, but they need a lot of work. Many of
Nashville's most prominent executives live right on Music Row.

Belmont Area

Belmont University sits at the south end of Music Row, in a wonderful
neighborhood. There are great small older houses that are still reasonably
priced in the $100,000 range, lower or higher depending on the shape they
are in. There is also a charming large apartment complex near the
university. There are small croppings of specialty stores and restaurants
sprinkled in with the homes, making it a very special neighborhood. The
Belmont Area is right off of Music Row, close to downtown and to I-440
which connects to all of the other interstates that will take you to your job.
Finding a house or apartment in this area would be ideal.

Fairfax Area

Just south of the Vanderbilt campus, this housing area is built around a
very special shopping area called Hillsboro Village. College students, music
industry execs, and just about everybody else are attracted to the great restaurants and specialty shops in this two-blocks-deep and two-blocks-wide area.
The little village is bordered on one end by Wedgewood/Blakemore, and the
other end by Fairfax Avenue. Fairfax ends at Hillsboro Village, and if you turn
into the housing area on Fairfax, you will wind up in a beautiful neighborhood. It has a wonderful park nicknamed "Dragon Park" (in honor of the
huge sculpture in the middle). The homes are a fairly nice size and in good
condition, which gives the neighborhood real estate a median value of
$250,000. The area has attracted investors who have renovated old apartment
buildings and turned them into very nice living spaces. The Fairfax area keeps
on going to West End Avenue on one side, and I-440 on the other.

West End Avenue

Sounds high rent, doesn't it? It is, when you are on the boulevard. But keep
going west and you will find smaller, charming houses that offer all kinds
of possibilities. You can rent a house or a guesthouse, there are apartments
mixed in with houses, or you can get a good deal on a house. The closer
you are to West End, the higher the cost will be.

Sylvan Park

If you keep going southwest, you will eventually wind up in Sylvan Park.
You can tell you are there because the streets are named after states for the
most part. This area is filled with old houses that need a lot of fixing up.
It is such a popular area, it's hard to find a good deal in Sylvan Park

anymore. There are some great duplexes here that aren't much to look at, but the price is right ($400 per month) and they are very roomy. If you are a golfer (and you should be, if you are in the music industry), McCabe Public Golf Course is practically in your backyard. Also, there are two eateries that are very popular with the music industry, the McCabe Pub and Sylvan Park Restaurant—both serve delicious southern home cookin'.

Downtown

If you are into cool lofts over old warehouses or high-rise apartments, you might find one downtown. There aren't many to choose from, but the Nashville Chamber of Commerce will be glad we mentioned it. A lot of effort has gone into the development of downtown and the prevention of urban sprawl in the city.

Edgefield Historic District

This is where you will find your best deals for a renovation project. Across the Cumberland River from downtown, the area has many historic homes, and they are protected by strict building codes. If you promise to renovate one of these homes according to their standards (if you buy one, you'll have to anyway), you can get a great deal and get funding for practically nothing. There are just glorious homes here, many having been restored by loving hands. The residents are very proud of their district, and sponsor a tour of the homes once a year. They also have beautiful Greenway Park and a special neighborhood hangout called the Radio Cafe, with its own writers' night. Some very special writers and artists perform here regularly, particularly Edgefield residents.

Belle Meade • Green Hills • Forrest Hills • Oak Hill

The high rent district. Belle Meade is the grandest neighborhood in Nashville, with some of the most beautiful homes you will ever see in our nation perched on acres of land. On your first visit to Nashville, be sure to drive through this neighborhood and gaze at the splendor. This is where you will find the old stone "slave walls," which were built by slaves around the plantations. Only parts of them still stand today. These neighborhoods are the most desirable living areas in the city. You can still find affordable housing in Green Hills, mostly huddled around Hillsboro Pike and I-440. The Villager is one of Nashville's most popular apartment complexes, because the price is right (starting at $500 per month). It's amazing that there are still apartments and condos for rent in this area, because it is probably the best geographic location in Nashville. You can get anywhere in fifteen minutes from this little area. Forrest

Hills and Oak Hill are further south and are mostly very large homes and properties.

Farther on Out

If you really try hard and stick with it, you will probably find something you are looking for in one of the neighborhoods above. If you just don't have any luck at all, then here are some more options.

Harding Place

Not to be confused with Harding Road, which runs briefly through Belle Meade, Harding Place starts at Harding Road and runs across the southern part of the city. There are lots and lots of inexpensive apartments and condos for rent, some in nice areas, and others in not-so-nice areas. "Nice" refers to appearance more than anything else. If you wander off Harding Road, north and south, you'll find many houses, but not neighborhoods, really.

Antioch • Bellevue • Rivergate

These are three areas that have grown up around mega-shopping malls. Antioch is in the southeast, Bellevue in the southwest, and Rivergate in the northeast. Lots of apartments, condos, houses—whatever you need. If you wind up working in one of these areas, then you might want to consider living there, too. But you'll be getting away from the mainstream. You'll probably find a writers' night somewhere in each of these areas, but you'll be driving into Nashville a lot in the evenings to go to the hot writers' nights and industry events.

This should be enough to help you in your search for a great place to live. If you are bringing your family, then you might want to go a little further out where you will find larger homes for less. A large percentage of music industry families live in Brentwood. Williamson County has a great school system (Nashville is in Davidson County), and you can probably get a big backyard and lots of kids in the neighborhood. Right now Cool Springs is a huge mega-mall, but huge homes are cropping up there as well.

Some people are taken with the history of Tennessee and wind up in historic Franklin, where a Civil War battle was brief and bloody. Others are interested in the vast farmland that is still available, and will settle on plots of land in Spring Hill or Fairview, or even farther out. There are lots of choices. One industry executive, the beloved Dale Franklin, lived in a barn! (An exquisite barn, that is.)

Before she passed away at too early an age, Dale founded three very important organizations: The NASHVILLE *entertainment* ASSOCIATION, Leadership Music, and SOURCE, a networking organization for top female music industry executives. If Dale could live in a barn, you can live wherever you want and still rise to the top. The more creative you are with your environment, perhaps the more creative you will be in your profession.

A ONE-YEAR GAME PLAN FOR SUCCESS ONCE YOU ARE SETTLED DOWN

This book has covered the ins and outs of Music Row from every conceivable angle. Now that you have made the commitment and actually moved here, it's time to get down to business. The first thing to do, if you haven't done this already, is get a day job. Some songwriters move here on a little nest egg they have put away, and plan to live on it for a year or two, expecting something to happen by that time. Even if you get a song put on hold tomorrow, it can take as long as two years before you ever see any money. The sales-to-collection-to-royalty payment process takes a long time. And, as was said previously, you don't want to put your own life "on hold" while you are pursuing your dream. Your dream *is* your life, living and working in Nashville and writing and creating great music at the same time.

Here is a list of milestones for a one-year period. "Every day" and "every week" doesn't necessarily mean weekends too! Take some time out to enjoy the wonderful perks of living in Nashville, like walking near Radnor Lake, attending outdoor concerts, and strolling through the many artisan fairs.

Every Day

- Keep a detailed journal. Write down every single thought and idea that pops in your head about the music industry, about songs, about almost anything. When you go out to the clubs at night or to a songwriters' workshop, write down whom you met and a little something about them to help you remember them later. Also write down names you heard that someone else mentioned, and what they said about them. That name might not mean anything to you now, but it could turn out to be a very important person that you want to meet. You'll have a written record of a friend who could introduce you.
- Write a song, or work on a song that you started. The more you work on your songs, the finer tuned they will become. Even if you don't think that songwriting is your strong point and you probably won't pursue a career in songwriting, you might be invited to collaborate on a song as an artist or a musician. You might be better than you think, and at least you will have had some experience in the process.
- Practice playing your instrument. The better you are, the better you will get your song across.

- Listen to the country radio stations: WSM, WSIX, and possibly KDF (they keep changing their format). It is an absolute necessity, even if you get frustrated with what you hear. This is what the Nashville record labels like and spend their money to produce.
- Watch the cable channel CMT (Country Music Television) enough to make sure that you have seen all the current videos. Write down in your journal the artist, the song, the songwriters, the record label, and you might as well write down the video producer and production company too. They don't select the songs or sign artists and musicians, but they are an important part of Music Row.
- Stop by the Acklen Station post office. Hopefully, you were able to get a P.O. box here, which is something you want even if you have most of your mail delivered to your residence. Everyone on Music Row has an Acklen Station P.O. box and they will stop by every day to pick up their mail. So you need to stop by there too. If you don't have a P.O. box, then mail a letter to family or friends. They'll love to hear all about Nashville.

Every Week
- Browse through a record store. Bring your journal with you and take notes on which artists are being promoted and what their CD label copy says. Record labels pay big bucks to have their CDs placed in strategic locations, like the listening stations or the end of the aisle. Listen to all the country product in the listening stations. Soak up as much information as you can.
- Buy one CD per week and study it inside and out. If this is too expensive to do, maybe songwriter friends will join you in developing a current country music library.
- Read the trades. If you can't subscribe to *Billboard Country Airplay Monitor*, go to the library or sneak a peek at the bookstore. Read the *Music Row* magazine from cover to cover and take notes in your journal.
- On Monday, Wednesday, and Thursday attend the NSAI, SGA, and TSAI workshops. Try for a minimum of one a week, but you really shouldn't miss one. There will always be an important somebody at each of these workshops that you will have a chance to meet face to face.
- Get out into the clubs and perform or observe as many open mics, writers' nights, and showcases as you possibly can. Make it a minimum of at least once a week (try to do more if you can).
- Collaborate on a song with a songwriter friend. This is a very important acquired skill and one you must develop! Don't skip this one!

- Make an appointment with an industry professional. Choose from PROs, publishers, and songwriter organization staff members. You will not be able to go back to the same people week after week, so you should have a long list of potentials. Once you meet with someone, plan to go back to see them in a month.
- Have lunch at a Music Row restaurant (see chapter 10). If they are too far away from your work, then stop by one of the hangouts after work on Tuesday (there's no songwriter workshop that night).
- For musicians only—browse through music equipment stores. Make sure your card is still on the bulletin board, or put another one back up there. Check out the other musicians who are listed there— make notes in your journal. You might have a good reason to call some of them and get to know them better. Remember that networking is the key to success, especially for musicians.

Every Month
- Review your journal. You'll be surprised to see that someone you wrote about a month ago is now a pretty good friend. Bring forward any names, ideas, or other important data that you want to be sure to remember. Some writers keep a separate song title or "hook" book. You can keep these ideas separate or in your journal—whatever works for you.
- Make a repeat appointment with someone you want to keep in close contact with.

Every Quarter
- Participate in an industry event. There are so many different industry events on Music Row, it would be wonderful to participate in every single one. But that would be very expensive and time consuming. Realistically, you probably aren't going to be able to do it all! So plan to do one per quarter, four per year.
- Invite key music industry professionals to your open mic, writers' night, or artist's showcase. Depending on where you are in your own stage of development, you may want to invite a few people just to get their feedback, or you may want to send invitations to your entire personal database listing. In any event, plan on four writers' nights/showcases per year; one per quarter.
- Record some guitar/vocal CDs of your songs. Please don't be tempted to do expensive full-blown demos until you really have something exciting happening with a song. Guitar/vocals are relatively inexpensive and will help you discover your songs' strengths and weaknesses.

- Evaluate your progress. Be really easy on yourself. If you got a repeat appointment, that's great progress. If you made some key contacts, that's progress. If you finished a new song, that's really great progress. If you managed to do some of the things on this list, that's more than most newcomers to Nashville get done.
- Make some short-term goals for the next quarter. Whom would you like to get an appointment with? Where would you like to perform on a writers' night? Whom would you like to co-write with?

Mid-Year Exam
- Have you established close relationships with someone at all three PROs?
- Have you met with all the publishers on your list of potentials?
- Have you identified your favorite open mic or writers' night hangout?
- Have you played a Sunday Writers' Night at the Bluebird Cafe? (This is a benchmark for writers who show growing talent and maturity.)
- Have you completed one song with a co-writer?
- Have you completed one song on your own?
- Could you pass a mini-quiz on who does what in Nashville? Are you getting to know who the decision makers are?

How do you really measure your progress? Everything you have read in this book, all of the interviews with songwriters and industry professionals, have told you that it is all about networking and developing relationships. If you are meeting people, getting out and performing, attending some industry functions and events, and getting in to see some top professionals occasionally, then you are doing great. If you are spending time fine-tuning songs in a home studio in your basement all by yourself, then you are not making any progress, *even if* those songs are awesome! In Nashville, the music business is a community effort.

Remember also that it's going to take a lot longer than you ever imagined. There are many wonderfully talented people that finally gave up after ten years of trying. There is no gold ring to try for—it's all about going for the ride. Just keep yourself out there and you'll do fine!

HOW TO SUCCEED WITHOUT MOVING TO NASHVILLE

If the decision to move to Nashville would cause hardship on you and/or your family, then it would not be a wise choice to move here. Your success will be measured by how content you are on a day-to-day level; it won't be about hearing yourself or your song on the radio for the first time, even though, admittedly, that is a pretty awesome experience. Doing something that you really truly love on a daily basis will be your greatest reward, even if you never get a song recorded or sign a record contract. That is only one step in the process.

One very gifted singer actually signed three different recording contracts at three different times; they all fell apart for different reasons. The first record company (Casablanca) completed an album, put it on the market, then went bankrupt for other reasons. The second record company completed the first single (they used to put singles out before they did an album), mailed it to radio, then the company was bought by a bigger company, and current developing artists were terminated. The third time the artist and record label couldn't come to terms on a producer; the artist was under contract to one producer, but the label wanted a different producer. You would think by this time the artist would have given up! But she made a great living as a backup singer both in the studio and on the road, and she wrote a few hit songs recorded by other artists. You've got to love what you're doing and keep on doing it, and don't get discouraged by the obstacles that stand in the way.

It doesn't make sense, either, to put your real life "on hold" and try your hand in the music industry for a few years. Songwriters have actually left their spouses at home for a few years while they came to Nashville to get established. One songwriter had a very unusual financial windfall—a lovely house on the beach *free of charge*. All he had to do was live there and take care of the house. He was considering giving that up in order to try to make it in Nashville. When life gives you a wonderful gift—a loving spouse, a beautiful house, a great job—it doesn't make much sense to give that up in order to go searching for another gift. Moving to Nashville to follow your dreams has to fit into your real world.

If you are struggling with "should I or shouldn't I," then you probably already have your answer. You shouldn't. Here is what you can do to pursue a career in country music and still live outside of Nashville.

Songwriters

Here's the real problem: Even if you read this book from cover to cover, especially the interviews, and clearly understand what it means; you still will be very, very surprised when you finally start interacting with people on a professional level. Things will be a lot different from what you thought they were going to be. That's why people have such a hard time breaking through the system when they are not residents. They don't have access to the right information. It's not really something you read about; it's something you experience. And it isn't really revealed to you on a one-week or two-week trip; it's unveiled slowly over time. So how to you get to the inside track in Nashville without living there?

Spend as much time in Nashville as you possibly can. Bring the family for vacations (as long as they understand that you'll be working and they'll be on their own). Actually, it will be easier to get appointments when you are from out of town. Publishers, producers, and A&R reps are always looking for fresh new material, so they are receptive to meeting with someone new. They also are very tuned into everything that is going on in Nashville and tend to meet with only the cream of the crop. When you live in town, everyone knows who's hot and who's not, and if you're not knocking them dead at the Bluebird then it's going to be hard to get into someone's office. If you don't live here, people won't expect there to be a "buzz" going on about you, but if you live here, then it is expected. That is the main reason it is so difficult for even very good writers to move to the next plateau of "hot" writer. Just good isn't good enough in Nashville. Spend your time in Nashville networking with as many people on as high a level as possible. Try to plan your trips around NSAI and SGA songwriter seminars; not just the workshops, but the three-day events. It's not about learning something, it's about meeting people, and the top executives participate in these seminars. Make it a goal to meet all those people listed in "In Charge."

Open a Nashville "office." Best choice: open a P.O. box and get an 800 number. Everyone here has a P.O. box and uses the Acklen Station post office (37212). When people see the return address on your CD, they'll think you live in Nashville. Of course, the 800 number gives it away that you don't. A 615 area code would be preferable, which you may be able to get through a cell phone. Second choice: use a mailbox service. Some of Nashville's top songwriters and artists use Star Station, Nine Music Square South, Nashville, TN 37203, Tel. (615) 321-3554 or *www.starstationonline.com*. This is a great company and is very popular with out-of-town songwriters (in-town songwriters, too). Publishers and producers will recognize the address and realize that you don't really have an office in Nashville, but even many of them use this mailbox and work from home in this age of cutbacks! Star Station has lots of other services that you might need when you are in town, including faxing, services, and they will forward the mail that is sent to your private mailbox. Instead of a P.O. box address, your address will be "Nine Music Square South."

Why do you need a Nashville address? To put on your CD and promotional materials. If your demo package is professionally done and your address is local, it will most probably get heard.

Find someone to drop off CDs for you. Even if you meet a publisher or producer in Nashville and they agree to accept your songs through the mail, the chances of your package ever getting to them are slim. CDs sent through the mail get rejected before they ever get to the person for whom they were intended. Maybe that songwriter you met at the Bluebird would be willing to drop off CDs for you in exchange for something. Maybe you could subscribe to a tip sheet and share the information with him. Or maybe you could include some of his songs when you demo your songs. Another idea would be to hire a Belmont music industry student for next to nothing. Songs that are dropped off usually get heard, if they are packaged correctly and look like all the other CDs sitting on the listener's desk. Songs that are mailed rarely get out of the envelope.

Look for a mentor. Eventually you will connect with someone on the inside who will take you under his or her wing. Nurture that relationship.

Be aware that top Nashville executives travel to other cities looking for new talent. If there is a music conference or songwriters' seminar somewhere in your vicinity, be sure to go! It isn't recommended that you skip a trip to Nashville in exchange for a conference because time spent in Nashville has more value, but music conferences are fun, and interesting, and loaded with top music executives.

Aspiring Artists

A talented artist has the best chance of making it outside of Nashville. In fact, if you don't write songs and just want to sing and play, there's no need at all to move to Nashville. Just concentrate on building up your fan base from where you live. Create a local and regional buzz about yourself and your music. Your live performance speaks for itself. However, here are some marketing ideas to get more exposure.

Hire a publicist. You will be amazed at all the different ideas they will come up with to help promote your act. They will also prepare professional packages for you, including bios, tear sheets (professional reproductions) of any print coverage you receive, like local newspaper reviews, etc.

If you don't have the money right now to hire a publicist, then be sure to prepare these materials yourself; a one-page bio, tear sheets on any print coverage, 8" × 10" glossy photograph, and a demo CD. Call and invite local music reviewers to come and see your act.

Play in the best club(s) in your area. The Nashville music industry is aware of the hot country clubs across the United States and will make a trip to see acts they have heard about. Get to know the club owner or manager and find out if they interact with the music industry at all (probably not, but it's possible that they might, or might be interested in trying to in the future.)

Be aware of the music scene around you. There may be other artists in your area who have attracted label attention. You might be able to open for them if the industry is coming to town to see them, or be sure to put on your own showcase on the same night. If you have several great live music venues located in one area, you might want to talk to your Chamber of Commerce about putting on a music conference. These are very popular and draw a decent crop of out-of-town visitors.

Start a fan club. Keep track of everyone who walks in the door to come and see your act. Get their name and address, and then start regular mailings of postcards with your tour schedule listed on the back. Mail these postcards to the database listings at the end of this book—they won't know who you are yet, but you just may stir their curiosity.

Get a booking agent. There might be one in your vicinity, or you might have to be your own booking agent when you are just starting out. Get booked in the regional areas surrounding your hometown.

Play at as many music conferences as you possibly can. Music industry professionals attend these conferences regularly.

Start a Web site. It doesn't have to be anything fancy; it's just a way to expand your fan base and help create a buzz about yourself, so when people hear about you they can look you up on the Internet.

Invite the music industry to your hometown. Once you have established a strong local following, have a great review written up in the local newspaper, have enough of a fan base to be confident of a packed house, and invite Nashville execs to come and see you.

Visit Nashville. Proceed with caution. Now you have to decide how you want to approach the Nashville record industry on its own turf. If your strong point is your CD, talk to a Nashville entertainment attorney about shopping it for you. If you are really confident in your live performance, then put on a showcase in Nashville. If you can possibly afford it on top of the expense of everything else, hire a Nashville publicist to help you get an industry turnout.

Aspiring Musicians

It's going to be tough to get a gig as a musician in the country music industry without living in Nashville, because it's all about networking. Your personality and how you interact with other musicians is just as important as how talented you are, so "you must be present to win!" Nevertheless, here are a few things you might try if moving to Nashville is out of the question.

Visit Nashville in January, February, and/or March. That's when auditions take place for touring bands. By May, all of the artists have hired their musicians. When you are in town, get out and play every single night. Try to meet as many other musicians as you possibly can.

Subscribe to Dick McVey's Musician's Referral Service. Call (615) 264-3637 or look it up on the Internet at *www.dickmcvey.com* ($30 application fee and $15 per month) The referral service operates in every possible way to secure employment for its musicians—a printed listing, a hotline, a Web site, e-mail, and fax. Once a month a printed list is mailed and faxed directly into the offices of over a thousand potential employers in Nashville, Branson, Myrtle Beach, and other areas. McVey has been helping musicians find gigs and artists find musicians since 1986.

19

Your Personal References

O ne of the most important things you can do to advance your career as a songwriter or artist/musician is to establish your own personal list of contacts you have made in Nashville (and other places) and keep it as up to date as possible. Right now, as you begin to pursue your dream career, you can use the information lists in this book as the basis for your own personal database.

CREATING A DATABASE

As you start to use the listings in this book, transfer them to your own computer using a file management software program that will allow you to sort by different categories such as last name, company name, or business category. Include an entry for business categories, like "Artist Manager," "Publisher," etc. You will be using your own personal database to invite people to your showcase or writers' night, and at first you might not want to mail to the entire directory. Another entry you might want to include would be one for general comments, like "met at the Bluebird Cafe," something to help you remember that person over time.

You can go ahead and start monthly mailings to Nashville even before you actually make a trip there or move there, especially if you are a performing artist. The most successful bands send a monthly or quarterly postcard of their tour schedule, even if they are not going to be anywhere near Nashville. That way, Music Row professionals will know a lot about you before they even meet you.

ABOUT BASIC LISTINGS

The listings in this book can serve as the basis for your own personal database. These are the top companies on Music Row and the ones you will want to contact about your songs or artist package. You should also use these listings to mail an invitation to your artist/musician showcase or a special writers' night at the Bluebird Cafe or Douglas Corner. For the most part, these companies have been around for at least a quarter of a century, and will probably be around for another decade. But people and locations change almost daily, and some of the contacts printed here will change before the ink even dries. You can fill in specific names for each company as you learn more about them and the people who work there.

All of the contact information you will need to start has been included in earlier chapters. Here I am just going to remind you of the categories you will want to add to your list, and refer you to the chapter of this book in which the information appears.

Nashville's Top Artist Managers

Contact information is in chapter 6, "Nashville's Top Managers and Entertainment Attorneys," pages 77-99.

If you are looking for the manager of a specific artist, you can find that information in *Music Row's* "Artist Roster" edition. When pitching songs to artist managers, you need to specify whom the CD is going to and for which artist.

Nashville's Top Music Publishers

Contact information is in chapter 5, "Nashville's Major Music Publishers" and "Nashville's Hot Independent Music Publishers," pages 47-77.

If you do a little research in *Music Row's* "Publisher Special," you will find individual names in both the listing section, and in the text and advertisements.

Nashville's Top Record Companies

Contact information is in chapter 6, "Nashville's Major Record Labels" and "Nashville's Independent Record Labels," pages 79-99.

If you do a little research in *Music Row's* "In Charge" edition, you will find a complete listing of everyone who works at the label, including the A&R department.

Nashville's Top Record Producers

Contact information is listed in chapter 11, "Nashville's Top Producers," pages 145-162.

REFERENCE DIRECTORIES

The people and companies here do not need to be entered into your own personal database, as you will be contacting them only if and when needed. Please keep in mind that any directory undergoes major changes every six months, so by the time you start to use this directory, some people may have moved. We have tried to include only those companies that have been doing business in Nashville for a long time and are known to provide excellent services. These directories only include complete contact information for those services that have not been included earlier in the book. Complete contact information for many Nashville organizations and services is already included elsewhere in the book and is listed in the table of contents.

For a more comprehensive and up-to-date directory of Nashville services, please consult the *Nashville Source*. To order, call (615) 251-1600 or visit *www.nashvillesource.com*. It is very reasonably priced and has been published for over thirteen years, although it is now under new ownership.

SECTION I: RECORDING SERVICES

It is strongly recommended that you use Nashville recording facilities to produce your songwriter or artist demo. You will not only get a superior product, which is comparable to the best demos being pitched on Music Row, but you will meet and interact with important music industry professionals. There is a wide range of pricing from one studio to the other, and it is not necessary to spend a lot of money on your demos. Be sure to shop around for the best deal.

Nashville's Best Demo Studios

See the listings in chapter 11, "Nashville's Top Demo Studios," pages 145–162.

CD Duplication Services

Cassette & CD Express
116 17th Avenue South
Nashville, TN 37203
Tel: (615) 244-5667
Fax: (615) 242-2472

Nashville Tape & Disc Corporation
1302 Division Street
Nashville, TN 37203
Tel: (615) 244-2180
Web site: *www.ntdc.com*

Complete cassette and CD manufacturing, as well as in-house graphic design.

Nashville Tape Supply
115 16th Avenue South
Nashville, TN 37203
Tel: (615) 254-8178
Fax: (615) 256-1155

We Make Tapes
115 16th Avenue South, Suite 101
Nashville, TN 37203
Tel: (615) 244-4236
Web site: *www.wemaketapes.com*
    Founded in 1979 by Scotty Moore, former lead guitarist for Elvis Presley. A one-stop shop for CD, DVD, cassette, and video duplication and supplies.

Writers Tape Copy Service
1905 Division Street
Nashville, TN 37203
Tel: (615) 327-3196
    CD and cassette tape duplication business of NSAI Hall of Fame and SESAC Songwriter of the Year Ted Harris.

SECTION II: SERVICES YOU WILL NEED TO COMPLETE YOUR WRITER/ ARTIST PACKAGE

As you no doubt know, quick copy companies do just about everything, including graphic design, word processing, color copies, printing, etc. They also sell fancy stationery, envelopes, folders, whatever you need. Creating your own writer/artist package is something you probably will have done at home before you even come to Nashville, but here are some services close to Music Row.

Copying/Printing Facilities

For your basic needs near Music Row:

Copies Unlimited, Inc.
120 20th Avenue South
Nashville, TN 37203
Tel: (615) 327-1758
Web site: *www.midtownprinting.com*
    If you want very nice, print quality CD covers and promotional materials, this is the place to go.

Kinko's
2308 West End Avenue
Nashville, TN 37203
Tel: (615) 327-2120
    If you can do it yourself on their Macintosh computers and copiers, this Kinko's is somewhat close to Music Row.

The UPS Store
Hillsboro Village
1708 21st Avenue
Nashville, TN 37212-3704
Tel: (615) 846-6269
    Formerly known as Mail Boxes, Etc., they have mail boxes for rent, as well as copy services, computer rental, etc.

Label Systems

Blank forms for your own computer. Design your own CD covers, inserts, and business cards.

Ace Label Systems
7101 Madison Avenue West
Golden Valley, MN 55427
Tel: (800) 383-8631
Web site: *www.acelabel.com*

Avery Dennison Office Products
P.O. Box 5244
Diamond Bar, CA 91765-4000
Tel: (800) 252-8379
Web site: *www.avery.com*

Great Photos

Alan Mayor Photography
3807 Murphy Road
Nashville, TN 37209
Tel: (615) 385-4706
    You will see Alan at every music industry event with his camera, capturing the moment. If you want to see his vintage photos, his book *The Nashville Family Album: A Country Music Scrapbook* can be found on *www.amazon.com*.

Teddie St. John
1534 Rock River Road
Nashville, TN 37128
Tel: (615) 506-7068
    Teddie specializes in pets and children, but her head-shots are the best you'll find anywhere if you can talk her into taking your picture.

Great CD Covers and Inserts/Business Cards

Latocki Team Creative LLC
2210 8th Avenue South
Nashville, TN 37204
Tel: (615) 298-3533
E-mail: *Luellyn@latockiteamcreative.com*
    Luellyn has created promotional materials for almost every major star in Nashville, and some who soon will be. She is very creative and understands an aspiring artist's budget.

Nterdesign
Tel: (615) 460-3888
E-mail: *nterzian@bellsouth.net*
    Nancy Terzian is an aspiring artist herself. You will often see her at Billy Block's Western Beat. She is a gifted graphic artist and can create an image for aspiring artists.

Great Bios/Artist Packages list

Beverly Keel
4487 Post Place, #114
Nashville, TN 37205
Tel: (615) 898-5150
E-mail: *bkeel@mtsu.edu*
    Beverly is the Nashville correspondent for *People* magazine, and also writes for *www.rollingstone.com*.

Robert K. Oermann
P. O. Box 120893
Nashville, TN 37212

Tel: (615) 383-5380

E-mail: *oermann@earthlink.net*

Bob Oermann is a multimedia personality in print, TV, radio, graphic arts, and public speaking. He writes the record reviews and other special articles for *Music Row* magazine. He was a judge on the season debut of *Nashville Star.*

SECTION III: PUBLICATIONS

Tip Sheets

Music Row Publications's Row Fax
1231 17th Avenue South
Nashville, TN 32132
Tel: (615) 321-3617 Fax: (615) 329-0852
E-mail: *news@musicrow.com*
Web site: *www.musicrow.com*

Tennessee Songwriters Association International Monthly Newsletter
P. O. Box 2664
Hendersonville, TN 37077-2664
Tel: (615) 969-5967
E-mail: *ASKTSAI@aol.com*
Web site: *www.clubnashville.com/tsai.htm*

Trade Publications

American Songwriter **Magazine**
50 Music Square West, Suite 604
Nashville, TN 37203
Tel: (615) 321-6096
Web site: *www.americansongwriter.com*

Billboard Country Airplay Monitor
49 Music Square West
Nashville, TN 37203
Tel: (615) 321-4290
Web site: *www.billboard.com*

Music Row Publications, Inc.
1231 17th Avenue South
Nashville, TN 32132

Tel: (615) 321-3617
Fax: (615) 329-0852
E-mail: *news@musicrow.com*
Web site: *www.musicrow.com*

Nashville Music Business Directory
9 Music Square West
Nashville, TN 37203
Tel: (615) 255-1068

The Nashville Source
1808 West End Avenue, Suite 702
Nashville, TN 37203
Tel: (615) 251-1600
Web site: *www.nashvillesource.com*

Other Helpful Publications

Nashville Music Guide
P. O. Box 100234
Nashville, TN 37224-0234
Tel: (615) 244-5673
Web site: *www.nashvillemusicguide.com*

Nashville Scene
2120 Eighth Avenue South
Nashville, TN 37204-2204
Tel: (615) 244-7989
Fax: (615) 244-8578
Web site: *www.nashvillescene.com*

The Nashville Yellow Pages
Web site: *www.yp.bellsouth.com*

Tennessean and *The Rage*
1100 Broadway
Nashville, TN 37203
Tel: (615) 259-8000
Web site: *www.tennessean.com*

Section IV: Recommended Reading

Allworth Press publishes some great books that cover everything you
need to know about writing and publishing, performing arts, business,

money and law, and just about everything else in the creative fields. They can be reached at *www.allworth.com* or (800) 491-2808. Here are just a very few offerings:

How to Pitch and Promote Your Songs, Third Edition, by Fred Koller. New York: Allworth Press, 2001.

A step-by-step guide to being your own publisher, targeting the right markets, building your own catalog, creating a demo package. The author is a highly respected Nashville songwriter whose credits include Kathy Mattea's hits *Goin' Gone* and *She Came from Ft. Worth.* Writing from an insider's point of view, he discusses the way the music business works (particularly in the Nashville country music market) and the strategies that have worked for him in getting songs cut. Geoffrey Himes of the *Washington Post* says, "Any songwriter with hopes of selling a song to a recording artist should read this book."

Creative Careers in Music, Second Edition, by Josquin des Pres and Mark Landsman. New York: Allworth Press, 2004.

Talented people of all levels can find profitable careers in today's thriving music industry with the help of this definitive guide. From songwriters to producers, solo artists to band members, a wide variety of careers in the music business are fully described, outlining the skills and training required for each and ways to target the right markets and income sources. The book thoroughly examines today's record business, detailing the pros and cons of starting your own label, major-label versus independent-label careers, and where and when to find professional help.

Making It in the Music Business, Third Edition, by Lee Wilson. New York: Allworth Press, 2003.

Both a practical business manual and a prized legal companion, this authoritative guide contains solid information and advice that songwriters and performers need to make it in today's competitive music industry. This updated edition covers current copyright law and protection, copyright infringement and how to avoid it, trademark law, business law for bands, the roles of bookers, managers, music publishers, and music lawyers, and the provisions of music publishing, management, and booking agreements.

Making and Marketing Music, Second Edition, by Jodi Summers. New York: Allworth Press, 2004.

This thorough guide explains everything musicians need to know to make and market a hit album, from raising money, securing a record deal, and distributing on major and independent labels, to the latest strategies for promoting and selling music on the Internet.

The following list of great books on the music industry was compiled and reviewed by NSAI Staff member Deannie Williams. They are available from the NSAI Bookshop, which can be found on their Web site, *www.nashvillesongwriters.com*

All You Need to Know about the Music Business by Donald S. Passman.

This is a very good book about the business side of the music industry. Its layout makes this book particularly useful. It is designed so that if you need just a little information on a specific topic, you only need to read key sections; this is for the reader on the "Extremely Fast Track." If you want to know a little more, you can read the sections for the "Fast Track" reader. The next level (with a little more depth) is the "Advance Overview," and lastly there's the "Expert Track" if you want to know the most. Topics covered include songwriting deals, publishing, record deals, royalties, and much more.

Music, Money, and Success: The Insider's Guide to the Music Industry by Jeffrey and Todd Brabec.

Jeffrey Brabec is an entertainment law attorney and vice president of business affairs for Chrysalis Music Group. His twin brother, Todd Brabec, a former recording artist and entertainment law attorney, is director of membership at ASCAP in Los Angeles. Together, the two have written a detailed examination of the music business. In particular, the book extensively explores the business aspects of alternative sources of songwriting income, such as television, motion pictures, commercials, and theater.

How to Be Your Own Booking Agent and Save Thousands of Dollars by Jeri Goldstein.

If you are a performer or working with an artist, this is an excellent book on booking gigs. The author—who has been an agent, manager, and promoter—lays out information in an extremely organized and systematic manner. This book covers the ins and outs of finding gigs, developing press kits, negotiating contracts for live performances, and dealing with the media.

Music Publishing by Randy Poe.

Randy Poe is the president of Leiber & Stoller's publishing companies. An excellent overview of music publishing, this book is for the songwriter who knows little about publishing but wants to learn. This is a clearly written, easy-to-understand book. It contains basic explanations of copyrights, sources of income, etc. It is not a book about pitching and placing songs.

The Songwriters' Guide to Collaboration by Walter Carter.

Co-writing is extremely important in Nashville. Over ninety percent of songs recorded are the result of a collaboration. *Songwriter's and Musician's Guide to Nashville* talks a lot about co-writing, but says nothing about what to do when a collaboration has gone sour. Songwriters should read this book before they begin co-writing. This book deals with the legal, psychological, and emotional aspects of co-writing. It explores proper etiquette in a collaboration as well as ways of finding a co-writer.

The Nashville Number System by Chas Williams.

The Nashville Number System is a way of notating song charts for musicians when they play on demos or at performances. In this notational system used principally in Nashville, numbers are used to correspond with chords. The first half of the book explains the notation, and the second half gives examples of actual charts from a few songs. The book is not a music theory book. It requires some knowledge of chords, but even with a moderate knowledge of music theory, this book will probably enable you to write out a simple chart.

The Craft and Business of Songwriting by John Braheny.

A practical guide to creating and marketing artistically and commercially successful songs. John Braheny was the cofounder and director of the Los Angeles Songwriters Showcase (LASS). The book is divided into two broad areas—the craft and the business. The subjects under craft include creativity and inspiration, subject matter, the media and the listeners, writing lyrics, constructing a song, writing music, and collaboration. The topics under Business include protecting your songs, knowing where your money comes from, publishing, self-publishing, demos, marketing yourself and your songs, additional markets, and getting a record deal.

Freshman Year in Nashville by Marc-Alan Barnette

This is a humorous guide to the first year in the Nashville community. Marc-Alan is writing from firsthand experience. He has a great reputation on Music Row, and spends a lot of his time helping aspiring songwriters and artists through NSAI, Belmont and Middle Tennessee universities, and many other speaking engagements. And he puts on a great show! Look for him in Nashville live venues, particularly at the It's All Good Café.

Nashville Entertainment Association Online, LLC, a Web site by Sherry Bond

If you have specific questions about the Nashville music industry, the place to go online is *www.nea.net.* The Nashville Entertainment Association was a trade organization started by legendary record producer Jimmy Bowen, and helped aspiring artists and musicians in Music City for two decades. They closed their doors in 1998, but their Web site remains, continuing to give detailed, insider advice about Music Row.

Index

Books from Allworth Press

Allworth Press is an imprint of Allworth Communications, Inc. Selected titles are listed below.

Making It in the Music Business: The Business and Legal Guide for Songwriters and Performers, Third Edition
by Lee Wilson (paperback, 6 × 9, 256 pages, $19.95)

Making and Marketing Music: The Musician's Guide to Financing, Distributing, and Promoting Albums, Second Edition
by Jodi Summers (paperback, 6 × 9, 240 pages, $19.95)

The Secrets of Songwriting: Leading Songwriters Reveal How to Find Inspiration and Success
by Susan Tucker (paperback, 6 × 9, 256 pages, $19.95)

The Art of Writing Great Lyrics
by Pamela Phillips Oland (paperback, 6 × 9, 272 pages, $18.95)

How to Pitch and Promote Your Songs, Third Edition
by Fred Koller (paperback, 6 × 9, 208 pages, $19.95)

Creative Careers in Music, Second Edition
by Josquin des Pres and Mark Landsman (paperback, 6 × 9, 240 pages, $19.95)

Career Solutions for Creative People: How to Balance Artistic Goals with Career Security
by Dr. Ronda Ormont (paperback, 6 × 9, 320 pages, $19.95)

Gigging: A Practical Guide for Musicians
by Patricia Shih (paperback, 6 × 9, 256 pages, $19.95)

Profiting from Your Music and Sound Project Studio
by Jeffrey Fisher (paperback, 6 × 9, 288 pages, $18.95)

Rock Star 101: A Rock Star's Guide to Survival and Success in the Music Business
by Marc Ferrari (paperback, 5 × 8, 176 pages, $14.95)

The Quotable Musician: From Bach to Tupac
by Sheila E. Anderson (hardcover, 7 × 7, 224 pages, $19.95)

Please write to request our free catalog. To order by credit card, call 1-800-491-2808 or send a check or money order to Allworth Press, 10 East 23rd Street, Suite 510, New York, NY 10010. Include $5 for shipping and handling for the first book ordered and $1 for each additional book. Ten dollars plus $1 for each additional book if ordering from Canada. New York State residents must add sales tax.

To see our complete catalog on the World Wide Web, or to order online, you can find us at **www.allworth.com.**